A HISTORY OF
INDIGENOUS SLAVERY IN GHANA
FROM THE 15TH TO THE 19TH CENTURY

AKOSUA ADOMA PERBI

A HISTORY OF
INDIGENOUS SLAVERY IN GHANA
FROM THE 15TH TO THE 19TH CENTURY

SUB-SAHARAN PUBLISHERS

Revised edition, published in Ghana 2007 by
SUB-SAHARAN PUBLISHERS
P. O. Box 358
Legon, Accra - Ghana
E-mail: saharanp@africaonline.com.gh

© Akosua Adoma Perbi 2004

This printing 2022

ISBN   9988-550-32-4 (soft cover)
           978-9988-550-32-5
ISBN   9988-550-95-2 (hard cover)
           978-9988-550-95-0

Credit for pictures
Ministry of Tourism and Diasporan Affairs.
Prof. Kofi Anyidoho.
Mr. Samuel Ntewusu.
Dr. Yaw Bredwa Mensah.
Mr. R. B. Perbi.
NUFU Norway Project No 34\2002 Ghana History\Development.

* The symbol on the cover is 'epa' in the Akan language, an Adinkra symbol signifying chains or bonds.

Book design and layout by Anne Yayra Sakyi
Cover by Kwabena Agyepong

DEDICATION

This book is dedicated to my husband Kofi Baah and my children Yaw Perbi, Amma Asamoabea, Adwoa Konadu and Nana Nketia.

CONTENTS

FOREWORD

A little over a decade ago, a reviewer of historical writings in Ghana lamented the fact that slavery was a marginal topic in the otherwise well documented historical studies of Ghana. The problem of colonialism and its impact on Ghana naturally seemed more pressing than the story of slavery even though very little was really known about how it was carried on. I have no doubt, therefore, that this book on the History of Slavery in Ghana will be welcomed by historians looking for in-depth studies of domestic slavery in pre-colonial Ghana.

It will also be of interest to the general public for what it reveals about this topic which is generally approached with circumspection in Ghanaian societies even though its contemporary relevance is evident in the judicial cases that have continued to plague our courts. The shackles of slavery can be broken but not its stigma or its intangible aspects which survive, for example, in the memory of those who make consanguinity the right to the assumption of chiefship. Any one who is not aware of this or ignores it in certain contexts because of personal ambition may be "advised" to go back home to the Elders and listen attentively to them as they recall their family history.

But the merit of this book does not lie only in the interest it will have for readers. Due to the painstaking manner in which the author collected a wide range of data in all the ten administrative regions of Ghana with the help of her field assistants, it is a veritable source of historical and cultural data not only for historians but also scholars in cognate disciplines. They include oral data from so-called slave descendants, cultural sites and trade routes as well as documentary evidence from an array of court records in the administrative regions and colonial government reports.

This body of data enables the author to make a number of analytical and often insightful observations, for one of her objectives is to bring to the study of slavery the experiential perspectives in terms of which salient aspects of its practice in a particular milieu might be interpreted. Accordingly although the focus of her research has been on Ghana, she is also concerned about slavery in its wider historical and comparative contexts so that her readers can appreciate the similarities and differences in the concept, forms, and ethics of indigenous slavery, which existed in Ghana long before the trans-Atlantic slave trade. As she points out in her book the trans-Atlantic trade became a major enterprise that far exceeded the bounds of domestic slavery both in the manner in which slaves were acquired and the treatment meted out to them.

The range of her data also enables her to make meaningful statements about the pragmatic aspects of domestic slavery. Although the most important reason for slavery in the domestic context was the practical need for a labour force in agriculture, mining, trade and industry, and a variety of services in homes, palaces and shrines, the roles and duties assumed by slaves beyond those of production made them an integral part of domestic, social and cultural life. From the evidence provided by the author, including written protests against the abolition of slavery submitted by some chiefs to the colonial Government, they participated in and made contributions, on their own level, to the shaping, maintenance and transmission of culture in pre-colonial Ghana. Coming from other Ghanaian societies and cultures, some of them had special knowledge and skills they could contribute to the particular areas of culture in the households to which they were affiliated. Thus some of them learned to be drummers, horn blowers etc, jobs which entailed not only mastery of techniques but also of local languages, repertoire and the oral traditions associated with them.

Another point that emerges from the work is that the institution of domestic slavery had important repercussions on attitudes and values of the communities among whom slaves lived. This is evident not only in the institutional arrangements cited in the work, but also in the references to this process in the oral literature and other sources. It was held for example that "a town that does not assimilate people from other lands never grows big "(*anana-ansaa kuro nyɛ kɛse da*). In other words, the growth of settlements and towns could be precipitated by the presence of people from other lands (*ananafoɔ*) if they were assimilated or integrated into the existing social structure. Because this became the "rule" rather than the exception, an adowa singer asks the rhetorical question:

> Where does one not find odd yams in a barn alongside
>> the regular ones?
> In which Asante town does one not find people
>> from other lands?
> (*Oputuo bɛn na awurukuo nni mu?*
>> *Asante kuro bɛn na ɔnana nni so?*)

Assimilating people from other lands called for the re-definition of forms and modes of affiliation, status, rights and privileges, fields of social action, ethical and artistic values and so on, some of which allowed some descendants of slaves to rise in rank, acquire wealth, become indispensable as creative adjuncts and ceremonial support or providers of artistic goods and services.
The converse of all these is also evident in oral literature. As the author shows, assimilation was not always complete. There were disabilities and impediments. For example although one may enjoy the privilege of royal association, one must not assume that this could be converted into the status of royalty.

> There is a difference between sons of chiefs,
>> and sons of chiefs, and "mixed up" sons of chiefs.
> (*Ɛsono ahene mma na ɛsono ahene mma na ɛsono frafra ahene*
>> *mma*)
> Real chickens are eating grains of millet
>> Ruffled feathered chicken, are you one of them?
> (*Nkokɔmma redi ayuo,*
>> *Na Boafo asɛnse, wowɔ mu bi?*)

Slaves expected to be treated as human beings and not just as a source of labour. At the Apɔɔ festival held in the Brong Ahafo region during which participants are allowed to sing songs of insult or provocative songs in order to get rid of whatever ill feelings they may be harbouring, those who come from the ward representing those in servitude may say to the royal clan in song:

> Allow the black slave to sleep
>> in the early hours of the morning
> *(Momma dɔnkɔbire nnya nhemanna)*

Slaves have the right to enjoy a good night sleep like anybody else. A person of royal blood who does not pull his weight at the battlefront or in a communal undertaking is reminded that

> If the man of royal blood in the ranks does not fight hard
>> The slave runs away from the battle field.
> *(Ɔdehyeɛ anko a, akoa dwane)*

Statements such as the foregoing are still cited in a variety of social contexts. In the light of the foregoing and the contemporary relevance of certain aspects of slavery in Ghanaian thought, I believe that what is needed is not only *historical knowledge* of domestic slavery as revealed in the events and circumstances surrounding its practice in Ghana but also *historical understanding* of slavery as a formative factor in the social, political and economic development of pre-colonial Ghana.

As will be evident from this Foreword, my own interest in this topic, including slavery in Akan thought as manifested in cultural practices and cultural symbols, comes from my encounter with it in my research in ethnomusicology and oral literature over the past sixty years. I am sure it is because of this and not just my natural paternal interest that Akosua asked me to write it. It is certainly a pleasure to do so.

Emeritus Professor J. H. Kwabena Nketia
International Centre for African Music and Dance, University of Ghana

ACKNOWLEDGEMENTS

I owe a debt of gratitude to a host of people. First to my husband and children who had to make sacrifices to enable me achieve my goal. Second to my parents for moral, material and physical support. Third to Prof. G.P. Hagan, former Director of the Institute of African Studies, Legon and now the Chairman of the National Commission on Culture, Ghana, for drawing my attention to the importance of embarking on research in indigenous slavery in Ghana, because it had been an area of neglect in many Academic Disciplines especially History.

To Professors M. Klein, R. Addo-Fening, J.K. Anquandah, D.E.K. Amenumey, J.K. Fynn and M.A. Kwamena-Poh for their encouragement, diligence, corrections and suggestions. To Professors Sheila Walker and Kofi Anyidoho for making it possible for me to do research in the U.S.A. and Britain from 1993-94 when I became affiliated to the African Studies Centre, University of Texas.

I am grateful to Mr. Paul Jenkins and Mr. Peter Hanger of the Basel Mission Archives in Switzerland for sending me all the documents relating to slavery in Ghana in the Swiss Archives. To all friends and relations who provided accommodation, food and sometimes transport during my field work and visits to the archives in the various regions of Ghana, I place on record my heartfelt thanks. All my numerous students in the Department of History, Legon between 1990 and 2002 deserve to be acknowledged for voluntarily doing field work for me.

Finally but not the least, I would like to express my deep appreciation to Sub-Saharan Publishers for making this dream a reality.

INTRODUCTION

The issue of slavery has engaged the attention of scholars world wide for almost a century. And yet as Miller and Smith state, the subject of slavery "continues to fascinate our historical imagination".[1] Two main reasons can be given for this state of affairs. First, the subject is of contemporary relevance and importance. Second, new sources, new ideas, new methods and new approaches keep emerging. One cannot foresee in the light of current developments that the curtain will be drawn on the subject. Indigenous slavery cannot simply be written off or stored in the Archives as an institution of the past because some historical facts about the institution are relived and revisited in the everyday life of the Ghanaian steeped in his/her traditions and culture.

This book focuses attention on indigenous slavery in Ghana. Ghana refers to the political entity located on the southern coast of West Africa on longitudes 1° East and 3° West along the Atlantic coast and between latitudes 4.5° North and 11.5° South of the Equator. It covers a land area of 239,460 sq. km. During the colonial period it consisted of the Gold Coast Colony, Asante and the Northern Territories (See Map I). It is bordered in the south by the Gulf of Guinea; on the west by La Cote d'Ivoire; on the north by Burkina Faso and on the east by Togo. Currently it has a population of about 18,304,700 million and is divided into 10 administrative regions (See Map II). Indigenous slavery is referred to as *Domestic Slavery* in the British Colonial Records. The Oxford Dictionary defines indigenous as "native (to); belonging naturally (to)". The Webster Dictionary defines indigenous as "originating in and characterising a particular region or country". Both definitions are relevant to this book so far as the subject is concerned. Although the word indigenous has recently come under attack, I would still like to use it in this book to distinguish the slavery I would be discussing from the slavery of the Atlantic and External worlds. P.E. Lovejoy who has written a lot on African slavery used the words **Indigenous African Slavery** in the Journal, *Historical Reflections* in 1979.[2] Martin Klein who has also contributed a lot to the literature on slavery in Africa used the words *indigenous slavery* in his book on slavery in Africa and Asia (1993).[3] In this book, Indigenous Slavery will cover the institution of slavery as it originated, developed and existed in Ghana. It pre-dated the Atlantic slave trade, co-existed with the Atlantic slave trade when it was introduced into Ghana in the sixteenth Century, and survived it up to the early part of the twentieth Century.

Indigenous slavery has not received detailed attention in the historiography of Ghana. While there is a lot of material on the Atlantic slave trade and slavery, the material on the indigenous slave trade and slavery is very scanty. It is this gap in our knowledge that partly inspired this research.

The geographical areas in Ghana which have received some coverage so far as both the indigenous and the Atlantic institution of slavery are concerned have been mainly the coastal areas and Asante. In 1978 I submitted my M.A. thesis on *A History of Domestic Slavery in Asante 1800-1920* to the Department of History, University of Ghana, Legon. Asante was chosen because it was the greatest slave trading and slave owning state in pre-Colonial Ghana and at the height of its power exercised authority over nearly the whole of modern Ghana as we know it today. It provided an ideal area for the study of indigenous slavery in Ghana. My period of research at that time (1975-1978) and my continuing interest in the subject of indigenous slavery made me increasingly aware of the need to study the other areas of Ghana as well and to examine in some greater detail those areas which have received some coverage. This thought has been sustained over the years by my interaction with scholars both in Ghana and outside Ghana.

This book, therefore, aims at covering the whole of Ghana as far as possible in the hope that a comparative analysis would enable us to identify common trends and divergences and the factors that account for them.

So far as the time frame of indigenous slavery is concerned, this book covers the fifteenth to the nineteenth century. The subject is considered mainly in themes. The fifteenth century begins with the arrival of the first Europeans (the Portuguese) on the shores of Ghana. This period marks the beginning of direct trade between Ghana and Europe. From this time onwards more documentary evidence becomes available on various aspects of Ghanaian life. It also coincides with movement of peoples into Ghana and increased movement of peoples within Ghana to form states and kingdoms. With the political processes of state formation went the evolution of social, cultural and religious practices of which the institution of slavery was a part. At the end of the nineteenth century Ghana and virtually the whole of Africa was ushered into an era of colonial rule and another phase of history began. The British Colonial Government, among other things, turned its attention to the indigenous institution of slavery and made frantic efforts to abolish it. The fifteenth to the nineteenth century, therefore, seem to me the most appropriate period to study a history of indigenous slavery in Ghana because indigenous slavery evolved, took form and became institutionalised during this period.

This book begins with the general perceptions of slavery and an assessment of their relevance to the Ghanaian situation. The second chapter looks at slavery and the slave trade up to the 18th century. It traces the historical beginnings of indigenous slavery and how slavery became institutionalised. Chapter three examines the sources of slaves for domestic use from the 15th to the 19th century. Chapter four discusses the local use of the male and female slaves in Ghana. Chapter five highlights the social setting in which the slaves found themselves in Pre-Colonial Ghana. The sixth chapter looks at slaves and succession to political office. In chapter seven the trend and effects of the abolition of the indigenous institution by the British Colonial Government are examined.

By examining these topics I hope I have given a holistic view of the indigenous institution of slavery and I have provided a better understanding and knowledge of the dynamics of slavery as practised in Ghana during the Pre-Colonial period. These topics will also enrich our understanding and appreciation of some aspects of present day traditional political institutions and social practices. I used four main methods of approach in the research work for the writing of this book. First, I collected oral material through field work in all the ten administrative regions of Ghana from 1990 to 2002. The transmission of oral tradition in Ghana is done at the traditional political and social level through various persons and means. All these methods were utilised as far as practicable. The resource persons have been the traditional court historians at the kings, chiefs, and queenmothers' palaces; household heads and the elderly men and women in individual households; ordinary men and women well versed in their family history. Questionnaires, interviews, note writing and observation were used to collect the oral tradition. The data was subjected to coding and analysis. I collected primary sources consisting of Archival material, Court documents, Chieftaincy Reports, Traders' Journals, Christian Missionary Records, Travellers' Accounts and European Colonial Reports. The National Archives of Ghana has eight archival centres and I was able to work in all the eight centres. I also visited the Kyebi Palace Archives of the Okyenhene and the Manhyia Archives of the Asantehene. I also got material from the Information Services Department, the National Council on Women and Development and the Law Reform Commission all in Accra, Ghana. Third, I gathered as much material as was available in the libraries of Ghana and the U.S.A. I was in the University of Pittsburgh, Pennsylvania, U.S.A. from September to October 1990 and December 2000 to January 2001. From September 1993 to May 1994 I was at the University of Texas, Austin, U.S.A. From 18th to 20th April 1994 I was at the Pennsylvania State College Library. From August 2000 to July 2001 I was the Fulbright-Scholar-in Residence at Manchester College, Indiana, U·S.A. I was able to gather more information not only from their library but also other libraries in the U·S.A. using the inter-library loan facility. I also spent a week in the month of May 2001in the African Studies Library of the Urbanna-Champagne University Illinois, Chicago, U.S.A. Four, I used a multi-disciplinary approach. The subject and the nature of the research as well as the multiplicity of the ethnic groups in Ghana required such an approach. Disciplines employed to enhance this research work included Archaeology, Geography, Linguistics, Sociology, Music, Dance, Drama, Poetry and Proverbs.

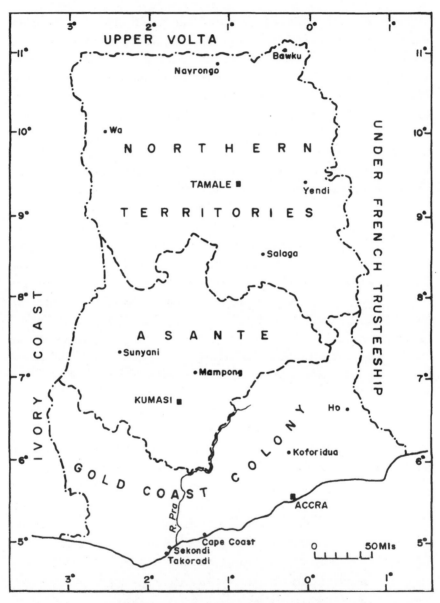

Map I   ADMINISTRATIVE DIVISIONS OF COLONIAL GHANA

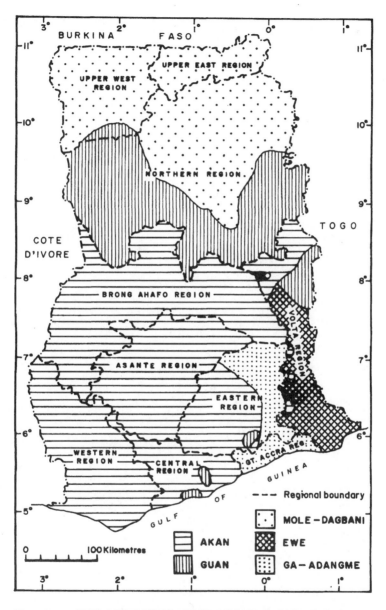

Map II **THE ADMINISTRATIVE REGIONS AND THE MAJOR ETHNIC GROUPS IN CONTEMPORARY GHANA**

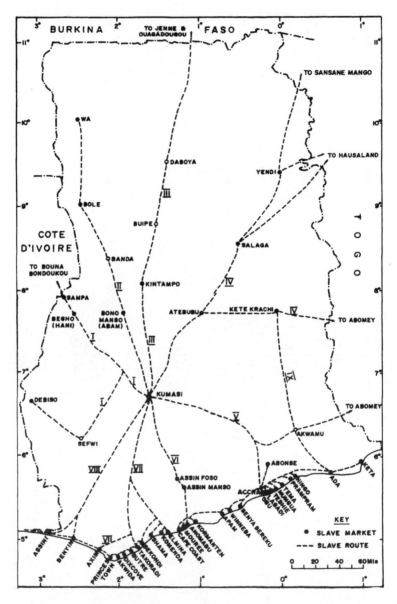

Map III   SLAVE MARKETS AND SLAVE ROUTES IN
PRE-COLONIAL GHANA

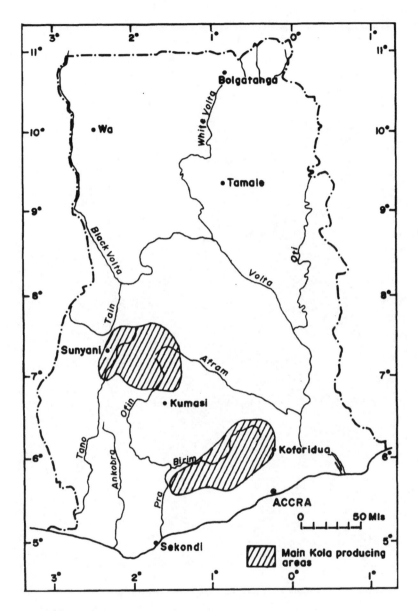

Map IV   THE KOLA NUT PRODUCING AREAS IN
          PRE-COLONIAL GHANA

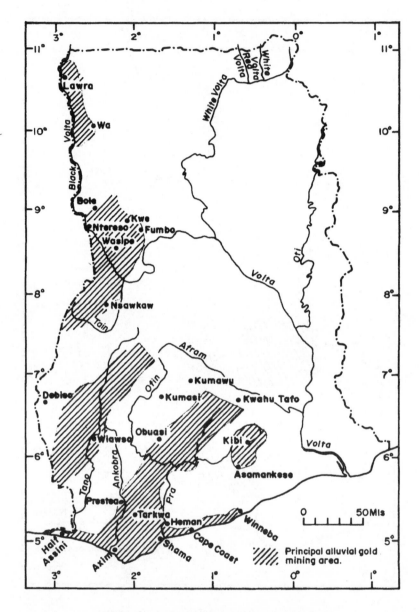

Map V PRINCIPAL GOLD PRODUCING AREAS OF
PRE-COLONIAL GHANA

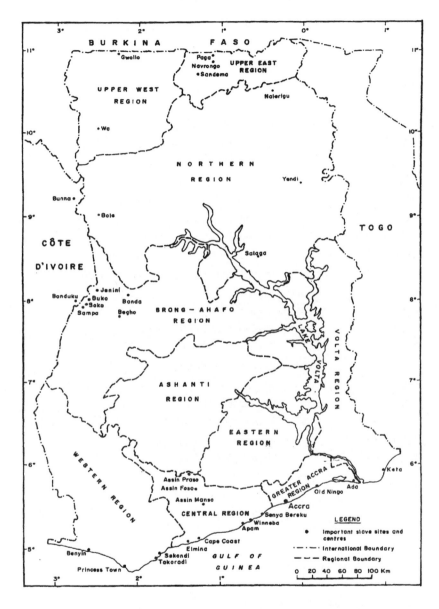

Map VI   MAP OF GHANA SHOWING IMPORTANT SLAVE
          SITES AND CENTRES

ABBREVIATIONS

A.S.H.	—	Ashanti Stool Histories, Legon.
B.M.S.	—	Basel Mission Archives, Switzerland.
G.L.R.	—	Ghana Law Reports.
G.L.R.D.	—	Ghana Law Reports Digest.
I.A.S.	—	Institute of African Studies, Legon.
J.A.H.	—	Journal of African History
N.A.G.	—	National Archives of Ghana, Accra.
P.R.O.	—	Public Record Office, London.
P.C.L.	—	Perry Castenda Library, Texas, Austin, U.S.A.
R.A.C.C.	—	Regional Archives Cape Coast.
R.A.H.	—	Regional Archives Ho.
R.A.K.	—	Regional Archives Kumasi.
R.A.K.D.	—	Regional Archives Koforidua.
R.A.S.	—	Regional Archives Sunyani.
R.A.S.D.	—	Regional Archives Sekondi.
R.A.T.	—	Regional Archives Tamale.
T.H.S.G.	—	Transactions of the Historical Society of Ghana.
W.A.C.A.	—	West African Court of Appeal.
W.A.L.R.	—	West African Law Report.

GENERAL PERCEPTIONS OF SLAVERY:
THEIR RELEVANCE TO THE GHANAIAN SITUATION

The work of Miers and Kopytoff has virtually become the 'Bible' of Historians. The work, made up of contributions from Historians and Anthropologists, underlines the inconclusive debate among scholars in the field of African Studies as to the best definition to give to African slavery.

Miers and Kopytoff in trying to define African slavery make it explicitly clear that it is a difficult assignment. They remark:

> Any discussion of African 'slavery' in English is necessarily bedevilled by the fact that the word conjures up definite images in the Western mind. Anglo-Americans visualize slavery as they believed it was practised on the plantations of the Southern U.S. and the British Caribbean.[1]

In their attempt to find an appropriate word for 'slavery' in the African context, Miers and Kopytoff only ended up using the same word *slave* but put in inverted commas. Other contributors opined that the indigenous African word for 'slave' should be used for the African Society being studied or discussed in order to avoid using the western meaning of 'slave' for the African meaning of slave. Other scholars have used descriptive expressions to define African slavery.

Consequently, there are terms like "lineage slavery; state slavery; palace slavery; individual slavery; agricultural slavery; industrial slavery and military slavery".

Miers and Kopytoff outline four main characteristics of slavery from the western point of view. First, that the slave is a *commodity* to be bought and sold and inherited. Second, that he/she is a *chattel* and is, therefore, totally in the possession of another person who uses him/her for private ends. The slave consequently has no control over his/her destiny, no choice of occupation or employer, no rights to property or marriage and no control over the fate of his/her children. Third, the slave can be inherited, moved or sold without regard to his/her feelings and may be ill-treated sometimes, even killed with impunity. Four, his/her progeny inherits his/her status.

Lovejoy in his detailed study on "The ideology of slavery in Africa" begins with the general definitions of slavery. He states that slavery, as a specific form of exploitation, had a number of characteristics which distinguished it from other forms of exploitation. First, slaves were *property*. As individuals they were owned, and while they were also recognised as human beings, their fundamental characteristic was that they were commodities. Several other authors seem to agree with this characteristic and it appears to be the most popular. Second, slaves were by origin *outsiders* who lacked kinship ties and who had been denied their heritage through judicial or other sanctions. This characteristic is also shared by other scholars. Third, slaves were completely at the disposal of their masters. The labour power of slaves could be used however desired; even their sexuality, and by extension, their reproductive capacities were not theirs by right; for children who were born to slaves inherited slave status unless specific provisions were made to ameliorate that status.

The Western conception of slavery can be summarised by these variables. First, the slave is a commodity; second, the slave is a chattel; third, the slave is inheritable; fourth, his/her progeny inherits slave status, slavery is, therefore, perpetual and hereditary; fifth, the slave is property and sixth, the slave is kinless, marginalised and an outsider.

In collecting oral traditions during field work from 1990 to 2002, in all the ten regions of Ghana, it became clear, as had been indicated by earlier writers, for example, Rattray, that in pre-colonial Ghana various conditions and degrees of voluntary and involuntary subordination of one person to another were recognised. Five separate terms were distinguishable. There was the *servant* ("akoa" in Akan, "subövi / suböla" in Ewe, "abaawa" (female), "tsulö" (male) in Ga, "tumo / bilchin" in Dagbani); the *pawn* ("awowa" in Akan, "awubame" in Ewe, "awoba" in Ga, "talima pabu" in Dabgani); the *slave* ("donko" in Akan, "kluvi" in Ewe, "nyön" in Ga, "dabli" in Dagbani); the *war captive* ("dommum" in Akan , "avalélea" in Ewe, "gboklefonyo" in Ga, "tuhugbaaii" in Dagbani), and the *slave under capital punishment* ("akyere" in Akan, "kluvisi wotso kufiana" in Ewe, "nyön ni abaa gbe le" in Ga, "dabli kuba" in Dagbani). A servant could serve in a household. Hence the word servant could be used figuratively to describe the people subject to a stool/skin and, therefore, to a king or chief. It could also be used to describe the relationship between two chiefs - one superior and the other inferior. The superior chief would refer to the inferior chief as his servant. The term servant, therefore, covered varying shades of subjection. This distinction between servant and slave buttresses Jordan's point that servant and slave were not the same and that servant was more a generic term than slave. The pawn was a person given to a creditor by a debtor as security for what he/she owed on the understanding that on repayment, the person would be returned to the original owner. Such a person was picked from the debtor's family. In Ghana the slave was a person who had been bought in cash or kind or acquired through various means by someone or a group of people. The slave was taken away from his/her home, his/her family, his/her state and his/her country into another home, family, state or country. The fourth category, the war captive as the name implies, was acquired through warfare. He/she was distinguished from the slave because he/she could be redeemed. The captive, the slave and the pawn invariably performed the same tasks. They all enjoyed certain rights but the captive and the pawn could be redeemed while the slave could not. Finally the fifth category, the slave under capital punishment, was the slave who instead of suffering imme-diate capital punishment for an offence of which he/she had been found guilty was held over till the appropriate time for the punishment to be carried out. Until then the slave was required to go about his/her normal duties.

When one examines slavery in the Ghanaian context from the documentary and oral data collected, one observes that some of the Western characterisations of slavery as outlined above approximate to the Ghanaian practice. Among the selected ethnic groups studied, the slave was regarded as a commodity, in the sense that the slave could be bought in cash or in kind. The slave could be a medium of exchange at the slave market. The slave could also be given away as a gift.

The characterisation of a slave as *chattel* was however, not part of the Ghanaian slavery experience. In Ghana the slave was regarded as a human being and was entitled to certain rights and privileges. These rights will be examined in detail in chapter five of this book when the social setting in which slaves found themselves among the various ethnic groups in Ghana is discussed. The position of a slave in Ghana was "that of a person in a state of servitude guarded by rights".

Another characterisation worth examining is the view of slavery as a perpetual and hereditary condition. Jordan states that the concept of slavery as a perpetual and hereditary phenomenon was the rule rather than the exception in America. Elkins for example thinks that from the time the first Africans arrived in America, specifically in Virginia in 1619, until the 1660s, English Common Law recognised various servant categories, none of which included perpetual and inherited chattel bondage. However, as soon as slavery became firmly entrenched in America, one of its marked features was that it was perpetual and hereditary. In 1663 Maryland and Virginia enacted the following laws:

> All Negroes or other slaves within the province, and all the Negroes and other slaves to be hereafter imported into the province, shall serve durante vita; and all children born of any Negro or other slaves as their fathers were for the term of their lives.[2]

The situation in the Caribbean seems to have been no different from that of America. Richard Ligon writing about Barbados in 1657 observed that:

> The land is divided into three sorts of men viz., masters, servants and slaves. The slaves and their posterity, being subject to their masters for ever, are kept and preserved with greater care than the servants, who are theirs but for five years, according to the law of the land.[3]

Oral tradition in Ghana relates that a slave was a slave for life as were his/her descendants, but there were exceptions to this rule because there were avenues for social, political and economic mobility.

Slaves, whether male or female who got married to free men or free women and especially to those of royalty, had their slave status virtually annulled. Children born out of such marriages became free members of the free parents' lineage. Slaves who were elevated to important political positions in Ghanaian society also had their slave status cancelled for all practical purposes. However, their children and their descendants did not automatically enjoy the same status as the elevated slave unless the king or chief responsible for the elevation of the slave said so.

Among the Asante, an Asante slave could be manumitted after he had gone through certain ceremonies. The Fantes also made provision for manumitting Fante slaves. Among all the ethnic groups selected for this book, a slave could gain his/her freedom if he/she ran to the shrine of the traditional priest or to the royal mausoleum.

Another point to discuss is the property status of slavery in Ghana. The Oxford Dictionary defines a slave as:

> a person who is the property of another and bound to serve him/her; a person compelled to work very hard for someone else; Somebody completely in the power of, under the control of....[4]

The Webster Desk Dictionary defines property as "something owned"; "right of possession". In pre-colonial Ghana there were three main types of property recognised by customary law - stool /skin property; family property and private property. Private property was anything that had been acquired by a person's own efforts and with privately earned money. Slaves were often regarded as part of a person's private property. A list of a person's private property would include gold dust, cloths, crops or trees, domestic animals, personal effects and slaves. In dealing with Ghanaian property rights so far as human beings are concerned, one would need to understand the relationship in the African and Ghanaian context of the rights that a person or group exercised over others. In Ghana as in many other African societies, there were rights people enjoyed in almost all social relationships. Children had the right to support and protection from their parents and the parents had the right to demand obedience and respect from the children. Husbands expected domestic services, respect, obedience and loyalty from their wives whilst the wives in return expected material support, protection and respect from their husbands. Masters and mistresses demanded obedience, respect and loyalty from their servants and slaves; servants and slaves expected material support, protection and care from their masters and mistresses. Kings and chiefs expected obedience, respect and loyalty from their subjects and the subjects in return expected protection and justice.

These demands and expectations were connected with the property rights of persons over others. It is in the light of these recognised property rights that slaves in Ghana became entitled to a number of privileges. There were traditional rules regarding the treatment of slaves and these rules served as 'checks and balances' in the property relationship between masters/mistresses and their slaves. These traditional rules regarding treatment of slaves will be discussed at length in chapter five of this book. In contrast with European and American conception of property rights of the masters under which slaves were treated like chattel, property rights in Ghana and existing traditional rules prevented the treatment of slaves as chattel. Elkins contends that in America, the rights of property and all other civil and legal rights were everywhere denied the slave. Filler notes that the slave code established in

America preserved the individual slave holder's right in his slave as property. In Ghana, some slaves could inherit property on the death of their owners. Faithful slaves who traded for their owners were sometimes given capital by their owners to begin some trading for their own use and benefit. De Graft Johnson recorded in 1927, the cases of slaves who acquired property of their own and became very wealthy. In one of those cases because of his wealth and the value of the public services the slave performed, a stool was created for his adoptive family.[5]

There was a saying among the Akan of Ghana that "A slave's life is in his master's hand" (In Akan: *Akoa nkwa ne ne wura*) and yet no slave owner had the right of life and death over the slave. Only the king or chief exercised that right over slave and free person alike. This privilege of kings and chiefs was clearly stated in 1880 at the trial of Nifahene Kwaku Amo of Asiakwa, when he was accused of sacrificing 3 slaves in March 1874 during the funeral celebration of his predecessor Chief Duodu. Nifahene Kwaku Amo defended his action by stating that before the imposition of colonial rule, Customary Law permitted kings and chiefs to kill slaves for ritual and other purposes. A slave, whatever his/her offence could not be killed by his/her owner. To kill a slave was 'murder' and the offence was liable to be punished. Even the Elders in the traditional political system did not have the power to kill their slaves.[6] This was in contrast to what prevailed in Europe and the Americas where slave owners irrespective of their rank had the power of life and death over their slaves. The Constitution of Carolina drafted in 1669, for example, provided that:

> Every freeman of Carolina, shall have absolute power and authority over his Negro slaves of what opinion or religion whatsoever.[7]

I agree with Garth White's contention that defining slavery as a property-based relationship is not a misnomer in the African context. White continues as follows:

> Admittedly, the concept of property must be included in defini-
> tions of slavery, but if it centres on ownership and the legal saleabil-

ity of the slave, it would not be sufficiently wide to cover the range of variation of African slavery.[8]

I would now consider the sixth characterisation of a slave as kinless, marginalised and an outsider. The study of selected ethnic groups in Ghana revealed that whenever a slave was acquired, he/she was integrated into the family. It was the first traditional rule with respect to the acquisition and treatment of slaves. The slave in Ghana invariably became part of his/her owner's household and part of the owner's family, lineage and clan. He/she was given a new name – the family name or any name the owner cared to give him as part of the process of integrating him/her into the family. What happened in Ghana pertained in many other African societies.

An important aspect of African slavery which Miers and Kopytoff highlight is its relationship to kinship. Kinship relations and kin groups are dominant elements in most African social systems and kinship usually defines both the idiom and the metaphor for social and political relations. Miers and Kopytoff state:

> What gives African slavery its particular stamp, in contrast to many other slave systems, is the existence of this slavery to kinship continuum.[9]

Lovejoy points out that within the African context several ideological frameworks are distinguishable. One ideological framework employed a system of symbols related to a kinship idiom. The kinship idiom personified social relationships. Consequently, slaves who lacked any kin could be incorporated as if they were related by blood. The second ideological framework was based on Islam; a third was abolitionist and questioned the legitimacy of slavery.[10] All these three ideological frameworks were relevant to the Ghanaian situation but the kinship idiom was the most dominant. Islam did play a role in slavery in pre-colonial Ghana, especially in what is today the Upper East, Upper West and Northern Regions of Ghana but it did not destroy the indigenous institution. The influence of Islam on the institution of slavery in Ghana was, therefore, not as predominant as it was in other parts of Africa, particularly in Northern Nigeria. Although Islam began to spread peacefully into Ghana from the 15th century onwards, it did not affect social and political institutions till later in the 17th century. The states of Dagomba, Gonja, Mamprusi and Wa, for example, had evolved their basic social and political institutions before Islam made any substantial impact on these states. In these states, therefore, Islamic features were added to the traditional systems. Trimingham and others have often stressed the ability of Islam to co-exist with traditional systems. Oral and documentary data collected from the Upper East, Upper West and Northern Regions of Ghana from 1990 to 2002 emphasised very clearly the indigenous aspect of the institution of slavery. With respect to the third ideological framework propounded by Lovejoy, basically questioning the legitimacy of slavery, it was the British colonial authorities in Ghana who raised this issue. Their attitude to slavery, the policies they adopted and their attempt to abolish slavery will all be examined in detail in chapter seven of this book. Watson points out that there are two modes of slavery – open and closed. African societies practised the open mode of slavery, while Asian societies practised a closed mode of slavery. In Asia it would have been inconceivable for a slave to be accepted into the kinship system of their owners.[11] By practising the open mode of slavery, slaves in Africa were not only incorporated into the lineage of their owners but they also enjoyed certain rights. The Western conception of a slave as an outsider and a marginalised person reflected in the fact that the slave had no place in the kinship system. He/she was alienated from all rights or claims of birth and he/she ceased to belong in his/her own right to any legitimate social order. He/she was a genealogical isolate, denied all claims on and obligation to his/her parents and living blood relations; to his/her remote ancestors and his/her descendants. He/she was culturally and legally isolated. The slave was a socially dead person. While this was true in Europe, America and Asia, it was different in Africa as a whole and in Ghana in particular.

I agree with White's contention that in Africa a key factor in assessing a person's status was the network of relationships between himself, consanguinal kin i.e. blood relatives - whether by biological fact or social fiction - and affinal relatives – i.e. relatives by marriage. This is true even today.

In an article on *'Mobility in pre-colonial Asante from a historical perspective'*, I indicated the importance of the family, lineage and clan in the past and present Asante social and political structure. In identifying an Asante, two main questions were asked in the past and these questions are still asked today. The first question was "where do you come from?" (In Asante: *wofiri hen?*). The second question was "what household do you belong to?" (In Asante: *wofiri fie ben mu?*). The first question sought to find out what Asante town one came from. The second question probed deeper into the person's family, lineage and clan affiliation. According to oral data collected from 1990 to 2002, these questions are still asked today both among the Akan and non-Akan groups in Ghana. The importance of kinship was and is still fundamental to the traditional social setting and the political structure of Ghana. I disagree with Wilks' assertion that kinship and lineage were not central to Akan-Asante society.[12] They were very fundamental not only to Asante society but to all Akan and non Akan groups in Ghana. All the selected ethnic groups studied in this book indicated that the slave had to be made part of the family. The family was the core of the Ghanaian social system.

H.S. Klein relates that slaves in the Western world were not unique in either the work they performed or in their lack of control over their own lives. Peasants, serfs, even clansmen and kinsmen, were often in temporary conditions of servitude. There was often little to distinguish slaves from other workers in terms of the labour they performed or the rights immediately available to them. But where slavery came to be recognised as an important institution, it was the lack of ties to the family, to kin, and to the community which finally distinguished slaves from all other workers. It was in fact, their lack of kin, community and land which made slaves so desirable in the pre-industrial world.[13] Of course in the African and Ghanaian context, slaves were made part of the kinship group. The slave in Ghana did not originally belong to the family that acquired him/her. He/she was bought or acquired through various means.

Though an outsider, the slave in Ghana unlike a slave in the Western World, invariably became part of the family of the person who bought or acquired him/her through outright adoption or marriage. It is important, however, to note that despite their integration or incorporation into various families and households in Ghana, slaves and their descendants never forgot that their membership of their new families was by adoption rather than by consanguinity. When the British Colonial Government passed laws abolishing slavery in Ghana, some freed slaves were quick to seek and to go back to their consanguineous families. Family members of enslaved relatives also went out looking for them. Hence an Akan proverb says "when a slave is playing with his master's son, he remembers his status as a slave" (In Akan: *Akoa ne ne wura ba edi agoro a, na n'akoa wo ne tirim*). Not even elevated slaves or those highly favoured by their owners ever forgot their servile origins. When one examines chieftaincy reports, court records and archival material from the period of abolition of indigenous slavery to the present, one finds that some families in Ghana have continued to regard the freed slaves and their descendants as adopted members of the family. This distinction becomes pronounced during traditional political, constitutional and social crises. On the other hand there are other families in Ghana who have completely integrated or assimilated the slave descendants and do not draw any distinctions of birth or adoption. During field work, there were some households who refused to respond to the questionnaires being administered because they had 'sworn oaths' not to talk about slavery in the family.

Since the 1970s, scholars in the field of African studies have examined some of the Western definitions, classifications and perceptions of slavery and have tried to apply them to the African situation. It is clear from the above discussion that not all the definitions, classifications and perceptions fit the Ghanaian or African situation. I cannot help but agree with Watson when he points out that slavery is a complex social institution which cannot be defined or pigeon holed with reference to a single attribute. I would like to submit, in the light of all that has been discussed in this chapter, that slavery in Ghana must be examined and appreciated from the Ghanaian perspective, definitions, classifications and perceptions of slavery. One should look at slavery in Ghana as having its own unique and peculiar features.

SLAVERY AND THE SLAVE TRADE
UP TO THE 18TH CENTURY

S lavery and the slave trade have been immemorial institutions and practices in almost every continent in the world. Orlando Patterson, G. Macmunn, H.S. Klein, W.K. Scarborough and others, agree that slavery is a world wide, immemorial institution. Orlando writes:

> There is nothing notably peculiar about the institution of slavery. It has existed from before the dawn of human history right down to the twentieth century, in the most primitive of human societies and in the most civilized. There is no region on earth that has not at some time harbored the institution. Probably there is no group of people whose ancestors were not at one time slave or slave holders. Slavery was firmly established in all the great early centres of human civilization.[1]

The earliest known legal documents concerned not the sale of land, houses, animals, boats and such like, but the sale of slaves. In Mesopotamia for example, the sale of slaves was known from 2300 B.C.[2]

Oral and documentary records in Ghana describe slavery as an "immemorial institution". In 1837, Maclean stated before the Committee of Merchants that slavery had been in existence in Ghana from time immemorial and as such the government of Cape Coast Castle of which he was the head could not be held answerable to the British public for recognising 'domestic slavery'.[3]

It is difficult to ascertain exactly when the indigenous institution of slavery began in Ghana. Perhaps, as succinctly put by Orlando Patterson above, the institution of slavery is as old as the beginning of human habitation on Ghanaian soil.

SLAVERY AND THE EVOLUTION OF HUMANKIND

The general belief held by historians and anthropologists is that slavery was not important when humankind depended on food gathering, hunting and fishing. Goody, however, cautions that even among hunters and gatherers there were exceptional instances where slavery occurred, and he cites the example of the Northwest coast of America. Archaeological evidence indicates that Ghana has had a fairly long pre-history, probably going back to around 50,000 B.C. at the least. There was human habitation in Ghana from the early Stone Age, the Middle Stone Age through the late Stone Age to the New Stone Age. The economy was marked by food gathering, fishing and hunting. The available records do not indicate whether during this period of foraging, slavery was practised in Ghana.

Humankind evolved from an economy based on foraging to one based on farming. The Neolithic or New Stone Age, as this stage of human development is known, enabled people to live in ways different from their previous ways of life. They could settle in one place for quite long periods, make permanent villages and give up a good deal of their wandering in search of game and wild plants. From about 2000 B.C. to 500 B.C. a little cultivation began to be practised in Ghana. Scattering of seeds collected through gathering produced plants and eventually crops, and man became aware of the possibility of cultivating crops. From about 500 B.C. to the 1st Century A.D. the art of cultivation was learnt and practised. This period marked the beginning of actual farming in Ghana. There was, however, no sudden break with the past because gathering, hunting and fishing continued to be important means of livelihood. The move from foraging to the era of domestication of plants and animals was gradual and evolutionary rather than revolutionary but it produced far-reaching results.

It led to the development of sedentary habitation, growth of larger populations and the rise of complex societies and civilisation.

Iron working became important in the country during this same period and the country experienced further remarkable changes in its living conditions. The use of iron implements for farming instead of stone tools, facilitated agriculture. The use of iron weapons brought a new source of military power and contributed to state formation and development. It is to the Neolithic period of Ghana's history that one must look for the earliest evidence of slavery. Technological advancement and dependence on agriculture created the need for labour. The available evidence indicates that around the 1st Century A.D. farming was done by individual households consisting of blood relations, pawns and slaves. The earliest evidence of slavery is, therefore, likely to be found in the field of agriculture.

The likely mode of acquisition of slaves in the Neolithic period in Ghana is however problematic. The use of pawns gives some clue to the possibility of voluntary servitude. Slaves might have also been acquired through warfare or commerce. One of the results of sedentary habitation during the Neolithic period in Ghana was the evolution and formation of village communities, chiefdoms and States. Around 1000 A.D. there emerged in Ghana complex settlements in the form of states and towns. In the course of these political developments, conquered peoples were enslaved and incorporated into the various political units which were being formed. The acquisition of slaves through warfare was an ancient practice. From ancient times it became the custom for conquering armies to enjoy absolute and unconditional rights over the property of the vanquished, including the right either to destroy or to preserve it for their own profit. The retention of captives taken in battle was a recognised practice among every people before the beginning of written history. The ancient records of the Assyrians, Egyptians, Phoenicians, Hebrews, Persians, Indians and Chinese are all full of references to slaves and the types of labour for which they were usually employed. With the Greeks and the Romans, the institution of slavery reached new heights.

Another possible source of slaves used in Ghana during the early Neolithic period was commerce. Indeed, commerce followed agriculture in the evolution of humanity. From the 1st Century A.D. onwards, commerce became part of the evolving Ghanaian traditional economy. Intensive farming resulted in the production of enough food to maintain specialists to work at making tools and weapons. This division of labour encouraged trade. The trade was at first within the state (intra-state), then it came to involve a number of states (inter-state) and soon it involved many states and many regions (long-distance). Commodities which were exchanged within the state and between states were fishing products, food crops, game, tools and ornaments. Trading became more complex when Ghana added an international aspect to the trade. Ghana became part of a wide network of African trade routes spanning northwards across the Western Sudan to North Africa (the trans-Saharan trade) and southwards along the coastal belt from Senegal to Nigeria.

The trans-Saharan trade had been going on for centuries before the birth of Christ. Its origin could be traced to the days of Carthage when the North African Berbers began exchanging salt, for which there was an insatiable demand in the Western Sudan, for gold which was very plentiful in the region. The trade continued throughout the era of Roman domination in North Africa. The earliest 'markers' on the trans-desert caravan trails were put there by Berbers who lived there more than 2500 years ago. But the trade became much bigger and more important for many people after the rise of powerful Muslim states in North Africa after about A.D. 650. The trade reached its height around A.D. 1500. Ghana became important in the trans-Saharan trade because of its richness in gold. From about the 10th Century A.D. gold from Ghana was exchanged for slaves, hides, ostrich feathers and other products from the Western Sudan as well as cowries, perfumes, beads and horses from North Africa. Bono Manso and Begho in modern Brong Ahafo Region of Ghana became important centres for this trade from A.D. 1000 to A.D. 1750. The Mande Dyula were the professional merchants in this trade.

In addition to the imports from the Western Sudan and North Africa, Ghana developed trade along the southern coastal belt from Senegal to Nigeria. In the 15th Century A.D. Ghana exchanged gold for slaves, beads, cotton cloth from the Benin State in Nigeria as well as the famous 'quaqua' cloth from Dahomey and Ivory Coast. The Portuguese testified to the existence of a brisk trade in slaves and other goods between Ghana and its coastal neighbours. The evidence suggests, therefore, that between the 1st and the 15th Century A.D. Ghana received slaves and other goods through commerce with its African neighbours.

SLAVERY AND STATE BUILDING
FROM THE 1ST TO THE 15TH CENTURY A.D.

Indigenous slavery became institutionalised in Ghana during the Neolithic and Iron age periods with the increase in state building activities, especially from the 15th Century A.D. The better a state's political structure became, the stronger it was in a position to practise slavery. Not only was it in a position to conquer its neighbours and capture prisoners, but also it possessed the capacity to use the services of the prisoners internally or to trade in them. Gradually slavery became part of the internal structure of these well built states.

In the Northern part of Ghana, the valleys of the Black and White Volta and their tributaries became early sites of civilization, culture and political development. The states in this region inhabited by the Guan, Vagala, Sisala, Tampolense, Dagarti, Konkomba, Koma, Nafeba, Gbimba and Chamba had political organisations which were not centralised. The family heads exercised the power of government and together with the "Tendana" (owner of the land), they governed the tribal communities. Traditions assert that slaves were used in the economies of these states both at the state and individual levels.

Between the 11th and the 13th centuries, a group of invaders arrived in Northern Ghana from the Lake Chad region of Nigeria. Their leader Tohajiye (Red Hunter) settled in Gambaga and established political control over the indigenous people. Two of his grandsons, Sitobu and Mantambu founded the Dagomba and Nanumba states respectively. Another grandson, Tohugu founded the Mamprusi state. A grandson of the Mamprusi chief, the son of his daughter called Nedega and a Busanga hunter called Widraogo founded the Mossi Kingdoms of Ouagadougou and Yatenga. By the 15th century, centralised states had been established in the Northern part of Ghana by these invaders from the Niger Bend region and their descendants. As in the non-centralised states, slaves were used in the economies and administrations of the centralised states.

Just as the ancient civilization in the Northern part of Ghana thrived in the Black and White Volta basins, so the ancient civilization of the Akan thrived in the Pra, Ofin, Tano, Ankobra and Tain River basins. From the 1st to the 15th Century A.D. the Akan developed a distinct political and social organisation. The need for labour was great in an environment endowed with rich soils, numerous rivers, large fauna, iron and gold. The Akan used slaves in agriculture, industry, commerce and administration.

The Akan groups inhabiting the coast lands of Ghana witnessed state building activities and a wave of migrations. The autochthonous Etsi established political units in the forests and coast lands of the modern Central Region of Ghana. Among the several towns and villages founded by them were Abrem-Agona, Okurawa, Asoantse, Sembew, Akona, Ebu, Juaso, Bosomadwe, Moure, Anomabu, Egya and Kormantse. Their states such as Abrem, Eguafo, Effutu, Asebu, Jukwa, Okurwa, Ando, Sonkwa, Adowegyir and Acron were of considerable sizes. The Etsi kingdoms had coastal outlets such as Elmina, Komenda, Cape Coast, Moure, Anomabu, Kormantse and Egya. The Portuguese noticed on their arrival on the coast in the 15th century that the Etsi were one of the major traders in Ghana. Their economy was based on trading, salt-making and fishing and slave labour was employed.

Fante oral tradition tells of how various groups of Fantes moved from the ancient Bono kingdom and Takyiman in modern Brong Ahafo around 1300

A.D. to *"Akan man mu"* (Akan land), the area encompassed by the Pra and Ofin Rivers. From *"Akan man mu"* the groups dispersed and founded states in the forest and coast lands. Some of the groups drove out the Etsi, others assimilated them. From *"Akan man mu"*, the Borbor Fante settled at Mankessim from where various groups moved out again. Mankessim became the Fante capital and European documents referred to Mankessim as " Fantyn". The original core of the Borbor Fante comprised the states of Essiam, Ayan Denkyira, Ayanmain, Mankessim, Kwaaman, Ayan Abasa, Abura and Abeadze. The Fante, like all Akan groups, had centralised states and well established social and economic systems. The Borbor Fante knew of the institution of slavery in the modern Brong Ahafo Region, as well as in "Akan man mu" before they finally settled in the forest and on the coast. The institution of slavery is evident in oral and historical records right from the beginning of Fante state building activities. Slaves were used in the economy as well as in the administration of the Fante states.

The same was true of the eastern coast of Ghana. Ethnographic, historical, oral and archaeological data indicate the existence of an ancient civilization in the Accra plains. During the first four millennia B.C., the Accra plains were inhabited by Late Stone Age hunter gatherers who also did some fishing. It was during the final stages of the Late Stone Age that village settlements began to be established. During the Early and Middle Iron Age, especially between 500 A.D. and 1400 A.D., these village settlements expanded. The earliest industries evident in these villages were iron working and pottery making in which slave labour was probably employed. In the 15th Century A.D. state formation began to take place when a priest-ruler of Asere succeeded in amalgamating some thirty Ga settlements into a centralised Kingdom. It was, however, after the 16th Century A.D. that further centralisation took place among the Ga-Adangme. These centralised Ga-Adangme states were familiar with the institution of slavery. Evidence from the Portuguese accounts of Eustache de la Fosse and Pacheco Pereira who visited the coast of Ghana in the 15th Century A.D. suggests this. De la Fosse and Pereira talked about a maritime trade in slaves, cloth and beads between the Nigerian coast and

Elmina. The slaves acquired by the Ga-Adangme through this trade were used in the iron working, pottery making and fishing industries.

SLAVERY AND STATE BUILDING
FROM THE 16TH TO THE 18TH CENTURY A.D.

The 16th to the 18th Century A.D. witnessed greater political changes and developments in Ghana. Various ethnic groups built formidable states and kingdoms. In addition, a wave of migrations of people into Ghana and within Ghana by people determined to create strong centralised states precipitated the political process. The institution of slavery was strengthened and woven into the political, social and economic fabric of states during this phase. Between the 16th and 17th Centuries A.D. Wadh Naba or Nabega led Mande invaders, already familiar with the institution of slavery, into Gonjaland in Northern Ghana, imposed his rule over the Gonjas and assimilated them. The newcomers established centralised political authority systems and turned Gonja into an important slave owning and slave trading state. The strategic position of Gonja on the trans-Saharan trade route also aided the development of the institution of slavery.

In the forest and woodland regions of Ghana the important political entities from the 16th to the 18th Century A.D. were Bono Manso, Takyiman, Wenchi, Adansi, Wassa, Aowin, Sefwi, Kwahu, Twifo, Assin, Akyem, Denkyira and Akwamu. All these Akan states were involved in slave trading, slave owning and slave dealing. On the coastlands the Borbor Fante were involved in wars of territorial expansion with their Etsi neighbours throughout the 16th and 17th Centuries A.D. The Borbor Fante attacked and defeated the Assin Etsi, the Etsi of Abrem, Eguafo, Fetu, Asebu, Sonkwa, Abeadze and Acron. By the middle of the 18th Century A.D. the Borbor Fante exercised political and economic control over the southern states from the mouth of the River Pra to the borders of the Ga kingdom. In the areas where the Borbor Fante established their states, the Etsi were effectively incorporated. The Etsi Kingdoms of Eguafo, Abrem, Fetu and Asebu which could not easily be subdued were allowed to survive on condition that they became an integral part of the Fante Confederation. The inland Etsi lost their political independence to Assin and Twifo. These wars of conquest and expansion, coupled with diplomacy, extended Fante territory eastward from the Bosumpra River to the Western frontier of Accra. Fante territory comprising twenty states became greatly involved in slave trading, slave owning and slave dealing.

In the Accra plains state building and migrations occurred between the 16th and the 18th Century A.D. The Ga Mashi, Nungua and Tema people subdued the Guan groups of Le, Kpesi and Afutu. The Le and Kpesi were assimilated but the Afutu group were able to maintain their independence and remained as the western neighbours of the Gas. The Osu people left the Osudoku settlement at Adangme and settled at Osu. In the 17th century the La people left their Adangme settlement at Ladoku and settled at Labadi (now renamed La). The Teshie people who were part of the La group broke away after a dispute and settled on land granted them by the Nungua people from the 18th Century A.D. onwards. Six principal Ga towns existed on the coast: Ga Mashi, the capital, Osu, La (Labadi,) Teshie, Nungua and Tema. In the Adangme area were the centralised states of Shai, Osudoku, Kpone, Prampram, Asutsuare, Ningo and Ada. In addition were the states of Manya Krobo and Yilo Krobo. Up to the 18th Century A.D., with the exception of the Ga Mashi, the Ga states were theocratic states ruled by traditional priests or *"Wulomei"*. Military attacks from the Akwamu, Asante and Anlo from the 17th century onwards, created problems of security for the Gas and caused them to adopt the institution of chieftaincy. The Ga Mashi led the way because they had begun practising a monarchical system of government at Ayawaso, their last settlement. The founder of Ayawaso, Prince Ayite, built a strong central government. All the Ga Adangme states integrated the institution of slavery into their political, social and economic organisations.

The Volta Region of Ghana witnessed the most widespread migrations during the 17th century. Ewe tradition talks of a series of migrations from Ketu in Nigeria and Notsie in Dahomey. Ewe tradition of some of the various groups relates that they met some Guan groups on their arrival in Eweland. Some of the Guan fled to other areas, others were assimilated by the migrants. By the second half of the 17th century, the migrants had founded a number of territorial divisions or *"dukowo"*. Each *"duko"* was under a king or paramount chief. All the states in Eweland lived as autonomous states right up to the 19th century. The Ewe states were familiar with the institution of slavery in their original homelands in Nigeria and Dahomey. As the states began to be formed, slavery became an integral part of the state's political, social and economic organisation.

The period between the 16th and the 18th Century A.D. was an eventful period in the history of Ghana. In addition to all the state building activities and migrations discussed above and the strengthening of the institution of slavery, the country witnessed the rise of the Asante state, the last and most prominent of the Akan states. In the fashion of the "volkerwanderung"[14] various Asante clans moved from Adansi in stages and at different periods northwards into *"Asanteman"* (Asanteland) from about the 14th to the 17th Century A.D. The earliest group was the Agona clan who founded Tafo. They were followed by the Ekoona, Aduana and Asenee clans who founded several settlements like Domaa, Amakom, Atwima, Kwabiri, Suntreso, Asokore, Kwaaman, Kenyaase, Kaase, Ejisu and Mampongten. The Bretuo clan followed and founded settlements like Mampong and Seniagya. The last group to move to *"Asanteman"*, the Oyoko clan, arrived in the 17th century. They founded several settlements, prominent among which were Nsuta, Juaben, Kokofu, Bekwai and Kumasi. All these settlements were ruled by their own chiefs and they practised all the political and social systems of the Akan with which they were familiar in their homeland in the Pra and Ofin basins. Naturally the institution of slavery was familiar to them. In *"Asanteman"*, the Oyoko clan remained a closely knit group and it is not surprising that it was through it that all the clans in *"Asanteman"* were welded together into one strong and big Asante nation. The second Kumasihene to reign after Kobia Amanfi, Oti Akenten (c1630-1660), set a precedent in *"Asanteman"* which was to be virtually followed by all his successors. He elevated hard working, loyal and faithful commoners and slaves serving in his court by giving them stools. This buttresses the point earlier made that the clans who settled in *"Asanteman"* were already familiar with the institution of slavery. The third Kumasihene Obiri Yeboah (1660-1697) created four stools for his faithful slaves. Osei Tutu (1697-1717), the fourth Kumasihene and the first Asantehene of the Asante union formed under the inspiring leadership of Okomfo Anokye, created nine stools for his loyal slaves.

Asantehene Osei Tutu rewarded Okomfo Anokye for his invaluable services to the Asante state with a gift of 300 slaves and 100 *Pereguans* (£800). Kumawuhene Okyere Boafo gave Okomfo Anokye 100 slaves and 200 *Pereguans* (£1600). These gifts of slaves would have been unthinkable if the institution of slavery was unknown to the Asante. Slavery became an important part of the Asante state right from its inception. Asante evolved well defined customs and attitudes towards slavery and made slavery an integral part of its political and social structure. For three centuries, Asante became the largest slave trading, slave owning and slave dealing state in Ghana. Asante society became so dependent on slave labour that the smooth running of the state and society was inextricably bound up with the institution of slavery. Slavery as an institution became part and parcel of Asante social and political life.

SLAVERY AND THE ATLANTIC TRADE

.The period from the 15th to the 19th Century A.D. saw the introduction of the Atlantic trade into Ghana with profound effects on the lives of Ghanaians and on the institution of slavery. The first Europeans to set foot on the shores of Ghana in 1471 participated in the existing indigenous southern coastal trade from Senegal to Ghana and acted as agents transporting slaves and other goods from various parts of West Africa to Ghana in exchange for gold. The Portuguese did this for almost a century. The Portuguese thereby boosted the already existing trade and increased the number of slaves Ghana would have otherwise received. The labour pool was increased and this strengthened the institution of slavery. Portuguese supply of slaves became a major means of satisfying the domestic requirements of the states and of individuals in Ghana. Pacheco Pereira reports that because the Kingdom of Benin was usually at war with its neighbours in the 16th century it possessed many captives. The Portuguese took advantage of the unsettled situation and bought a slave for 12 or 15 brass bracelets each or four copper bracelets. The slaves were brought to the Elmina Castle and exchanged for gold. In addition to slaves, the Portuguese brought cotton cloths, panther skins, palm oil and some blue shells with red stripes called "coris" from Benin to exchange for gold. According to Portuguese accounts these goods were highly valued at the Elmina Castle where the Elmina King's chief factor sold them to Ghanaian and other African merchants for gold.

Elmina and other coastal states became more prosperous as a result of the trade with the Portuguese and the other Europeans who followed them. Elmina tradition recounts how the originally small fishing village grew into a big state and great market as result of European trade. According to Feinberg, prior to the Portuguese arrival, Elmina was a small settlement but grew in size, population and wealth as a result of its close relationship with the Europeans resident in the castle. By the 18th century Elmina had become one of the largest and most prosperous towns on the Ghana Coast. The Dutch found the Elmina state confined to a small strip of land to the west of the castle but by 1813, the boundary of Elmina was fixed at the Sweet River to the east.[5]

The Portuguese introduced a new population of different ethnic background to the Ghana coast by bringing in Benin slaves from Nigeria. In Elmina these slaves came to be known as *"Alatas"* (Nigerians). They gradually became part of Elmina's political, military and social life. Of the ten *"Asafo"* companies, one belonged and still belongs to the *"Alatas"* and the company is known as *"Alatabanfo"*. The Dutch and the Danes seem to have followed the Portuguese tradition of going to Benin for slaves for employment as labourers of the European companies operating on the coast.

On the Accra coast, the Ga Mashi divided the non-Ga residents into three quarters. *"Otublohum"* was the quarter for the Akwamus who had ruled the Ga in the 17th and 18th centuries; the *"Abola"* quarter consisted predominantly of Fante fishermen, but also resident in this quarter were slaves who worked for the Dutch; the *"Alata"* (Nigeria) quarter comprised slaves from Benin in Nigeria who worked as labourers of the English Company. In the course of time these non-Gas became incorporated into the governmental structure of the Gas. The Ga Mashi system of succession was influenced by the presence of the Akwamu, resulting in the adoption of a matrilineal form of succession alongside the original patrilineal system. Titles and offices were conferred on non-Gas who exhibited outstanding qualities such as bravery and wealth. In the middle of the 18th century, Kodjo, a slave of the English Company resident in the *"Alata"* quarter rose to become a linguist. He rose further to become the first *"Alata Akutso Mantse"* (Alata quarter chief). He was provided with a chief's stool by Otublafo of the *"Otublohum"* quarter. Kodjo's influence was so great that he superseded the Mantse of Sempe, the original rulers and owners of the land on which James Fort was built, and the Mantse of Akanmadze. In the course of time, Kodjo's descendants became acknowledged as the *"mantse"* (chief) of the whole of James Town, comprising Sempe, Akanmadze and Alata.[6] The European presence had added another dimension to the indigenous institution of slavery.

In the interior states of Ghana, trade with the Europeans on the coast influenced the economic policies of some of the states. The Akan families and clans who dispersed from the region of the Pra and Ofin basins were people who had been enriched by their trading and agricultural activities. They moved to areas of great economic wealth and potential where they not only engaged in local trade but also established trade links with the Europeans on the coast. Because of their wealth, they also became powerful and so imposed their rule in the areas where they founded states. States like Akyem, Akwamu, Asante and Denkyira which subsequently emerged strove to secure effective control over the gold, ivory, kola nuts and other forest products of Ghana. They engaged in slave-raiding expeditions to provide slaves to work the gold mines in order to provide gold to the European traders on the coast in exchange for European goods.

The European presence on the coast definitely influenced the indigenous institution of slavery. From the 15th to the middle of the 17th century, the international economy of Ghana was based on gold exports. The intense demand for gold influenced the propensity for slave labour. European introduction of guns and gunpowder from the 1650s onwards further influenced the indigenous institution of slavery. There was a proliferation of wars in Ghana, mostly aimed at acquiring slaves for sale to the European companies and individual European merchants. Ghana became a major source of slaves. Daaku laments that between 1642 and 1650 the Gold Coast which had been a gold mine both literally and figuratively for the Europeans, now became a "slave mine" for virtually the whole of Western Europe.[7] In the 18th Century, European visitors to the country questioned why the country was called the Gold Coast, because in reality it had become part of the slave coast. Many of the townships which grew up around the European settlements on the coast became important ports through which slaves were sent out of the country. In the 1720s, a British trader called William Smith came to Ghana and exclaimed in amazement "why this is called the Gold Coast I know not!"[8] Ghanaian traders in the early 18th century began to ask for gold in exchange for slaves. It was really a case of "carrying coal to Newcastle". Ghana which had been receiving slaves from other African countries for internal use from the 1st to the 15th Century A.D. now became a major supplier of slaves. This trend exerted an impact on indigenous slavery. Although the trans-Atlantic slave trade was not responsible for creating the institution of slavery in Ghana, it did have a profound effect, both positive and negative, on indigenous slavery.

It is clear from the above account that by the 15th Century A.D. the institution of slavery was known and practised in virtually all the states that had been established in Ghana by this time. The institution began from Neolithic times. As more state building activities took place in Ghana from the 16th to the

18th century, slavery became woven into the state's political, social and economic organisation. The beginning of the trans-Atlantic slave trade in Ghana from the 16th century onwards added impetus to indigenous slavery. The period covered by this book witnesses the full development of indigenous slavery as an institution.

Chapter

3

SOURCES OF SLAVES FOR DOMESTIC USE
FROM THE 15TH TO THE 19TH CENTURY

Oral and documentary records on Ghana indicate five major sources of domestic slaves during the period of slavery and the slave trade. These were warfare, market supply, pawning, raids and kidnapping and tribute. The minor sources included gifts, convicts, communal and private sales or deals.

(A) MAJOR SOURCES OF SLAVES
(i) Warfare
Prisoners of war were enslaved and they constituted a large proportion of the total slave output. Oral data collected from 1990 to 2002 show 31% of the respondents indicating that warfare was a very important source of slaves. The percentages for the other sources of supply were as follows: market supply about 26%; pawning 10%; raids and kidnapping 10%; tribute 10%. These five sources accounted for 87% of total supply with the minor sources accounting for the remaining 13%.

This oral data is supported by documentary evidence. In 1681 an English trader at Komenda bought 300 slaves without much effort. A year later he could only obtain 8 slaves after combing the entire coastline from west to east. His informants told him that there was a shortage of slaves because the country was at peace.

The French trader Barbot observed in 1682 that when the inland countries were at peace there were no slaves available on the coast, but whenever there was war, it was possible to get 400-500 slaves in a fortnight or three weeks. According to him when the Akwamus were at war with the Akyems, the town of Ladoku, on the Adangme coast and its citizens have a considerable number of good slaves to dispose off; for whilst those two inland nations make war, most of the prisoners are conveyed to Lay and Accra and sold to the Europeans. "The Achim blacks commonly carry their prisoners to Lay and the Aquamboes to Accra. In time of war 400-500 slaves are loaded into ships in a fortnight or three weeks."[1]

Barbot noted that Accra, a tributary state to Akwamu in the 17th century, in time of war supplied as many slaves as were sold all along the rest of the coast. He observed:

> Slaves are for the most part people taken in war...the Gold Coast in times of war between the inland nations and those nearer the sea will furnish great numbers of slaves of all sexes and ages; sometimes at one place and sometimes at another, according to the nature of the war, and the situation of the country between which it is waged. I remember, to this purpose that in the year 1681, an English interloper at Commenda got 300 good slaves, almost for nothing, besides the trouble of receiving them at the beach in his boats, as the Commenda men brought them from the field of battle, having obtained a victory over a neighbouring nation, and taken a great number of prisoners.[2]

Twenty three years later, the Dutch trader Bosman confirmed that "most of the slaves that are offered to us are prisoners of war which are sold by the victors as their booty".[3] Bosman went on to assert that the chief occupations in Ghana were commerce, agriculture and warfare. He remarked:

> The most potent negro can't pretend to be insured from slaves; for if he never ventures himself in the wars it may easily become his lot.[4]

Throughout the 1700s and 1800s prisoners of war were a vital source of slave supply. An English traveller called Gordon remarked in 1874 that prisoners of war constituted the largest proportion of all the slaves exported from the coast. Daaku affirms that all the available evidence suggests that it was the victims of wars and raids that provided the bulk of slaves. Indeed European traders on the coast noted that wars "made gold scarce but Negroes plenty".[5]

In the early decades of the 19th century, Asantehene Osei Bonsu told Dupuis that it was Asante custom to take back home large numbers of captives after success in war. He explained:

> I cannot make war to catch slaves in the bush like a thief. My ancestors never did so. But if I fight a king and kill him when he is insolent, then certainly I must have his gold, and his slaves, and the people are mine too. Do not the white kings act like this?[6]

The wars which were fought in Ghana from the 15th to the 19th century were primarily wars intended to deal with specific acts of provocation or wars of expansion, conquest and self defence. Slaves were accidental by-products of these wars. Pieter de Marees found wars calculated to deal with specific acts of provocation so rampant in Ghana in the early 1600s that he cynically re-marked:

> As they are haughty and jealous of one another they easily find a reason to make war on one another. But the wars do not last long; they are started with great speed and also quietly ended. They very easily make war on one another and are so haughty that one will not tolerate the other; and consequently they immediately challenge one another to take the field and wage a battle.[7]

In 1661 Mueller noted that though the states in Ghana were constantly at war with one another the wars were short-lived and dealt with specific provoca-tion. The Asebu were enemies of the Fante and Etsi; Eguafo was always at war with Adum while Accra frequently fought Agona and "Ecqueah". Fetu whose main enemy in the 1660s was Abramboe, either enslaved its prisoners of war for life or took some of them to a distant part of the coast to be sold. Abrem, described as "good warriors" on the Dutch map of 1629 fought numerous wars with its neighbours particularly the Eguafo, Fetu and "Akanists".[8]

In the northern part of Ghana the Mole-Dagbani states comprising Mamprusi, Dagomba, Gonja as well as the Mossi states embarked on wars of conquest and expansion right from the founding of the states from the 11th to the 18th Century A.D. In all these wars captives were enslaved and these states became important slave suppliers. The strategic position of these states contributed immensely to this role. They were positioned between the Niger bend and the Volta River and this enabled them to play a "middleman" role in the trade between the desert, savannah and the forest belt. To the north of them they exported slaves, gold and kola nuts, while to the south they exported slaves, horses, cattle, donkeys, sheep, farm implements, copper bars and coloured native cotton cloth.

Southern Ghana experienced seemingly interminable wars of conquest, expansion, and defence in the 17th century. In 1658 Valkenburg, the Dutch official at Elmina reported a long drawn out war between the states of Twifu, Adansi and "Akan". Twifu was the first Akan state to crystallise in the forest region of southern Ghana into a political entity under the hegemony of the Aduana clan. After the death of the fifth king, a succession dispute broke out and this led to the breakaway of a section of the royal family led by Otomfo Asare. They eventually founded the Akwamu state. This breakaway weakened Twifu which was ultimately conquered and annexed by the Denkyira towards the end of the 17th Century A.D. Twifu was succeeded as the leading state in the forest by Adansi which in turn lost the leadership of the congeries of Akan states in the Pra and Offin basin to Assin during the second half of the 17th Century. By 1660, Assin had extended its sway as far south as the coastal regions occupied by the Etsi and the Abramboe. These struggles and battles led to large-scale enslavement of people. Indeed Dapper reported in 1670 that "the kingdom of Akanien are rich in slaves and gold and are great traders as well".[9] The Akan states in the Pra and Offin River basins had become great suppliers of slaves mainly as a result of the numerous wars they had engaged in.

From the middle of the 17th century onwards, the Akwamu state embarked on a multiplicity of wars during which captives were enslaved. With the conquest of Accra in 1680 Akwamu came to control directly the maritime trade in gold and slaves. The Akwamus embarked on frequent wars against the Akwapims. They also conquered the territory between Accra and the Volta. Wars were also fought in Krepeland and Kwahu.

The Akyem state was a slave holding society throughout the 17th and 18th centuries. Barbot remarked in the 17th century that "the blacks of Akim are very proud and haughty and rich in gold and slaves".[10] Reindorf said of the Akyem that "they neither sold nor killed their prisoners as the Akwamu did, but kept and naturalised them".[11] The gold and slave trade was Akyem's most important economic activity in the 17th and 18th centuries. The gold trade dominated the economy of Akyem until about the third decade of the 18th century when it was replaced as elsewhere by slaves as the dominant export-able commodity. According to Romer the Akyem sent only a "few slaves" but plenty of gold to the coast during the early part of the 18th century. In 1731 a combined force of Akyems and Accras numbering 40,000 marched to Akwamu. Although the Akwamus sustained heavy loses they were not de-feated. The Akyems and the Accras made many prisoners and gained large spoil. In January 1733, King Akwonno of Akwamu laid siege to Accra for four months. The king of Accra sent two of his chiefs to Akyem to ask for help from Baa Kwante, Frempong Manso of Akyem Kotoku and Owusu Akyem. After a sharp combat with the united forces of Akyem, Accra and Akwapim, Akwamu was defeated and many prisoners taken. Akwamu was driven back from the Akyem peak to beyond the Volta. Owusu Akyem re-turned to Akyem with "very numerous Krepe and Akwamu captives".[12] Oky-enhene Baa Kwante (1727-1742) changed Akyem's policy of keeping the pris-oners internally and decided to sell some of them. Thereafter the slave trade became popularised. Trade caravans from Akyem to the coast carried as many as 2,000 slaves.

Feinberg observes that:

> The 18th century in southern Ghana can be characterized as a time of turmoil. Warfare, the threat of war, or rumours of war were very prevalent. These were often confined to a particular area such as Agona or Juffer or Ahanta, but were sometimes widespread covering the whole "upper" or "lower coast".[13]

Reindorf recounts the numerous encounters between the Anlogas on the eastern, and Adas on the western side of the Volta from 1750 to 1776. In 1750 it was the Anlogas who were defeated. In 1776 the Anlogas won the upper hand when they formed an alliance with several ethnic groups and attacked the Adas. On both occasions prisoners of war were enslaved by the victors. On the latter occasion it is said that "one half of the population were killed, great numbers were made prisoners".[14]

Between 1822 and 1823 an expedition was organised by the Accras against Akropong. Over 100 people were brought to Accra. "Some were killed and the rest sold into slavery".[15] In 1829 a dispute arose between two towns at Krepe, Adahokoe and Ahodome. With the assistance of the people of Kpalime, the Ahodomes attacked the Adahokoes and "took prisoners in large numbers".[16] In that same year the Accras, Aburis, Begoros and Akwamus attacked the Krepes. Over 2000 Ahodomes, men, women and children were captured. Enslavement of war captives continued to be the norm in the wars which broke out in 1858 between the Gas and the Krobos; in 1866 between the Adas and the Awunas.

Fanteland also experienced more than its fair share of wars in the 18th and 19th centuries. In all these wars captives were enslaved. According to Van Seveshuyser "a majority of the states thought of nothing but war" because of a plentiful supply of firearms.[17] Baidoo-Debey adds that Elmina experienced "frequent and unbearable" attacks from its neighbours.[18] Between 1720 and 1721 Fante attacked Agona and Fetu. In 1726, 1738, 1740 and 1780 there were four attacks on Elmina by Fante with Anomabu, Eguafo, Asebu, Fetu and Abrem. In 1739- 40 the Fante war against Elmina was aimed at ruining Elmina and making the wives and children of Elmina slaves. The Fante were defeated by the Elmina people with the support of the Dutch. The 19th century wars in Fanteland were mainly attacks from Asante.

The newly created Asante confederacy was involved in numerous wars in the 18th and 19th centuries. Asante conquered and annexed Banda and Dagomba in the Northern Region; Takyiman in Brong Ahafo and Gyaman in parts of modern Brong Ahafo and modern La Cote d'Ivoire. During the same period Sefwi in the west and Twifu in the south were conquered. In the south east Asante attacked Akyem, Kwahu, Akwapim, Akwamu and Accra. According to Reindorf, Asante attacked Banda because Worosa, the king of Banda made a practice of seizing and killing Asante traders in his territory. Asantehene Osei Kwadwo declared war on him, defeated him and took plenty of prisoners. In 1742 two bloody battles were fought between Asante and Akyem. Akyem was defeated and Asante captured 4,000 prisoners.[19] Addo-Fening records that in 1764, Asantehene Osei Kwadwo destroyed Kyebi, the Akyem capital, executed more than 400 Abuakwas and sold others into slavery. Osei Kwadwo again defeated Okyenhene Obiri Koran (1765-1783) in 1772, chased him out of his kingdom in early 1773 and replaced him in 1775 by his younger brother Twum Ampofo.[20]

The wars in Ghana continued unabated in the 19th century. Reindorf relates that from 1807 to 1823;

> the Asantes were lords of all the countries between their kingdom and the coast. Most of the best kings and chiefs as well as the greater part of the population had been crushed and brought over to Asante as captives for life.[21]

In 1807 Asante waged war against the Fante for harbouring two Assin chiefs, Tsibu and Aputae. According to Governor White:

> Hundreds of men, women and children were carried up to the Ashantee country; some were sold to the ships and traders, and many have been sacrificed at the several customs made by the king, for relations and principal men killed in the war.[22]

In 1809 the Asante army defeated the Fantes at Kormantse and moved on to Winneba and Awutu, attacking and destroying the towns. As a result of these attacks, Asante opened a traffic in slaves between Accra and their war camp for a number of months. Between 1811 and 1816 Asante attacked the Fante again and sent many captives to Kumasi. According to Bowdich, as a result of the Asante invasion of Fante in 1811 and 1816 "thousands were dragged into the interior".[23] On 23 May 1817, Simon Cock, in his evidence before the Committee on African Forts stated that half of the inhabitants of Winneba had been carried away by the Asantes in 1816.[24] Between 1811 and 1816 Asante had several encounters with Akyem, Akwapim and Krobo. Vast numbers of Akyem, Akwapim and Krobo were made prisoners. The women and children of Abotakyi who had been harboured at Eburumaso were also captured and carried off to Asante.

In 1820 Asante attacked Gyaman. According to Reindorf, almost all successive monarchs of Asante from the time of Osei Tutu had to carry on war against Gyaman either to suppress rebellion or to obtain tribute. When the Gyaman king Adinkra, a tributary king to Asantehene Osei Bonsu made for himself a golden stool similar to that in Kumasi, he was attacked and killed. "Immense treasures and numerous prisoners were taken to Asante".[25]

In 1868 Asante invaded Krepe and took home a large number of captives. In 1873 Asante invaded the coast again and took away numerous captives to Asante. In 1892 Asantehene Prempeh I invaded the Nkoranzas and Mos and sent many prisoners to Asante.

The high incidence of warfare from the middle of the 17th to the 19th century, was fuelled to a large extent by the exigencies of the Atlantic slave trade. An increase in the supply of firearms, an insatiable demand for labour in the American mines and plantations as well as the extreme profitability of the trade in slaves provided added incentives for warfare. Christian relates that due to the demand for slaves by the various European factors on the coast, the Akwamus were forced to wage wars of aggression on their vassal states. Akoto states that Akwamu proper had little gold and ivory and since it could not conquer Akyem which was very rich in gold, it diverted its expansionist forces to the slave coast - east of the Volta - in an effort to control the slave trade.[26] In the 1720s the demand for slaves by the Dutch, English and Danes far outstripped demand for other commodities. The wars which the Akwamus fought were largely aimed at getting slaves to satisfy European demands.

The activities of the great Mandinka warrior Samory Toure in the northern part of Ghana in the 19th century, created an additional source of slave supply. Samory's expansionist activities and campaigns began around 1870 when he made Bissandugu his capital. From here he moved towards Bamako and his power was felt north of the Niger. Between 1870 and 1887 Samory built a great African empire out of the social and political crisis which engulfed the peoples of the Guinea coast and the southern savannah. In the 1890's Samory's forces moved to the northern part of Ghana. He defeated Gyaman in 1895 and moved on to Banda and Dormaa. He established his headquarters at Djimini in modern La Cote d'Ivoire and sent his son Sarantye Mori eastwards to make contact with the commercial towns of Bonduku, Bole, Buna and Wa. By late 1895 Samory's forces had occupied these towns and for eighteen months they spread throughout the north. Samory's agents entered into the Dyula trading network and opened new markets for slaves. In addition Samory established slave camps in the Northern and Brong Ahafo parts of Ghana and in parts of modern Burkina Faso and La Cote d'Ivoire. Samory obtained food, horses, ammunition, cloth etc. by exchanging slaves. He found slave trading and slave dealing very lucrative activities. Akan traders flocked to

Samory's slave camps to purchase slaves. Adansi oral traditions remember Samory as *"Samonoo nnonkofo wura"* (Samory the slave master).

In the 17th century the leading suppliers of slaves in Ghana were the Akwamu, Akyem, Denkyira and the Mole-Dagbani. In the 18th century the Akyem, Asante and Mole-Dagbani were the major suppliers. The greatest suppliers of slaves in the 19th century were the Asante, the Mole-Dagbani and Samory Toure.

(ii) Market Supply
Numerous markets were scattered across the length and breadth of Ghana during the period of slavery and the slave trade. The establishment of the markets also led to the development of an intricate network of trade routes connecting the markets within states, between states and between the various African regions and countries. In the 15th century the trans-Saharan routes facilitated trade and communication between Ghana and its neighbours. Map III shows the slave markets and the slave routes in Ghana. In the 18th and 19th centuries Asante's control and influence over peoples and states outside the modern boundaries of Ghana also helped to strengthen trade ties between Ghana and its neighbours. In the early 1870s, the priest of Krachi Dente in the Volta Region gave Captain Glover a list of ethnic groups who were either under Asante control or experienced some kind of Asante influence. Some of these groups were a hundred miles beyond the present boundaries of Ghana. Among these were Yendi, Sablagu, Karaga, Gambaga, Suguruku near Dahomey, Kopiala east of Ouagadougou and Gando east of Sansanne Mango.

From oral and documentary data collected one can identify over 60 slave markets the people of Ghana had access to during the period of slavery and the slave trade. Three of these markets were outside the boundaries of modern Ghana. In what is today Burkina Faso, oral traditions mention the Ouagadougou market. In modern La Cote d'Ivoire the Buna and Bonduku markets were important for slaves. In modern Upper East, Upper West and Northern Regions of Ghana there were 4 slave markets, namely Salaga, Yendi, Bole and Wa (See Map III). Salaga was the most famous of the markets not only in those regions but also in the whole of Ghana. In every region of Ghana, where field work was conducted, Salaga market was always mentioned as the first and most important market.

In what is today the Brong Ahafo and Asante Regions there were 5 notable slave markets at Kintampo, Atebubu, Bono Manso (Abam), Begho (Hani) and Sampa. In the Volta Region traditions describe the middle Volta and the northern areas as thriving areas for slaves and point to Kete Krachi as the most famous market in the region. According to Johnson, the traditions of Aveme Tokor mention slaves, salt, oil and pottery as some of the commodities traded at the Aveme Tokor market. A tradition of Ninapon suggests that this market was already in existence in the 1830s.[27] During the period of the Atlantic trade, Keta on the Volta Estuary became an additional market and port for slaves. The markets in the Greater Accra and Eastern Regions were in Kyebi, Gyadam, Anyinam, Krobo, Abonse, Ayawaso, Ladoku, La (Labadi) and Accra Central. In the Central Region, Cape Coast, Assin Manso, Assin Fosu, Agona and Moure were the important slave markets. In the Western Region Debiso, Takoradi and Sekondi were the notable slave markets. All the inland markets listed in modern Ghana so far add up to 33.

With the introduction of the Atlantic trade from the 16th Century A.D. onwards, all the European castles, forts and lodges on the coast and virtually every coastal town from Assini in the west to Keta in the east developed a slave market either around the fort or in the town. The coastal markets numbered about 30 (See Map III). All the inland and the known coastal slave markets number 63. If one added the 3 markets outside Ghana the grand total would be 66.

The markets were supplied with slaves acquired through warfare, raids and kidnapping, tribute and from the personal stocks of individual and professional traders. It seems quite clear from the detailed account given on warfare in Ghana that the kings and chiefs who waged wars had three options as to the disposal of the war prisoners. In the first option they could use them domestically in the state; in the second option they could send them directly to the coast to be exported through the Atlantic trade; and the third option was to sell them at any internal market of their choice. Ward records that Denkyirahene Boa Amponsem made Denkyira the principal state for the Dutch traders. Its gold was abundant and remarkably pure, and its wars with neighbouring kingdoms made it as important a source of slaves for Elmina as Akwamu was for Accra. Ward further relates how the internal markets were swelled with slaves obtained through raiding and warfare.

> The great slave market at Manso, near Cape Coast was largely kept supplied from the Ashanti wars. The Banda war brought thousands of slaves into the market at Manso.[28]

During the Komenda wars of the 1700s, abundant prisoners were sent to the coastal markets for sale. The Akwamu and the Akyem wars of the 18th century, and the Asante wars of conquest and expansion from 1700-1896, contributed in a great measure in swelling the slave markets particularly those in the southern part of Ghana.

Towards the end of the 17th century and in the first few decades of the 18th century, slave raiding and kidnapping became an established occupation among the Akwamu, Akyem, Kwahu and Fante in Southern Ghana; among the Krepe in the Volta Region and among the Mole-Dagbani and Mossi states of Northern Ghana. The markets in the north and south received their supply of slaves from this source also.

States in Ghana which received tribute in slaves and other goods from conquered states often satisfied their domestic need of slaves first, before disposing of the surplus on the slave markets in the north or south.

The Hausa traders from modern Nigeria and the Mossi traders of Burkina Faso were the professional long distance traders. Together with Samory Toure they supplied the markets in the Upper East, Upper West, Northern, Brong Ahafo and the Volta Regions with slaves.

The Slave Routes

Map III identifies nine main slave routes in Ghana during the period of slavery and the slave trade. These routes are based on oral and documentary data collected from 1990 to 2002. These routes have been labelled I-IX on Map III.

Ghanaians were free to ply any of these routes to visit any market of their choice for their slave supply. Kumasi was the centre from which all the slave routes in Ghana radiated northwards and southwards. These routes were also trade routes for the other goods required for the import and export trade of Ghana. It is paradoxical that Kumasi which was the cross-roads of all the trade routes had no known slave market. Traditions however talk of a few slave transactions between individuals living in Asante. Kumasi's commanding position in Ghana's trade could be attributed to two factors. The first factor was its strategic position. It was not far from the point where the forest and savannah met. The second factor was political. As a result of the wars of conquest, expansion, aggression and retaliation that Asante engaged in, virtually the whole of modern Ghana came under its control. Asante became the great overlord recognised by nearly every state. Political power re-enforced economic and social authority. What follows are brief comments on the nine routes identified on Map III.

Route I was the route that linked Kumasi with the Sampa slave market in the modern Brong Ahafo Region. Sampa was further linked to the Buna and Bonduku slave markets of modern La Cote d'Ivoire. A small branch of this route was connected to the Debiso slave market in the modern Western Region. Route II linked Kumasi to the Wa and Bole slave markets in the Northern Region of Ghana. Route III linked Kumasi to the Kintampo slave market in the modern Brong Ahafo Region and with the central provinces of Buipe and Daboya in the Northern Region. This route provided traders and travellers access to Ouagadougou in modern Burkina Faso and Jenne, in the Western Sudan. Route IV connected Kumasi to the Atebubu slave market in modern Brong Ahafo Region and to Salaga and Yendi slave markets in the Northern Region. From Yendi there were two routes. One route went to Hausaland in modern Nigeria and the second route went to Sansanne Mango. Another branch of Route IV linked Atebubu to Kete Krachi. From Kete Krachi another route went to Abomey in Dahomey (modern Republic of Benin).

Southwards Route V connected Kumasi to Accra. There were several minor southerly branches of this route linking the Ga-Adangme coastal towns of Ada, Ningo, Prampram, Tema, Nungua, Teshie, La (Labadi) and Osu, as well as the Gomoa town of Senya Breku and the Effutu town of Winneba in the modern Central Region of Ghana. Route VI also led southwards from Kumasi to Assin Fosu, Assin Manso, Anomabu and Cape Coast, in the modern Central Region. In Daaku's opinion, Anomabu was the most important slave market on the coast, while of all the inland markets Ward considers Assin Manso to have been the "great slave market".

Route VII connected Kumasi to Elmina in modern Central Region and Takoradi and Axim in modern Western Region. Branches of this route led to the Ahanta and Fante coastal towns of Komenda, Shama, Sekondi and all the towns between Sekondi and Axim. Route VIII linked Kumasi with the Nzema towns of Assini and Beyin and the whole of the south-western province of Ghana.

Route IX connected Kete Krachi slave market to Akwamu, Ada and Keta. It was a very important route in the modern Volta Region. Kete Krachi was generally regarded as the limit of the navigable part of the River Volta. The Krachi Falls made trans-shipment of goods necessary there. It was therefore a good place to control river traffic. The slave routes from Kumasi, to the mouth of the Volta River passed through Akwamufie, whilst the salt route from Ada passed through Akuse and Amedeka and converged at Akwamufie.

Finally there was a long coastal route beginning from Grand Bassam in modern La Cote d'Ivoire, passing through the Nzema, Ahanta and Fante coastal towns, to the Ga-Adangme towns and through Keta to modern Togo, Benin and Nigeria. This route was the one discovered and later used by the Portuguese when they arrived in Ghana in 1471.

Organisation of the Slave Trade

Ghana's social and political organisation allowed every Ghanaian to engage in the slave trade. Consequently there was private as well as official participation in the trade. With respect to private participation, anyone who had the means could go to any of the markets to purchase slaves for private use. Official participation involved the kings and chiefs. They usually had officials who traded on their behalf. Among the Akan the chief trader was called the *'Batahene'* and he led a team of traders known as *'Batafo'*. They were usually drawn from the *'Gyase'* (Household) division of the palaces. Slaves from warfare, raids, kidnapping and tribute were often held by kings and chiefs because the taking of captives involved state decisions and state prerogatives. Daaku relates that although anybody could sell slaves, not every member of the state was entitled to receive slaves caught in war. Since declarations of war and peace were reserved for the kings and their elders, it was they who benefited most from them. All captives were held by the kings in trust for the state and it was customary for them to reward faithful service and bravery in war with a few slaves. Slave raiding also required a form of official backing since it normally caused inter-state wars.[29] Because of the involvement of kings and chiefs in the slave trade, some of the European travellers and traders created the erroneous impression in their records that it was only kings and chiefs who were involved in the slave trade.

Private and official traders took the slaves they had acquired to any market of their choice, bearing in mind the market conditions and prices being offered at the various markets. At the markets the slaves were sorted out according to their sex and age, priced and exchanged for an assortment of goods. In the Upper East, Upper West, Northern, Brong Ahafo, Asante and Volta Regions slaves were exchanged for cowries, kola nuts, ivory, rubber, iron, copper, textiles, shea butter, livestock, foodstuffs, salt, tobacco, knives and occasionally gold dust. Private and official traders who wanted to buy slaves from the markets also went to any market of their choice with a wide variety of goods to exchange for slaves. In what is today the Eastern, Greater Accra, Central and Western Regions of Ghana, slaves were exchanged for commodities like salt, dried and smoked fish and foodstuffs. With the introduction of the Atlantic trade European goods like guns, gunpowder, cloth, liquor, hardware, provisions etc. became available both in the inland and coastal markets. In dealing directly with the European merchants on the coast, the Ghanaian traders in addition to European goods demanded money in the form of cowries, Pound Sterling or gold dust.

Traders' recollections of their visits to some of the slave markets in the 18th and 19th centuries indicate that the average price for a full grown man was 120 Heads of cowries; a boy of 15 years old 100 Heads of cowries; a small boy or girl 70 Heads of cowries; and a grown up girl 120 Heads of cowries. In 1889 a German traveller called Blinger visited the Salaga market and made this startling revelation:

> 300 cowries are sold for a male slave, 400 for a female slave, 1,000 cowries for a horse, 500 for an ox, and 150 on a sheep.[30]

In 1929, the British anthropologist, Rattray, was informed that a female slave cost 2 shillings while a male slave cost 1 shilling and 6 pence.[31] This was at a time when the indigenous slave trade had been abolished by the British colonial government and a few daring traders were clandestinely continuing with the trade. What is striking in the prices of slaves is that throughout the period of slavery and the slave trade, the price of female slaves in Ghana was more often than not higher than that of male slaves. There was a higher premium on female slaves because of their sexuality and reproductive roles. The Ghanaian experience is confirmed by recent literature which indicates that although the slave population of Africa consisted of men and women, boys and girls, the preference, so far as indigenous slavery and trade were concerned, was for women and girls, whilst in the Atlantic trade the preference was more for male slaves than female slaves. The males were needed in the Americas to perform 'back-breaking' tasks.

Inspite of the services of official traders, ordinary citizens vied with one another to carry royal commodities. The reason was that they enjoyed privileges as 'the king's men' that ordinary traders missed. In addition to the head load that was allotted to such a person, the carrier added his own trade goods. By custom the market was opened first to the royal traders before it was flooded with the commodities of other traders. Thus by carrying the load of the king or chief, a carrier was assured of a ready market. In addition to the above privileges the carriers were exempted from the normal tolls.

The indulgence of the kings and chiefs through whose territories the trade routes passed to the various slave markets had to be assiduously cultivated. Sometimes kings and chiefs had to undertake high level negotiations with neighbouring states for easy passage for their subjects. In 1715 for instance, Ofori, king of Akyem Abuakwa paid about 800 Pounds Sterling to King Akwonno of Akwamu to enable Akyem traders pass through Akwamu to the coast. Ward describes the slave trade in Ghana as follows:

> a vast organization of wholesale dealers, brokers, depots for the collection of slaves. The slave trade, like the cocoa trade of today, was a trade in which the small men could share. The purchasing power of the people depended on it.[32]

SALAGA: THE MOST FAMOUS SLAVE MARKET

Limitation of space precludes a detailed examination of all the 63 slave markets in Ghana. Instead Salaga, the most famous of all the slave markets, will be briefly examined as a classic example of a slave market in Ghana.

Salaga in the Gonja kingdom of Northern Ghana was founded in the 16th Century A.D. by Mande horsemen. In 1744 Asante forces made a successful expedition through eastern Gonja and on to Dagbon. The division of Kpembe in the Gonja kingdom of which Salaga was part became a tributary state of

Asante. Asante maintained a firm control over the Salaga market enabling it to derive much profit from the trade. Salaga was regularly visited by Asante representatives in the market season to collect market dues and tribute and remind other traders of Asante military authority. It is to the credit of Asante that in 1896 the king of Ouagadougou told Ferguson that "20 years ago when Ashanti was in power, the Gonjas and Dagombas dared not break the market regulations".[33] In 1882 when Lonsdale visited Salaga and tried to find out how Salaga became an important market, his informants could not tell. All they could recall was that during the period of Asante domination the importance of Salaga was three times greater than what it was at the time of Lonsdale's visit.

Some travellers and traders who visited Salaga during the closing decades of the 19th century attributed Salaga's importance as a market to its strategic position. In the 1890s Klose observed:

> Its geographical position is even better than that of Kete; it lies still farther north in the Niger bend and nearer to the Niger and is quite near the source rivers of the big Volta stream. Because of its distance from the coast it is independent of it.[34]

In 1888 Von Francois testified to the commanding importance of Salaga. This, he said, made it the trading emporium of the Upper Volta and Niger area. He remarked:

> Three natural waterways coming from afar meet in the neighbourhood of Salaga. The Black Volta from the west, the White Volta from the north and the United Volta thrusts directly south to the sea. Salaga lies in an area in which natural communications meet.[35]

Salaga had a great advantage over all the slave markets in Ghana as a result of its strategic position. It was linked to the western and central branches of the trans-Saharan trade routes and consequently connected to two of the four main routes linking West Africa to the Sahara and North Africa.

Traders from Ghana and outside Ghana flocked to the Salaga market. The Mossi traders from modern Burkina Faso brought slaves, livestock, cotton, sheabutter and mats to Salaga. The Hausa traders from modern Nigeria brought slaves, livestock, cowrie shells, woollens, carpets, silks, leatherware, silverware, iron pots, copper and brassware. Traders from Gyaman in modern La Cote d'Ivoire brought woven and sewn cloths while traders from Timbuktu supplied shawls and tobacco. There were also traders from Kano and several other towns of the Niger River Region as well as traders from North Africa. No wonder Von Francois remarked in 1888 that Salaga market was

> the best place for the anthropologist, ethnographer and linguistics student who wants to study the people of the Niger. Not only all the products of the Niger bend, but also all the tribes of the Niger come together here.[36]

Oral data collected during field work in all the ten regions of Ghana from 1990 to 2002 indicate that Salaga market was regularly visited by traders of virtually every ethnic group and state in Ghana. It appears, however, from traders' journals and travellers' accounts that the principal traders were the Akan of Asante, Brong, Kwahu and Akyem. This was because one of the major items of trade highly demanded in Salaga was kola nuts. The kola nuts grew only in the forest areas and these were the areas inhabited by the above mentioned Akan people. The nuts were in great demand in West Africa and North Africa. A few writers mention the qualities and uses of the kola nuts which help to explain its popularity as a commodity. Bonnat, for example, found in the nut three remarkable qualities – the power to sustain the body without food and without a feeling of hunger; the absence of thirst when no water can be obtained; and the removal of all sleepfulness. These qualities were of immense value to the trans-Saharan traders plying the long caravan trails. Cohen explains that since Islamic orders forbade smoking and drinking of alcohol, Muslims found kola a substitute for cigarettes and drinks.[37] The nuts were also exchanged as gifts, used as drugs for certain illnesses and offered to guests at ceremonies. The nuts had stimulating effects. Kola nuts continued to be an important commodity in the northern trade well into the 20th Century A.D.

In addition to kola nuts, Ghanaian traders from the south brought to Salaga market ivory, rubber, sometimes gold dust, salt, tobacco, calico, dried fish and European goods like liquor and cloth from the coast. The items from the coast were either bought directly on the coast by Akan traders, or they were brought to Asante by Fante traders; or they were transported via the land routes and the Volta River by the Fantes and other traders in the Volta area. The period of trading in Salaga was the dry season which lasted from December to April. Traders who arrived in Salaga at the beginning of the rainy season had to wait at Yendi. One reason was that there were no kola nuts for sale during the rainy season.

Salaga market was divided into two sections. One section was for foodstuffs like yams, rice, maize and goods like textiles etc. The other section was for 'human ware'. There were also two principal sessions in the market. The first session was often a morning market and it was conducted under shades and stalls. The second session was the market held in the open air. Some of the commodities for sale were laid on mats. It was often in the second session that slaves could be found. They were chained together in groups of 10-15 by the neck and waist of one to another and they waited in the open air, under the burning sun for purchasers. Other slaves were fastened to a long rope with iron shackles on their legs.

During the closing decades of the 19th century, two Ghanaian missionaries who visited Salaga were amazed at the plenitude of slaves at the market. Theophil Opoku observed that more than 800 slaves were brought to the market by the professional Mossi and Hausa traders and they readily found purchasers. On 14th March 1877, David Asante witnessed the arrival of Mossi and Hausa traders accompanied by 400 slaves. Five days later, he saw another group of 350-400. He was informed that in the 'olden days' travellers estimated an annual turnover of about 15,000 slaves in Salaga market alone.[38] It is not surprising that the traveller Klose remarked: "It is only thanks to the slave trade that Salaga has become so famous".[39] Wolf observed in 1889 that:

the slave trade is especially energetically carried on in Salaga. The whole importance of Salaga is so closely connected with it that the possible attempt of a power to suppress it would lead to a great war.[40]

After Sir Garnet Wolseley's invasion of Asante in 1874, Salaga reasserted its independence from Asante. Dr. Gouldsbury reported that before the fall of Kumasi there were hundreds of Asantes resident in Salaga. According to Opoku, they comprised officials, weavers and traders. An entire quarter of the town had been occupied by Asantes and the doors of the Lampour mosque had been made by Asante carpenters. In 1876, Dr. Gouldsbury wrote that:

> As soon as the intelligence arrived at Saraha [Salaga] that the white man had taken Coomassie, and that the Ashantee forces were scattered and broken, the Sarahas seized all the Ashantees in their country (and they were counted by hundreds), and killed everyone of them, thus taking reprisals for bitter wrongs they had for years helplessly and hopelessly groaned under.[41]

After the burning of Kumasi by Wolseley, Asante trade with Salaga declined and the bulk of it was diverted to Kintampo and Atebubu. Between 1874 and 1904, Kintampo and Atebubu assumed the role of the Salaga market. Hausa and Mossi traders came to these markets with slaves, livestock, blankets and other goods to exchange mainly for kola nuts. Many of the traders involved in the Salaga trade became involved in the Kintampo and Atebubu markets. In 1904, Hausa traders at Atebubu announced their retirement from the kola nut trade. One of the reasons was that the abolition of the slave trade had deprived them of the means of porterage. The slave trade shifted to Kete Krachi. The Germans encouraged slave traders to pass through Northern Togoland to Kete Krachi. They allowed Mossi and Hausa traders, Samory and Babatu slave caravans, kola nut and rubber traders to buy and sell slaves at Kete Krachi, a practice which had been forbidden in British territories.

(iii) Pawning

Pawning was basically the act of offering a person as security for money borrowed. The pawn became a pledge, a mortgage or a security for what a person owed. The pawn worked for the creditor who fed and clothed him/her until the debt was paid. Pawning had been a common practice in Ghana right from the beginning of the formation of states and kingdoms. It was also a very common practice in most African societies.

Several factors brought about pawning. The major factor was indebtedness. In 1602, Pieter de Marees made this observation:

> The slaves found here are, firstly, poor people who are enslaved because they are unable to earn a living; secondly persons who owe their king some fine which they are unable to pay, so that they are condemned to slavery by the king as a form of payment. Thirdly, there are young children who are sold by their parents because they do not have the means to bring them up or feed them. The slaves are obliged to serve people under whom they were put throughout their lives...[42]

In the 1680s Barbot reported that some people became slaves in Ghana "through extreme want in hard times" and some were "insolvent debtors".[43] Pawning was not slavery but pawns who were not redeemed found themselves in slavery. So long as the debt remained unpaid the pawn remained with the creditor. If he/she died before the debt was repaid, the borrower had either to clear the debt or provide a new pawn. If the money was never repaid the pawn and his/her descendants ended up as slaves. In 1751 the Dutch were asked by one of their soldiers to free his mother, who though originally a pawn had recently been sold as a slave and was being held in the Elmina castle.

Christian records that among the Akwamu, men and women who owed debts were sold into slavery during the 17th and 18th Centuries to recover the debts. According to Ward petty chiefs could sell into slavery people who lost their cases in their courts and could not pay their fines. Ordinary citizens could sell their debtors.[44]

Addo-Fening states that in Akyem Abuakwa indebtedness became a major cause of slavery in the 19th Century. Litigation, funerals and consultation fees for the priests of the various gods, put many people into debt and such debtors were often forced to pawn themselves or their relatives. In extreme cases debtors sold themselves or their relatives outright into slavery.[45] Pawning was practised by kings, chiefs and individuals. There is an interesting record of King Addo Dankwa of Akropong pawning his nephew called Adum to the Asante taxmaster Owusu Afriyie in the 1830s. King Addo Dankwa had promised General Amankwa of Asante that he would be punctual in paying the annual tribute to the Asantehene; and when he defaulted on one occasion he pawned his nephew with the hope of redeeming him as soon as possible. In the 1860s the Basel missionaries reported several cases of pawning in Akyem Abuakwa. At Kukurantumi one of the Christian converts, Moses Yaw Badu who had been pawned for 4 pounds to pay funeral expenses of a relative was saved from bondage by a kind-hearted man who advanced him the money to pay his debt and work it out.[46]

In the late 1890s the Kumasi Ankobeahene (Chief of Internal Security) called Yaw Chein pawned 9 people in the town of Odumase, one of whom was his own son. In 1907 a Wenchi girl was pawned by her father Yaw Moshi to an Asante woman.[47] Table I on the next page shows the extent of pawning as a component of slavery based on the questionnaires administered in the field from 1990-2002 in all the ten regions of Ghana.

It will be noticed from Table I that slaves obtained through warfare ranked first, with a total of 95; slaves obtained through direct purchase particularly at the slave markets ranked second, with a total of 80; slaves obtained through indebtedness or pawning ranked third with a total of 29; slaves obtained through raids ranked fourth with a total of 19.

TABLE I   HOW SLAVES WERE OBTAINED IN THE PAST

SAMPLE AREA	100	200	300	400	500	600	700	800	NA	TOTAL
UPPER WEST	4	—	3	5	4	2	—	—	3	21
UPPER EAST	1	1	—	4	—	2	—	—	4	12
NORTHERN	8	—	2	—	1	—	—	—	4	15
BRONG-AHAFO	6	—	3	—	4	—	—	—	7	20
ASANTE	9	2	—	7	—	2	—	—	31	51
WESTERN	16	1	4	7	—	3	1	—	30	62
CENTRAL	7	1	8	5	4	1	1	1	5	33
EASTERN	14	2	5	21	—	3	3	2	21	71
GT. ACCRA	7	—	—	5	—	1	1	—	16	30
VOLTA	7	—	6	14	1	3	—	—	30	62
Unidentified	16	—	1	8	—	2	—	—	4	31
TOTAL	**95**	**10**	**29**	**80**	**10**	**19**	**6**	**3**	**155**	**407**

Meaning of the Codes:

100 — *War*		95
200 — *Capture*		10
300 — *Pawning/ Debt*		29
400 — *Purchase*		80
500 — *Barter*		10
600 — *Raids*		19
700 — *Gift*		6
800 — *Betrayal*		3
NA — *No answer*		155

At the beginning of the 20th century, when the British colonial government decided to abolish pawning, there were protests from Asante. In 1908 the chief and Elders of Manso Nkwanta insisted that pawning should be maintained because the "institution was essential to the poor".

(iv) Raids and Kidnapping

Table I shows that eight out of the ten regions in Ghana indicated through the questionnaires administered between 1990 and 2002 that raids contributed significantly to slave supply. The regions which indicated otherwise were the Brong Ahafo and Northern Regions (see Table I). It is clear however from documentary sources that all ten regions of Ghana were involved in slave raiding and kidnapping.

In Southern Ghana Barbot indicated in the 1680s that some slaves were

> sometimes stolen away, out of their own countries by robbers, or spirited by kidnappers, who often carry away many children, of both sexes, as they find them about the country, being sent to watch the cornfields of their relations.[48]

Reindorf records how after the conquest of Accra by the Akwamu in 1680, cultivation was confined close to the towns because of the incessant inroads and kidnappings by the Akwamus. "Accra was in an unsettled state by the incessant kidnapping and plundering by the Obutus and Akwapims". Reindorf also noted:

> The kings of Akwapim who tried in vain for several years by inroads and kidnapping to subdue the Akra, were more successful with the Krobos and Shais, who were their neighbours and depended on them for the lands they cultivated. We must admit that the Krobos themselves were first rate kidnappers...[49]

In 1707, Sir Dalby Thomas described the people of Abrem on the Fante coast as "but a poor inconsiderable people... not having 500 arms in the country and yet very troublesome even kidnapping Asante traders".[50] Around 1710 acts of robbery and 'panyarring' were committed against the servants of the Dutch Company by the Fante. The neighbours of the Elminas subjected the town to constant attacks and protracted sieges aimed at capturing the town. The roads leading to the farms and trade paths became dangerous to tread, because the Fantes laid ambush and kidnapped them. Life became insecure because Elmina could be attacked at any moment of the day. A British report of 1760 noted that when trade was bad the Fante went to Akyem, Akwapim and beyond to raid for slaves. The Fante became so notorious as slave raiders and kidnappers that Rev. Quaque of the Anglican Church at Cape Coast thought that the commonest method of acquiring slaves during the period of slavery and the slave trade in Ghana was through raiding.

Reindorf relates how the people of the Volta Region, the Akwapim Ridge, the Ga-Adangme and the Effutus engaged in slave raiding and kidnapping. Between 1733 and 1777 'men stealing' was very prevalent among the Akwapims. Accra women were also not safe at Mlefi and other Volta towns when they went there to buy corn because of raids and kidnapping. Around 1740 there was a great famine in Accra and people were obliged to travel to Ningo and the Volta towns to buy corn. This led to a terrible increase of 'panyarring and man-stealing', and many Accra women were sold. Some were lucky enough to be redeemed by their relatives, but others were kept in captivity for life. The Ningos would kidnap people from 'any town' into slavery.

One of the reasons why permanent peace between the Anlogas and the Adas proved impossible in the period 1782-1784 was the 'panyarring' or forcible seizure of men and property belonging to other people in payment of long-standing debts. From 1749-1809 the Effutus kidnapped Accra women and children into slavery. In the late 1830s Okuapemhene Addo Dankwa looking for means to pay his annual tribute to Asante and redeem his nephew pawned earlier, sent word to the Krobos that they should open a new market for pots because the Akwapims needed earthenware vessels. He sent about 14 heads of cowries as a bait to the market of Kwagyefo. The Krobo women responded to this call by sending plenty of pots to the market. The Akwapims who were hidden in the bush captured 77 women. King Addo Dankwa paid the Asantehene with 70 of them and sold the remaining.[51]

Although Asante obtained most of its slaves through warfare and direct purchase at the slave markets, it was also involved in some slave raiding. Ward states that Asante obtained a majority of its slaves through warfare and raiding. The Tribu people, between Kwahu Dukoman and Adele, east of the Volta River, told Cornevin that they were not much troubled by Asante raids because their chief gave a present to the chiefs of the Asante armies so that they would not advance into the state. Kpando tradition relates that the Peki people were raided annually by the Asante when the river was low. Consequently Kpandu and Nkonya people claim they moved away from sites nearer the river to higher and safer sites to avoid such raids.[52] In 1884 the king of Adansi asked the British colonial government to use its good offices to bring back his children who had been kidnapped and carried off into slavery by an Asante man. Raiding and kidnapping were also practised by the Akyems. Kidnapping was resorted to on a small scale for the procurement of slaves for sale outside the state. In pre-colonial times two aggrieved members of the Kyebi royal family settled in one of the Accra villages and made it a habit of seizing and selling Akyem traders into slavery.

Of all the southern states of Ghana, the Akwamu state earned the greatest notoriety for slave raiding and kidnapping from 1530 to about 1870. At their first capital in Nyanoase, the Akwamus plundered, raided and kidnapped passing traders as well as their neighbours. Reindorf asserts that "The Akwamus lived upon war and plunder ever since the kingdom was established at the foot of the Akim peak".[53] Between 500 and 600 slaves were sold to European slave dealers by the Akwamu king through raiding and kidnapping every month during the 16th century. The Akwamu carried on the same policy beyond the Volta. "Many towns were devastated by repeated attacks, kidnapping, extortion etc. Many parents were bereft of their children".[54] Between 1530 and

1730 any Akwamu who met his countryman on the coast "would, very often entice him to the forest and sell him".[55] At their new home in the Volta gorge, the Akwamu possessed the same characteristics of plundering, fighting and trade which had characterised their activities at Nyanoase. They soon made their influence felt in the Ada hinterland through marauding attacks and closing of the paths. It was as a result of the marauding attacks of the Akwamu upon Akyem Kotoku traders at Dodi that Dompreh, chief of Akyem Kotoku invaded Akwamu. This invasion developed into the third Krepe war.

In the second and third decades of the 18th century, special organisations emerged in Akwamu concerned solely with raiding and kidnapping free men and free women into slavery. These organisations terrorised the countryside at night and seized any unfortunate persons who might be around. They were then sent secretly to the coast for sale. Kings Akwonno (1703-1725) and Ansa Kwao (1725-1730) had their own bands who raided neighbouring territories especially the Krobo lands. Members of these bands or organisations were nicknamed "siccadingers" by the Europeans.

According to Ward, one of the causes of the clash between Akwamu and Accra in 1733 was the Akwamu practice of

> waylaying and robbing Akim and Fante people and selling them as slaves to the Dutch. This practice was locally known as panyarring.[56]

Between 1839 and 1842 the Akwamus reduced Krepeland to such a "deplorable and wretched condition" through raiding, kidnapping and warfare. Akoto states that the Akwamu raided their subjects whenever they needed slaves. Bands of warriors seized people and sold them into slavery. Sometimes inhabitants of whole villages were seized and sold.

With respect to Northern Ghana, District Commissioner Cardinall reported in 1927 that the Upper East, Upper West and Northern Regions of Ghana were permanent reservoirs for slave hunting and slave raiding expeditions. He noted with dismay what he called "islands of anarchy" in the Mossi and Dagomba states. Cardinall stated that slave raiding had only recently ceased and that every year the Kokombas engaged in slave raiding and kidnapping. The Dagbon people raided the Dagarti, "Grushie", Kanjarga, Frafra, Kusasi and Lobi peoples. It is Braimah's contention that under Asante domination, the Northern peoples made sacrifices by going to war to obtain slaves to pay to the Asante representatives. It was common sight to see the Kpembe contingent in "Grushie" country hunting for slaves to give to their Asante masters. The "Grushies" suffered a lot from raids and kidnapping. The climax of slave raiding was in the 1880s and 1890s.

Around the 1880s the Muslim raider Mossa caused a lot of havoc in the Upper West, Upper East and Northern Regions of Ghana. He was followed at the same period by the Zabarimas. They conquered and controlled a vast area stretching from Ouagadougou in modern Burkina Faso to Wa in Ghana. Some of the leaders who made their mark were Alfa han dan Tadano, Alfa Gazare dan Mahama, Babatu or Mahama dan Issa and Isaka Karaga dan Aljima. Of these four Zabarima leaders, the one whose name is often mentioned in oral traditions in Ghana is Babatu. As a result of their conquests and raiding activities, the Zabarimas opened two important slave centres at Kasena and Walembele. Kasena was their capital town. The victims of slave raids were sent to other slave markets as well, particularly the Ouagadougou market. The Buwala clan of the Sissala remember another slave raider called Ali Giwa, who was one of Babatu's captains. Ali Giwa raided the towns between Banda and Tumu and created so much distress among the Debi towns that when the British offered them colonial protection they accepted it whole heartedly. As a result of British protection they composed a song: *"Ali Giwa bra tulo ko na naraa tsugagbaga"* (Ali Giwa return and see whether people are still slave trading). In other words they were now free from slave raiding and trading because their new overlords were the British.

(v) Tribute
Tribute paying was a very common practice in pre-colonial Ghana. Reindorf

records that between 1500 and 1660, the old kingdom of Accra extended on the coast to Aharamata, north of Aneho, in modern Togo. The chiefs there were tributary subjects to the Accra king Mankpong Okai and sent him annual tributes and presents. It was the Denkyirahene's insatiable demand for tribute from Asante and other conquered states which provoked the Asante to rebellion that ended with the battle of Feyiase in 1701.

According to Christian, after 1730 the Akwamuhene demanded tribute from the Akwamus who remained in the old Akwamu empire after their defeat. The Akwamu remnants were at Asamankese, Akwatia, Kade, Kwaaman, Tafo, Nkoronso, Maase, Otwereso and Apapam. The chief of Asamankese for example had to send an annual tribute of 500 slaves to the new Akwamu capital in the Volta gorge.

In pre-colonial Ghana, the Asante state stood out as the most demanding state so far as tribute is concerned. Almost all the states Asante conquered from 1700 to 1896 were regarded as tributary states. Wilks asserts that there were many politicians in Asante who held the view that the prosperity of the nation was virtually bound up with the maintenance of the flows of tribute from outlying provinces to the capital. Gyaman, which was conquered by Asante in the 18th century paid tribute in slaves and gold until the early 1900s when the indigenous slave trade and slavery were abolished by the British colonial government. In 1817 Bowdich observed:

> most of the slaves in Coomassie were sent as part of the annual tribute of Inta, Dagomba and their neighbours to Ashante.[57]

All the coastal states from west to east paid tribute in slaves. The exact numbers are however not given in the records. Major Chisholm writing to Sir Charles Macarthy on 30th September 1822, mentioned a meeting at Abora in the Fante state of representatives from Elmina, Accra, Wassaw, Assin and other tributary states of Asante to discuss the alteration in the mode of payment of tribute to the Asantehene. Chisholm wrote:

The slave trade was at its height when these states were brought under the Asante yoke and the taxes imposed on them were receivable in slaves. The great reduction in the value of human beings and the want of purchasers for them, made the king ask for gold or European goods in their stead.[58]

To the north of Kumasi, the states of Gonja and Dagbon paid tribute in slaves and other goods. In 1882 Lonsdale reported that Gonja paid 1,000 slaves yearly to Asante. Wilks relates that in the early 19th Century, Gonja paid 500 slaves, 200 cows, 400 sheep, 400 cotton cloths and 200 cotton and silk cloths annually to Asante. Apart from the slaves received from the Gonja province as a whole, Salaga in the Kpembe division of the Gonja state had to supply Asante with slaves. This must have been due to Salaga's importance as a great slave market. In 1873 Glover reported that Salaga "paid a great sum yearly in money and also some 600 slaves". The missionary Buss was told in 1878 by the 'Crown Prince' of Salaga that in their relationship with their Asante overlords:

> slaves and money were exacted at will and Salaga alone had to provide a quota of 1,000 slaves, cattle and money.[59]

The Salaga people expressed this tribute in song as follows:

> Every year, we had to send 1,000 of our brothers to the Kumasi knife, and to the Kumasi king all our money without grumbling.[60]

Lonsdale also reported that Dagbon paid a yearly tribute to Asante of 1,500 slaves. Other authors like Wilks, Reindorf, Ferguson, Fuller and Cardinall estimate between 500 and 2,000 slaves a year. In addition to slaves, Dagbon paid 1,000 cattle, 1,000 sheep, 1,000 fowls, 400 cotton cloths and 200 silk cloths to Asante annually. South of Kumasi, the southern province of Akwapim paid 1,000 slaves and 300 bags of snails annually to Asante. The Akyem Abuakwa state paid 500 slaves to Asante. Between 1835 and 1838, Akroponghene Addo Dankwa resorted to pawning, kidnapping and raiding in order to obtain slaves to pay the annual tribute to Asante. Many small Ewe chiefships sent 12 men to Kumasi annually. The numerous small districts within the outer provinces to the east of the Volta also paid tribute in slaves to Asante. Kpandu and Nkonya traditions say they paid tribute in slaves to Asante. Ajade tradition claims that the Buem people submitted and paid tribute to the Asante forces in the 1880s.

(B) MINOR SOURCES OF SLAVES

(i) Gifts
One of the commonest minor sources of slaves was in the form of a gift or gifts. In 1700 the Akwamu king opened negotiations with the Akyem who had attacked and sacked two Akwamu towns in 1699. The Akwamu king sent the Okyenhene a gift of 30 slaves, spirits and other goods. After the Denkyira war of 1701, Asantehene Osei Tutu rewarded Okomfo Anokye with 300 slaves; Mamponghene Amaniampong gave Anokye 100 slaves and Kuma-wuhene Okyere Brofo gave Anokye 100 slaves too. In 1730 Akyem bought Asante neutrality with a gift of 500 slaves when it was preparing to attack Akwamu because of the special relationship that existed between Akwamu and Asante. Around the same time Obodai Nyonmo of Aneho, in modern Togo asked for assistance from the king of Accra against his enemies with an inducement of presents of slaves and precious beads. Between 1749 and 1809 Asantehene rewarded General Koranteng Pete who led the conquest of Yendi, with 300 slaves.

Before they embarked on their wars between 1817 and 1823, many Asante chiefs consulted the traditional priests in Accra for traditional medicine through the Accra king. On their return from such wars they sent large presents of slaves to the king of Accra and the traditional priests. In 1829 Captain Aforo was sent by King Akoto of Akwamu to Accra with 12 slaves and some money as presents to King Tackie and his chiefs. A year later, Chief Ankrah of Accra rewarded every chief who had taken part in the Krepe expedition with slaves. Those who benefited from this gesture were the chiefs of Ada, Shai, Osudoku, Krobo, Aburi and Begoro.

Gifts of slaves were exchanged not only between states but also within families. As early as 1602 De Marees observed that it was a usual practice on the coast of Ghana that when the king's children married they were given a slave each as a gift to serve them. Bowdich found a similar practice in Asante where members of the royal family received gifts of slaves from the chiefs.

In Asante it became a customary practice that whenever a new political office or a stool was created, the Asantehene presented the beneficiaries with a number of gifts including slaves. Asantehene Osei Tutu, set this precedent in Asante and all his successors followed suit. In 1817 Bowdich observed that when Agyei was made a linguist of the Asantehene he was presented with a house, wives, slaves and gold. It also became customary to reward people who excelled in the state with slaves.

(ii) Convicts
Convicts were sometimes sold into slavery. In 1705 Bosman reported that the brother of the king of Komenda committed an offence and he was sold into slavery, together with his wife and children. Common prisoners who could not raise a ransom were sold as slaves. If a female slave committed adultery, she was also sold.

In the early decades of the 19th century, Kyebi and Gyadam were the most important slave markets in the Akyem Abuakwa state. The slaves were prisoners of war as well as convicts. In the 1870s, Okyenhene Amoako Atta I (1867-1887) was accused by the British colonial government of selling slaves at Anyinam. The slaves were prisoners of war, pawns and convicts.

(iii) Betrayal
Another minor source of slaves was betrayal or treachery. An interesting example can be found in Romer's account of what happened at the

Christiansborg Castle in Osu in the early part of the 18th century. Romer was an employee of the Danish Guinea Company. One day while on duty an Akwamu man visited the castle and inspected the goods in the store house. He told Romer that he liked the fine goods on display and it was a pity he had nothing for payment. He then left the castle and returned about half an hour later with his wife, apparently to help him select the goods. Little did she know she was going to be exchanged for the goods. After they selected the goods, a pre-arranged scuffle occurred between the castle servants and the Akwamu man in the course of which the man's wife was seized and chained. As noted earlier in the early 19th century, Akroponghene Addo Dankwa tricked 77 Krobo women into slavery by pretending that the Akwapims needed a market for earthenware pots. Ramseyer recalls how the Asante General Adu Bofo tricked a large number of Apollonians into slavery. In the late 19th century, Ferguson reported that the Brong still recalled incidents of betrayal into slavery. Ramseyer, Bonnat and traditional sources relate how the Wusutas were betrayed by Adu Bofo during the 1869 war in Krepeland and were brought to Kumasi and sold as slaves.

(iv) Communal and Private Sales/Deals

There were cases in Ghana where whole towns and villages were sold into slavery. Traditions assert that the town of Ankaase and its inhabitants were sold to the Asantehene. On 30th June 1926 the story was told of the punishment by the Asantehene of the Adontenhene of Kumasi around 1794 for peculation. The punishment took the form of forfeiture of four villages belonging to the Adontenhene. The four villages comprising Dunyani, Essasu, Anwhea and Abira were conferred upon the stool of the ancestor of Chief Kwaku Dua. Between 1916 and 1920 the people of Dunyani, near Kumasi, struggled to liberate themselves from Etipemehene Kwaku Dua who persistently maltreated them on account of their slave status.[61]

Private slave transactions often occurred within states. An old woman from Akwapim recalls vividly how individuals moved slaves from house to house like any trade ware looking for purchasers. She even recalled names of some families who bought slaves through this means. In Asante where there were no slave markets, selling of slaves was carried out on a person to person basis. Oral traditions refer to two main ways in which Asantes were sold. The first was purchase by cash and the clinching of the deal by an additional payment as 'stamping fee' of sorts. This was referred to in Akan as *'wa te no trama.'* The payment of the additional sum rendered the purchase irrevocable. Asantes bought by *'trama'* bore the yoke of slavery till they died. The second was through pawning *('awowa')*.

On 17th July 1907 the chief of Agogo complained to the Asantehene that two of his daughters had been sold by his brother Akumia at Agogo and Bompata respectively. Eight days later it was reported at the Asantehene's court that a woman from Biposo had been sold to a man at Nsuta for 4 Pounds Sterling. On 5th August 1908, one Kwame Boateng reported that his grandmother Efatoo Safour had bought a woman called Efua from the chief of Offinso. In 1921 it was revealed at the Asantehene's court that attempts by an Nkawie citizen to redeem a fellow Nkawie man called Yaw Boakye from slavery was rejected by the Chief Linguist of Bantama because Boakye had been bought by his ancestor not from Nkawie but from an ancestor of one Yaw Nkrumah, a Bantama Safohene.[62]

(C)   THE EFFECTS OF THE ATLANTIC SLAVE TRADE ON THE INDIGENOUS SLAVE TRADE

The institutionalisation of the Atlantic slave trade in Ghana from the middle of the 17th Century A.D. onwards did not supersede the indigenous slave trade. The two systems existed side by side and sustained each other. Sources of slave supply for the Atlantic slave trade remained the same as for the indigenous trade. Warfare remained the major source for both trade systems. Up to the middle of the 17th century, slaves formed a minor import 'commodity' for Ghana. Ghana's major export item then was gold. Ivory also featured prominently in Ghana's list of exports. In the indigenous long distance trade, kola nuts, salt, dried and smoked fish remained the major commodities from Ghana. From the middle of the 17th century, however, slaves overshadowed gold and ivory as the most important 'commodity' in the Atlantic trade and Ghana became a major source of slaves. The period of heaviest exports was from the late 17th to the early 19th century, the period of the development of sugar plantations in the West Indies. This great shift from gold to slaves affected the indigenous system of slavery and the slave trade in many ways.

In the first place the greater demand for slaves for the external market resulted in an increased tapping of the indigenous sources of slave supply. This period of great demand for slaves also coincided with the introduction of guns and gunpowder into Ghana. Incessant wars of conquest, expansion, aggression and retaliation became a feature of the Ghanaian experience. Fynn and Addo-Fening remark:

> Following the large scale introduction of guns and gunpowder from the 1650s onwards and the subsequent proliferation of numerous wars aimed at acquiring slaves for sale to the agents of the European Companies as well as Interlopers, Ghana became a major source of slaves.[63]

The Akyem state which had hitherto been concerned only with the indigenous slavery and had even refused to sell slaves into the Atlantic system became an active participant in the Atlantic slave trade. The gold trade which had dominated the economy of Akyem until about the third decade of the 18th century was replaced by slaves as the dominant exportable 'commodity'.

Akwamu became a typical example of a state which geared all its energies into the supply of slaves for the Atlantic market. It is very clear from the records that the Akwamus waged wars of aggression against its vassal states namely, the Akwapim, the territory between Accra and the Volta River, Krepeland and Kwahu, as part of a general economic policy to capture slaves for the

Europeans on the coast. Bands of warriors seized people and sold them into slavery. A 'witch hunt' for slaves was conducted within the state itself. Akoto records:

> The rulers created 'palaver' in order to find cause for arresting subjects and selling them into slavery. Sometimes inhabitants of a whole village were seized and sold to European traders. Cruelty meted out on the subjects were all means to acquire more slaves.[64]

Wilks relates that when in the middle of the 17th century, five European nations established a presence in Accra to trade in gold and slaves from the interior, Akwamu sought direct access to the coast. With the conquest of Accra in 1680, Akwamu according to Ansah gained control of the maritime trade in gold and slaves.

Akosua Bonsu relates how the small Kormantse town on the Fante coast became a very important slave trading post as a result of the Atlantic trade.

> Rulers and subjects strove to benefit from the slave trade. The routes between the coast and the forests which were used for the gold trade were converted into slave routes.[65]

A second way in which the Atlantic trade affected the indigenous system was in the scale of wars, raids and kidnapping it precipitated. Oral and documentary records relate how large areas of land in the northern part of Ghana were desolated and depopulated by domestic slave dealers. Cardinall referred to 'islands of anarchy' in the Northern Region. In the Volta Region many towns were devastated by repeated attacks. Districts were depopulated and whole tribes were thinned out. Daendels, governor-general of the Netherlands Settlements on the Coast of Guinea, reported in a letter dated 17th June 1816 at 'Great Commany' of the Fante coast that "This district has been much depopulated by the slave trade so that the inhabitants have need of very little farmlands". Irene Odotei considers the depletion of the Ga population to have been a major effect of the wars and invasions of the Ga coast from 1680 to 1742. Some of the Ga sought refuge in the southern part of modern Togo, while many were captured and enslaved. The lamentations of the Kple song below shows the feeling of the Ga towards the dwindling of their population:

> Ani lomo be mo kwraa?
> Aha lomobii fee,
> Nyehe lomobii blublu.
> Oshi Adu kome, lome be mo kokwraa
> Aha Buadzabii fee;
> Naa, Buadza be mo,
> Aha komebii blublu;
> Aha kombii fee;
> Kome be mo kwraa.
> Nye ha Dodebii fee;
> Naa Dode be mo;
> Aha Dodebii fee;
> Naa nye ha Nkranpong fee,
> Nye ha foloi eha Nkranpong fee;
> Wo Atsimbii ameha Nkranpong fee Eta,
> Ameha Nkranpong bii blublu;
> Mua Nkranpong be mo.[66]

Translation:

> Does man have anyone at all?
> They snatched all man's children;
> you snatched all man's children;
> you snatched all man's children;
> Sakumo, men have no one at all.
> They snatched all Olila's children.
> Lo, Olila has no one.
> They snatched all Sakumo's children
> They snatched all Sakumo's children,

Sakumo has no one at all
You snatched all Dode's children
Lo, Dode has no one.
They snatched all Dode's children
Lo, you snatched all Great Accra.
You let uncircumcised people empty
all Great Accra;
Our Akims have emptied Great Accra;
They emptied all the people of Accra;
so Accra is empty.

The Atlantic trade with its resultant increase in wars, raids and kidnapping created a state of insecurity, panic and fear on a scale hitherto unknown. In 1714 Director General Harding lamented that

the kidnapping of people is becoming so common that no Negro whether free or slave dares pass without assistance from one place to another.[67]

John Atkins remarked that the raiders

lay concealed in the woods which surrounded the small villages and made the attack under cover of the night, seizing the people by surprise.[68]

The demand for slaves and the profitability of the Atlantic trade introduced greater brutality and harshness into the indigenous institution. The trade had the effect of making administration of justice in the native courts harsh and callous as enslavement became punishment for many offences which hitherto attracted only fines.

The Atlantic trade provided a ready outlet for what some states claimed to be a redundant slave population. The trade thus enabled such states to control and regulate the size of their domestic slave population. In Asante it became state policy not to allow slaves to outgrow the free population for fear that they would take over the kingdom. Asante had learnt a bitter lesson from the Bonduku war of the early 19th century in which some of its slaves joined the Bonduku against them.

The indigenous slave trade and the Atlantic slave trade were both profitable 'businesses' and states and individuals who had engaged in the indigenous trade embraced the Atlantic trade and reaped much profit. The Asantehene testified to the profitability of the two trade systems during the visit of Bowdich and Dupuis to his kingdom in the early 19th century. It is difficult to get any trade records from the chiefs' palaces or from individual households. Oral traditions assert that both the state and individuals benefited immensely from the two trade systems. Various families put up several houses and lived a wealthy kind of life, for example the Konny and Kabes families. According to Inikori and Engerman the literature on the costs and benefits of the Atlantic trade for Africa generally agree that those who raided and took captives, and the African traders who bought and sold captives, all realised private gains. They assert:

> No quantifiable evidence exists for detailed measurement of the private gains and losses. It is generally accepted that the export centers on the African coast benefited economically and demographically from the trade.[69]

The effects the Atlantic trade had on indigenous slavery became glaring after the Atlantic trade had been legally abolished by Britain in 1807. The traditional sources of supply of indigenous slavery became exhausted or blocked. As a result the supply had been drastically cut by the abolition of the Atlantic slave trade. In 1822 Major Chisholm informed Sir Charles Macarthy of a meeting at Abora in Fante land by representatives of Elmina, Accra, Wassaw, Assin and other tributary states of Asante to discuss the alteration in the mode of payment of tribute to the Asantehene. The Asantehene was demanding payment in gold or European goods instead of slaves because the tributary states were finding it difficult to procure slaves. In 1877 the Basel missionary Opoku visited Salaga and was told that the number of slaves brought to the market by Hausa and Mossi traders had drastically reduced and that in the 'olden days' travellers estimated an annual turnover of about 15,000 slaves.

The extent of Ghana's involvement in the Atlantic trade, the duration of the traffic (about 200 years) and the sheer numbers of victims had significant effects on the country. It has been estimated that between 1620 and 1807 Ghana alone provided about 16% of the total slave output required from Africa by the U.S.A. Between 1733 and 1807 Ghana supplied 13.3% of slaves needed by South Carolina. Between 1710 and 1769 Ghana provided 16% of slaves required by Virginia. In the total English trade Ghana supplied 18.4% between 1690 and 1807 and 12.1% of the total Atlantic trade for the period 1701-1807. The words of Gasper are a fitting conclusion to this section:

> The Atlantic slave trade left its mark on all the societies that it touched, directly or indirectly, in Africa, Europe and the Americas.[70]

The sign post showing the way to the Pikworo Slave Camp in Paga in the Upper East Region.

A tourist and a tour guide by the sign post indicating that Pikworo Slave Camp was a holding place for slaves in transit to the Salaga Slave Market.

This rock at the Pikworo Slave Camp was used in the past to punish slaves who misbehaved. A Tour Guide demonstrating how the slaves sat on the rock with their hands chained behind them.

The Slave Cemetery in Pikworo, Paga.

These stones served as entertainment for slaves as they knocked smaller ones against them to produce music (as in the insert) – Pikworo, Paga.

Hand dug plates in a rock at the Pikworo Slave Market in Paga.

The Gwollu Defence Wall in the Upper West Region.

A demonstration of how the people within the Gwollu Defence Wall fought against slave raiders.

Performers in the Sandema Fire Festival held every year in commemoration of the slave raids that took place in the area.

A dancer in Sandema in the Upper East Region with all the paraphenalia used in the slave raids.

The Nalerigu Defence Wall in the Northern Region.

Piled up rocks at Paga where the slave raiders stationed their guards to prevent possible attack on the Slave Camp.
One can see Navrongo by standing on the rocks.

Salaga Slave Market. The tree in the background replaced the original baobab tree (uprooted by a rain storm) to which the slaves were chained before sales began.

Hand-dug out plates by slaves on a rock in Salaga.

A house in Salaga which was used to keep slaves in transit to the Slave Market. This building is now being used by the Ghana Private Road Transport Union – Salaga.

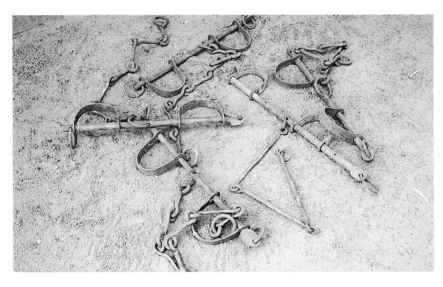

Chains and shackles used for the slaves on display at Salaga.

Dug out wells by slaves at Salaga.

Present day representation of these wells which are still in use.

Broken walls at Salaga, some of the slaves had their rest here.

*This pond served as the place where slaves were given their last bath
before they were sent to the Slave Market.*

The Slave Cemetery in Salaga.

The grave of Babatu, a famous slave raider in Yendi.

*A metal sword believed to have been planted by Ndewuna Jakpa,
a famous ruler and warrior in Northern Ghana on the Salaga – Kito road.
This metal cannot be removed. Legend has it that the day this metal
is removed will be the end of the Gonja kingdom.*

LOCAL USE OF SLAVES
FROM THE 15TH TO THE 19TH CENTURY

As has already been pointed out, slavery was a world-wide institution. Slavery in Africa did not begin with the Atlantic slave trade, and in Ghana the institution pre-dated contact with the Europeans. There were six major uses to which slaves were put from the 15th to the 19th century. First, slaves constituted a reservoir of labour for agriculture, trade and industry; second, slaves were used in the administrative sectors of the state; third, some slaves served in the military; four, slaves performed domestic chores in the palaces of chiefs, at shrines and in individual households; five, a special category of slaves was available for sacrifice in accordance with traditional beliefs and practices; six, personal slaves satisfied the private desires of their owners.

(A)   SLAVES AS FARMERS AND FISHERS

AGRICULTURE – Oral and documentary evidence from the 15th to the 19th century testify to the importance of agriculture in the national economy. Oral tradition of the Fante states stresses that before the arrival of the White man, people in those states were primarily farmers. They produced food crops like rice and yam, fruits and vegetables. When the Portuguese arrived on the coast of Ghana in the 15th century, they noticed a great deal of local exchange in agricultural products. In the 1600s De Marees was highly impressed by the contribution of hard working peasants to the availability of food in the markets. Peasant women supplied the markets with sweet potatoes, yams, maize, rice, oranges, limes, bananas and sugar cane. Barbot observed in the early 18th century that the markets at Great and Little Commany were well supplied with corn, roots and fruits. The food producers were Fetu, Abrem, Eguafo, Ahanta, Shama, Axim, Komenda and "Accanes". From 1700 to 1900 agriculture continued to be a primary occupation in Ghana. Reindorf ranked agriculture as the most important economic activity in Ghana in the 18th and 19th centuries. The importance of agriculture in the colonial period is also well documented.

From the 15th to the 19th century agricultural production in Ghana was almost totally dependent on slave labour. Labour in pre-colonial Ghana, as in most of Africa, was organised on the basis of households and slaves complemented the labour requirements of families. It is also clear from documentary evidence that it was the common people and slaves who undertook cultivation and other forms of manual labour. Agriculture became so closely associated with slavery that in 1875, Rev. Schrenk of the Basel Mission, who had been in Ghana for several years, observed that the pupils passing through his school objected to any form of agricultural work because it was associated with slaves. In 1883, Burton and Cameron, concluded, after examining labour conditions in West Africa as a whole, that the husband traded and fought battles and left sowing and reaping to his wives and slaves. The shift from the Atlantic slave trade to 'legitimate' commerce in the 19th century increased the number of slaves available for use in agricultural production.

> Too often an economy in which the slave was exported, was replaced by an economy in which the slave was employed in farming, or in collecting and transporting agricultural products.[1]

Indeed the development of legitimate trade in raw materials fuelled an extensive use of domestic slaves in local production to meet the demands of the international market. Farming expanded in scale and scope during the second half of the 19th century, partly to meet the demands of external markets. As farming expanded so too did the use of slave labour.

The results of oral data collected between 1990 and 2002 in all the ten regions of Ghana on the uses of male and female slaves during the pre-colonial period are shown below.

USES OF SLAVES IN PRE-COLONIAL GHANA

CODES: *M - Males*   *UW - Upper West*   *WE - Western*
             F - Females   *UE - Upper East*   *CE - Central*
                           NO - Northern   *EA - Eastern*
                           BA - Brong Ahafo   *VO - Volta*
                           GA - Greater Accra   *AS - Asante*

USAGE	SEX	UW	UE	NO	BA	AS	WE	CE	EA	GA	VO	Total
Agric.	M	17	13	10	13	37	52	12	38	23	54	289
	F	9	4	-	2	10	23	2	14	4	18	86
Total												**375**
Procreat.	M	-	-	-	-	6	-	1	1	-	2	10
	F	10	6	11	9	26	18	11	17	3	16	127
Total												**137**
Court Service	M	1	1	3	3	9	6	5	8	1	12	49
	F	-	2	2	-	2	1	2	3	-	-	12
Total												**61**
Commerce/ Industry	M	-	-	1	9	3	10	4	4	5	5	41
	F	-	1	2	5	1	3	2	6	3	18	51
Total												**92**
Miscellanous	M	-	-	-	-	1	-	4	-	1	1	7
	F	2	-	-	-	-	-	-	1	1	1	5
Total												**12**
GrandTotal	**M**	**18**	**14**	**14**	**25**	**56**	**68**	**26**	**44**	**30**	**74**	**396**
	F	**19**	**13**	**15**	**16**	**39**	**45**	**17**	**41**	**11**	**53**	**281**
		37	**27**	**29**	**41**	**95**	**113**	**43**	**89**	**41**	**127**	**677**

From the above data, it is clear that in terms of the utilisation of slave labour, agriculture ranked first with a total of 375 respondents. Although both male and female slaves participated, the employment of males was higher, 289, than that of females – 86. It is significant that this oral data is supported by documentary and oral records covering the period from the 15th to the 19th century. Agriculture involved farming, collecting, livestock rearing, hunting and fishing.

(i) Farming

Before the arrival of the Portuguese in Ghana the indigenous crops grown in the forest were root crops like the yellow and white yam. In the savannah belt the indigenous crops were the root crops and cereals like rice, Guinea corn and millet. Along the coast the indigenous type of rice known as *Oryza glaberlima* was grown. The introduction of a large variety of food crops from the New World by the Portuguese into Ghana enhanced agriculture. De Marees gives a list of some of these crops. They included sweet potatoes, oranges, lemons, sugar cane, pineapple, banana, red pepper, ginger, groundnuts and tobacco. In addition to this list were maize, melon, pawpaw, varieties of yam and rice. The foreign rice was known as *O. Satina*.

From the 17th to the 19th century the popular food crops grown in the savannah belt were indigenous and foreign varieties of yam, millet, maize, rice, cowpeas and beans. In the forest belt the indigenous and foreign varieties of yam as well as cassava and cocoyam were cultivated. Along the coast, fruits, vegetables and rice (both the indigenous type and the foreign variety) were grown, in addition to root crops. Two systems of agriculture emerged: local peasant agriculture and plantation agriculture. Male and female slaves were employed in both systems of agriculture. With respect to plantation agriculture, kings and chiefs as well as some individuals owned large tracts of land on which male and female slave labour was used. In the early 19th century, Bowdich was highly impressed by the numerous plantations he found in Asante owned by individuals as well as the kings and chiefs. Bowdich expressed surprise at the size and orderliness of the plantations. The plantation to him had much of the appearance of a 'hop garden well fenced in, and regularly planted in lines with a broad walk around.' At each wicker gate he saw a hut where a slave and his family resided to protect the plantation. These plantations were generally within 2 or 3 miles of the capital. On these plantations as well as others scattered across the length and breadth of the country, agricultural products consisting mainly of foodstuffs were grown.

In the northern part of Ghana some farmers grew maize, millet, guinea corn and rice. Along the coastal plains maize and rice were grown on large expanses of land. While only the indigenous variety of rice was grown in the northern part, the coastal plains cultivated both the indigenous (*Oryza glaberlima*) and foreign (*O. satina*) varieties. Axim and Ahanta, with their wet soils, heavy rainfall and high annual temperatures were regarded as the sole producers of the cereal. The land around the lower end of the Volta, periodically flooded by the river was another important producer of cereals. In the forests, yams, sweet potatoes, cocoyam, cassava and plantains were grown. A number of vegetables such as okro, onion, garden egg and red pepper were grown throughout the country. Fruits like pineapple, pawpaw, water melon and sugar cane were more popularly grown on the coast. Sugar cane was also grown in the Volta flood plain. Tobacco was grown in large quantities almost throughout the whole country. From the Neolithic period to the end of the 17th century, the method of cultivation was bush fallowing. Along the coast iron implements replaced stone implements, but in the interior, stone implements continued to be used. In the 18th and 19th centuries, bush fallowing continued to be practised and the farm implements employed both in the interior and the coast were the cutlass and the hoe. The plough was unknown, nor were animals used for farm work. From the second half of the 19th century plantation agriculture became export-oriented. Ghanaian agricultural exports between 1850 and 1874 were palm oil, gum, guinea grains and groundnuts. From 1874 onwards other agricultural products such as rubber, timber and cocoa were added. Male and female slaves cultivated food crops for home consumption and for local markets as well as cash crops for export.

(ii) Collecting

The dawn of the Neolithic Revolution did not bring an abrupt end to collecting of food and other plants. Collection went on side by side with cultivation. Each of the two great vegetation formations in Ghana, of savannah and forest had its characteristic wild food plant resources. Throughout the pre-colonial period, male and female slave labour was used in food collecting. In the savannah of northern Ghana some of the important trees whose fruits were collected were shea butter, baobab, tamarind and *dawadawa*. In the forest the two notable wild food plants were the kola nut and oil palm. Along the coast were the oil palm and the coconut tree. Of all the food plants listed above, the kola nut became the most important export crop in Ghana during the era of the trans-Saharan trade.

The kola tree grew wild (and still does) in the forest areas of Ghana. Its area of highest production was the forest belt in Asante stretching from the Pra River to Sunyani (See Map IV). Kola production was of the utmost importance in Asante and other Akan states in the forest like Kwahu and Akyem because it was in high demand by the peoples and traders in the savannah areas of West Africa and in North Africa. Three qualities in the kola nut made it a commodity in high demand. First, the nut was capable of numbing the pangs of hunger and thereby sustaining the body without food. Second, it was capable of suppressing thirst; and third, it had the ability to remove sleepiness. These qualities were of immense value to the traders who plied the trans-Saharan routes. The nut was a stimulant and a sustainable substitute for the Muslims who were forbidden by their religion to drink alcohol or to smoke cigarettes. The nut was also exchanged as a gift, used as a drug for certain illnesses and offered to guests at ceremonies.

Male and female slaves were employed in the picking, preparation, transportation and trading of the kola nuts. The slaves helped in gathering the nuts which fell on the ground when ripe. The gathering required much time and labour. After gathering the nuts, the slaves separated them from their covering or shells and cured them by burying them underground. After some time they were retrieved and packed into travelling baskets or sacks, covered with large leaves to keep them as fresh as possible and transported to the market centres, particularly the Northern and Brong markets. In the Northern markets, Salaga became the most important centre for the nuts and earned the name 'Bini Goro', the town of kola. The role of male and female slaves in kola nut production was so important that the traveller Freeman remarked in the 19th century:

> On the abolition of domestic slavery the kola industry in Ashanti will tend to die out, just as the rubber trade in Akyem languished as soon as the abolition of slavery was proclaimed there. Thus in one way the British annexation of Ashanti (with its accompanying abolition of slave-holding rights) will tend to destroy the caravan traffic by crippling the industry that created it.[2]

During the closing decades of the 19th century, the kola nut was not only exported northwards but also southwards to the coastal ports and sent overseas to Europe and the U.S.A. In the 1870s, Lagos emerged as the principal market in West Africa. Traders from Lagos came to Ghana to buy the fresh nuts and ship them to Lagos in large baskets lined and covered with green leaves. The kola nut continued to be an important export commodity well into the 20th century.

(iii) Livestock rearing

Some male slaves were employed in rearing livestock in both the northern and southern parts of Ghana. In the southern part, livestock rearing was usually a subsidiary occupation to farming. In the northern part it was often a separate occupation. The most important animals which were reared were cattle, sheep, goats, pigs, horses and asses. The horses and asses were reared in the tsetsefly free areas of northern Ghana. They were kept more as a means of transport than as beasts of burden. Male slaves sent the animals out in the morning to graze and returned them in the evening. They would look for watering points such as streams and dams and make sure that the animals were well fed and watered. They would watch them closely throughout the day, protect them and take good care of them. In the night they would pen the animals. They also helped milk the cattle.

(iv) Hunting

Hunting was practised both in the forest and the savannah areas of Ghana and was predominantly a male occupation. Some male slaves were employed in hunting for individuals as well as for the kings and chiefs. In a number of traditional histories it was the slave hunters of kings and chiefs who discovered new land for settlement. Hunting was a specialised skill and individual masters and members of royalty had to train their male slaves to enable them to be part of this profession.

Asante oral tradition relates that what is today the Ahafo District of the Brong Ahafo Region was the hunting ground for the king and chiefs of Asante. Male slaves employed the skills they had acquired from their training in the palaces in this region. Some notable hunters were Adu Boahen and Adu Bofo ('*Bofo*' in Akan means a hunter).

Hunting involved the catching of game for food and for sale as well as the killing of elephants for their tusks. The latter was a very dangerous and risky job and male slave labour was employed. Throughout the pre-colonial period, ivory was one of the important exports from Ghana. In the savannah areas hunting was usually done during the day. The hunters moved in groups for security reasons. They left their homes early in the morning and returned in the evening with their catch. In the forest areas hunting was done at night and in groups. The principal weapons were bows and iron-tipped arrows and spears. A few hunters used the long muzzle-loading gun. The hunters were often accompanied by dogs. The slaves brought all the game to their owners who distributed them as they saw fit. Traditionally the thigh of every game was given to the chief.

(v) Fishing

Fishing was an important economic activity all over the country. Along the coast of Ghana, fishing was a primary economic activity. Male slaves were employed both in inshore fishing which was usually done in the night and in pelagic fishing. In pelagic fishing, the hook and line or large fishing nets over 100 feet long were used. The Fante coastline was notable for the abundant fish it caught annually which formed an important commodity in local trade. Documentary records single out Axim, Shama, Mouree, Elmina, Asebu, Fetu and Komenda as important fishing centres. Of all these centres Elmina was the most important fishing town. Dapper pointed out in the 17th century that a fisherman was held in higher esteem than a trader amongst the townspeople.

In the Ga settlements farming was the traditional occupation but some sea fishing was done from the 17th century onwards. It was not until the late 19th century that sea fishing became a primary occupation on the Ga coast. A similar pattern prevailed on the coast between Kpone and the Volta with respect to sea fishing. In this area lagoon and river fishing were more popular. Male slave labour was employed in fishing in the inland areas in rivers and lakes. Fishing in the Afram River was for centuries one of the major props of the Guan economy. Lake Bosumtwe was also a popular fishing lake in Asante. In the early 19th century, Fante, Assin and Gyaman male slaves were kept in the settlements around the lake to fish for the king and chiefs. Apart from the Asantehene, several Kumasi chiefs had their lacustrine villages on the borders of the lake from which they drew a regular supply of fresh fish. In the early decades of the 20th century, a British Commissioner of Asante reported that the only example of the fishing industry in the region was that around Lake Bosumtwe. The fish from this lake was said to be greatly esteemed by the Asantes who even while living on the coast, still endeavoured to obtain this lake fish in preference to the salt water fish. Traditional methods employed in fishing in the inland areas from the 15th to the 19th century involved the use of canoes, harpoons, small cast nets, hook and line and basket traps. These methods continued to be employed in the 20th century.

Division of labour in the fishing industry was along gender lines. While the male slaves helped their masters to go fishing, their female counterparts helped their mistresses to smoke, dry or salt the fish for both home consumption and for the local markets. In the 1600s De Marees remarked on the diligence of coastal women whose husbands caught fish from the sea and gave it to them to process and sell. The women, assisted by their female slaves, carried fish over 100 or 200 miles into the interior to be sold.

(B)   SLAVES AND TRADE

From the 15th century to the end of the 19th century, male and female slaves traded for individuals as well as for kings and chiefs. They were involved in three major types of trade – intra-state trade, inter-state trade and long-distance trade.

(i) Intra-State Trade
Intra-state trade was trade conducted in a large number of markets scattered throughout a kingdom or state. Some of the markets in the northern part of Ghana were in Salaga, Wa and Bole. In Asante, markets were held in Atebubu, Kintampo and Kumasi. In the coastal areas Elmina, Cape Coast, Accra, and Keta were important markets. The markets were held either daily or periodically and the commodities sold were mainly foodstuffs. Male and female slaves served as carriers of trade goods while a few others sold and bought goods on behalf of their owners. Female traders overshadowed their male counterparts in this type of trade because it was a convenient adjunct to household and farming activities.

De Marees provides a vivid description of a typical intra-state trade at the Cape Coast market. The market vendors were mainly women (free and slaves), peasant and fishermen's wives. They were all well organised. They knew where they must stand with their goods or wares. Those who came to the market with fruits had their section on one side; others who came with wool, water and bread had their place to sit or stand on another side; there were different sections for chicken, fish, meat, palm wine, rice, kenkey and Dutch linen.

(ii) Inter-State Trade

Trade was not only conducted within states. It was also carried out between two or more states. There was trade between Asante and the Fante states in which Asante received dried or smoked fish or salt in exchange for gold. There was also trade between the Akwapim and the Ga states in which Akwapim supplied foodstuffs in exchange for salt and dried fish. There was also a lot of intra-state trade among the Fante states. Elmina exchanged fish for palm wine, maize and cattle from Fetu, Abrem and Komenda. From Axim, Elmina received fruits, rice and provisions in exchange for fish and gold. Elmina also received foodstuffs from Eguafo, Ahanta and Shama. It was estimated in the 18th century that the produce of the farmers of Elmina would only provide enough food for about three months. This situation forced the Elminans to rely on outside sources for their food supplies. Elmina had fish in abundance and this was a major item of exchange in the inter-state trade. As in the case of intra-state trade, male and female slaves were used as carriers, while others did business for their owners.

(iii) Long-Distance Trade

Long distance trade covered many more states and longer distances. This resulted in the evolution of a complex network of trade routes spanning the length and breadth of Ghana, and connecting Ghana with its African neighbours northwards, eastwards and westwards (See Map III). The trade southwards involved not only states in Ghana but also trade with Ghana's West African neighbours and with the European merchants on the coast.

It is evident from Portuguese records that in the 15th century, long distance traders in Ghana used slaves as carriers, vendors and buyers both within the country and outside the country. In the 16th, 17th, 18th and 19th centuries, traders and travellers into Ghana like De Marees, Barbot, Bosman, Atkins, Muller and Boyle also made similar observations. For example De Marees remarked:

> People of other places in the interior buy many commodities through

their slaves, whom they give a quantity of gold and send to the ships which always lie off the towns. Those slaves buy what the merchants desire, such as linen, woollen cloth, beviesen and beads and then send their slaves or blacks with these goods inland in order to sell them there.[3]

Muller noted that

when the Accani traders had finished making their purchases, they loaded them all into bundles which the slaves carried on their heads. From the sea they went to Assingrad, the first land in the great kingdom of Accani. This was where most of the Accani who lived in Fetu had their homes, wives, children, slaves, farms and cattle. This place was five days journey from Cape Coast, but since the slaves were heavily loaded they could not travel more than five German miles (about 23 English miles) in a day. The path to Assingrad was, therefore, about 115 miles. From here the traders went on through Alance. [4]

Barbot related that the busy Akan merchants carried all the goods they bought on the coast by land on their slaves' backs to the interior markets. Strangely enough, it is only Barbot who makes mention of slaves carrying loads on their backs. All the other traders and travellers cited above mentioned that the slaves carried the loads on their heads. This practice continued well into the 19th century. In 1844 Allen and Thomson met in Accra several traders from Asante with European and Ghanaian merchandise. Everything was borne on the heads of the slaves, both male and female. In the 1870s, Boyle met a convoy of female porters from the interior at Nyankomasi and Cape Coast with their loads carried on their heads. Some of the slaves became such efficient carriers that they earned the title of professional carriers. Such carriers could head load between 55-68 lbs worth of goods and cover an average of 20 miles a day. Most traders and their slaves could cover a total distance of between 100 and 200 miles. Human porterage was very vital in pre-colonial Ghana because there were no railways or motor vehicles. Indeed slaves were the main means of transportation. The trade routes along which the slaves passed "were pathways trampled into being by the feet of countless thousands of traders".

Long distance traders, both free and slave, male and female, moved together in caravans with guards, porters and drovers, as well as a leader, a guide, a treasurer and a quarter master. A caravan ranged from between 1000 to 2000 people. In Akyem Abuakwa, until the emancipation of slaves in 1874, slaves continued to form the core of the trade caravans. With emancipation, free born Akyem, Kwahu and New Juaben, joined freed slaves as porters and carriers. Trusted slaves could be appointed heads of the caravans and put in charge of all the business transactions. Slaves played such a crucial role in the long distance trade that Bosman concluded:

> Those who come from the inward part of the country to traffick with us are chiefly slaves. One of which, on whom the master reposes the greatest trust, is appointed the chief of this caravan. But when he comes to us, he is not treated as a slave, but as a very great merchant, whom we take all possible care to oblige as very well knowing that he being a peculiar favourite of his master, may at pleasure go to the English, Danes and Brandenburghers as well as come to us.[5]

From the description given in traders' journals and travellers' accounts of the organisation and mechanism of trade in Ghana during the pre-colonial period, it was no mean duty for a slave to be asked to transact business on behalf of the owner. The slave had to be familiar with the political situation, the range of tolls and the whims and caprices of the various kings and chiefs through whose territories they passed. The slave had to thoroughly survey the market in order to get a good bargain. The slave also had to make sure that his/her wares were exchanged for quality goods. Those who were asked to trade in gold were very privileged because Muller described gold trading as a 'specialised business'. Successful trading on the coast, for example, required that both

Ghanaian and European traders understood the trading language as well as the complicated system of gold weights involved.

From east to west, west to east, south to north and north to south of Ghana, slaves traded on behalf of their owners in agricultural products especially foodstuffs, fish, salt, hunting products, livestock, products of craft industries, gold, slaves and European goods. In the northern part of Ghana, slaves exchanged kola nuts, ivory and gold for products from the Sudanic belt of West Africa and North Africa. Some of these were cowrie shells, woollens, carpets, silks, leather ware, silverware, brass ware, honey, cloths, mats and shawls. On the coast of Ghana, gold, ivory and slaves were exchanged for European goods like guns and gunpowder, liquor, cloth and provisions. In 1882, Captain Lonsdale summed up the use of slaves in trading ventures in Ghana as follows:

> Traders of all parts of the interior use as carriers, principally slaves. The services of these slaves have been, according to the views of the owners, secured for an indefinite period by the payment of the money invested in their purchase, and the cost of their daily subsistence.[6]

(C)   SLAVES AND INDUSTRY

The important industries in Ghana which used slave labour during the pre-colonial period, were gold mining, iron working, salt-making, rubber production and the art and craft industries such as pottery, basketry, cloth-weaving, wood carving, metal working, soap making, bead manufacturing and polishing, and leather working.

(i) Gold Mining
It appears from documentary and oral evidence that the gold mining industry

attracted the largest labour of all the industries in Ghana. This is not surprising since Ghana had abundant gold which earned her the name 'Gold Coast' from the 15th century.

The gold mining industry in Ghana dates back to antiquity. Gold featured prominently among essential commodities of the trans-Saharan trade during ancient times. Gold was eagerly sought for in Europe from Roman times to the Middle Ages. West African gold gleamed on the crowns and in the coffers of the popes and kings of Christendom. The gold in Ghana was mainly found in areas inhabited by the Akan and this was why the Akan were drawn into the mainstream of the trans-Saharan trade. Archaeological evidence indicates that the ancient gold mines in Ghana were at Jinjini and Chemraso in Dormaa Ahenkro; Nsuhunu, Banda Nkwanta, Jenikrom, Awusu and Atuna in Takyiman area; and in a number of Adansi villages and towns such as Kenyasi, Jameskrom and Jeda. Gold was not only traded across the Sahara, but also within the country and with Ghana's African coastal neighbours. When the Portuguese arrived on the coast of Ghana in the 15th century, they were amazed at the abundance of gold they found on the coast, especially at Elmina. They observed that Elmina was the terminus of the central route from the interior to the coast, from which branches led into the various gold producing areas. They found Mande traders in Elmina who had brought goods like cloth and beads to exchange for gold and salt. They also found trade between Ghana and Senegal, Gambia, Ivory Coast, Dahomey and Nigeria in which Ghana exchanged gold for cloth, cotton, beads, slaves etc.

Between the 15th and 19th centuries, the Portuguese and the other Europeans who followed, exploited the gold resources of Ghana. It has been estimated that between A.D. 1400 and A.D. 1900, the Akan of Ghana produced a total of about 14 million ounces (400 million grams) of gold by traditional methods, and that an average of 40,000 miners may have been at work each year when the gold trade was at its height in the 17th century. Of the gold produced, roughly one-third was carried across the Sahara and two-thirds traded to Europeans on the coast of Ghana.

From ancient times to the closing decades of the 19th century, Ghana's gold was exploited from three geological formations. The first was alluvial gold derived from beds of rivers flowing along the Birimian rock formation. The second was derived from coastal sands found mostly between Apam and Axim. These sands were impregnated with particles of gold brought down, generally after rain, by running water from Birimian rocks. The third was from alluvial deposits, sometimes covered by a laterite crust, occurring on the gentle slopes of old valleys of rivers flowing in Birimian terrain. Ghana was also blessed with large deposits of gold found in the southern region in Birimian rocks, but gold from these rocks could not be exploited during the pre-colonial period because the techniques for separating the gold metal from the hard ore were unknown. (See map V for the gold producing areas).

Panning was the principal means of winning gold from the loose alluvium and the coastal sands and this was usually the work of women. Women, free and slave, as well as children, both free and slave, were involved in this industry. The alluvium was worked throughout the year, but the coastal sands were panned normally after a heavy downpour. Besides, the coastal sands yielded only small amounts of gold. Along the coast from Fante land to Accra, female slaves panned gold using stream placers. Oral traditions of the Ga state of Ayawaso relate that before A.D. 1600 their ancestors were mining alluvial gold for export and that it was only when the Ga found out that their Akan neighbours were producing superior gold that they stopped their own production and began to purchase and sell Akan gold. The same method of using stream placers to directly pan alluvial gold was used in the interior, along the streams and rivers. Wenchi traditions talk about stream placers being used to pan for gold in the streams and rivers of the Tain, Bisi, Atom, Adaagye and Botim. In Asante, slaves collected alluvial gold through panning on the Tano River. Gold was also made available during the rainy season. In the early 19th century, Dupuis observed that during the rainy season there was occupation for between 8,000 and 10,000 slaves for two months. In the Denkyira, Akyem and Assin states, female slaves panned for gold daily. Wilks has estimated that in the 19th century, in what is today the Brong Ahafo and Asante

Regions, a slave panning for gold on a rewarding stretch of river might be expected to win gold to the value of not less than one shilling and six pence a day, rising to three shillings or even five shillings. Valuing gold at a minimum of three pounds and twelve shillings an ounce, and placing output at one shilling six pence per diem, a labour force of 8,000 might be expected to wash 5,000 oz. per month during the rainy season. Barbot lists 24 Akan states which cover what is today the Brong Ahafo, Asante, Eastern, Central and Western Regions of Ghana in which gold panning was practised. In the early 19th century Issert mentioned that the king of Asante had innumerable slaves constantly at work for him in the mountains and that each of these slaves had to collect or produce 2 ounces of gold per diem. During the closing decade of the 19th century, Africanus Horton remarked that the Asante

> do not dig gold themselves, nor will they even pick up dust or coins that fall by accident believing that such are jealously disapproved by the ground fetish; but they have no scruple in making slaves work for them.[7]

The third source of gold from alluvial deposits required hard work. It was a dangerous and risky job because it required mining the gold. It was male slave labour which was predominantly employed to exploit this source of gold because it also demanded much time and labour. In the 1600s, De Marees reported that the gold sold on the coast was found in the earth in the interior in deep pits as well as from some mines not far from the beach near Fetu.[56] He considered this third source of gold as the best gold. He stated:

> The gold which comes straight from the gold hills, without having been worked or molten in the least, is considered the best, once the sand and gravel have been properly blown and knocked out of it.[8]

In 1601, Muller attested to the importance of gold and the gold trade at Fetu and in many of the Akan states. He also related that it was in the rich gold mountains that the best gold sold on the coast could be found. Rich gold was

---

obtained from the mines in Akyem, Denkyira, Aowin, Twifo, Assin, Wassa, Adansi, Kwahu, Tafo and Asante. "The gold of Akyem was and still is the purest and finest". The gold was sold along the coast from Fante land to Ga land. From the 15th to the 17th century it was Elmina which remained the most important port of the gold trade. From the 17th century onwards, Accra on the Ga coast also became important for its maritime trade, especially in gold. Van den Broecke said of Accra "to this place come down indeed the most and best gold of this whole coast". In the 18th century, Barbot described Accra as 'that golden country', whose people furnished the Danes, Dutch and English with more gold and slaves than did the whole Gold Coast.

The first and major part of the mining operations that the male slaves were obliged to carry out was to break through the hard lateritic crust, after which the compacted alluvium underneath the crust was easily dug out with simple hand tools. The slave miners then dug slanting pits with broad steps or deep holes to a depth of between 50 and 150 feet at places where the gold nuggets were found. These holes or steps were known in Akan as *nkron mena*. They ranged between 3-4 feet in diameter. Smaller holes for the feet were dug on the walls to facilitate climbing. To bring to the surface the dug up soils, small cans or baskets to which strong ropes were attached were lowered into the holes, filled up by the slaves inside and pulled up by the slaves on the surface. A mines shaft was narrow enough for a man to rest his back against the wall while his feet rested in the holes cut into the opposite wall. A number of shafts grouped together in an area were often interconnected by subterranean tunnels. The depth of a mine depended on the height of the water table, as there was no means of pumping out water; and on the degree of consolidation of the alluvium.[62] The gold-impregnated earth which was brought to the surface by the small cans or baskets, was crushed and panned. The gold won was of two types: pure gold dust and gold nuggets or rock gold. Gold dust commanded a high price in Europe; lumps of rock gold, some of which were reported to weigh as much as 200 "guineas", fetched a low price because a high proportion of their weight was taken by useless rock.

In the 17th century, Muller reported that no European had ever seen the gold mines "and they were always surprised when told of the skill with which the barbarians mined gold". Muller continued "many slaves lost their lives in mining accidents". The third method of mining gold described above, has been called "Residual Placer Type Mining" by the Archaeologist James Anquandah. In the early part of the 17th century, attempts made by the Portuguese and Dutch to set up gold mining installations in Ghana failed. It was not until the late 19th century that effective European mechanised exploitation of local alluvial and deep mines commenced. Gold production throughout the pre-colonial period was entirely in the hands of Ghanaian chiefs, kings and some individuals. The people of Ghana jealously guarded the secret of the locations of the mines. Attempts by Europeans to collect information on the mines failed, and where the Europeans found gold-bearing deposits on the coast, the localities were declared sacred by the indigenes in order to prevent mining by the Europeans. Failure on the part of the Europeans to observe the religious taboos always ended in great trouble. In 1694 for example, the Dutch brought out geologists from Europe to prospect for gold in a hill regarded locally as sacred, about half a mile from Fort Vredenburgh in Komenda. This resulted in a serious war between the Dutch and the Komenda. An Englishman called Joseph Baggs, who was in the service of the African Company imported mining equipment with which he planned to extract gold from Manku Hill, about 4 miles west of Winneba. His plans came to an end with his death in 1700. Gold mining was often a state controlled enterprise and restrictions imposed on foreigners by Ghanaian chiefs and priests also applied to the common people. Periodic collapse of mines added substance to the warnings of priests against desecrating holy places. Only slaves and authorised free men worked in the mines.

If one considers the fact that the gold mining industry which produced all the gold that was traded to Europe and the Islamic world from the 15th to the 19th century was indigenous and based mainly on slave labour, then the importance of slaves in this industry cannot be overemphasised.

(ii) Iron Working

Archaeological data indicates that iron technology played an important role in the affairs of Ghanaian and West African society. It is believed that iron working reached West Africa during the first millennium. By the 4th Century A.D. iron producing techniques had spread throughout the region. The earliest iron working sites in Ghana can be found at Hani (Begho) and Bonoso in the Brong Ahafo Region; New Buipe in Gonja; Adansi, Akyem Kotoku, and in the Accra Plains. From surface reconnaissance and oral traditions it is also known that many other village and town sites in Ghana established iron extractive industries between A.D. 1000 and 1500.

Local iron called *Atwetweboo* in Akan was smelted and used. From the 15th to the 19th Century A.D., local iron ore continued to be used in the traditional iron working industries and it was supplemented by iron provided by the European merchants on the coast. The local ore was found over extensive areas of the savannah of Northern Ghana, Brong Ahafo and Buem in the Volta Region. Until the 1920s, traditional blacksmiths provided the bulk of iron implements and weapons used in Northern, Upper East and Upper West Regions of Ghana. Male slave labour was employed in the building of iron furnaces and great earthworks characterised by trench systems, banks and deep interior ditches. The slaves also helped to smelt and mould the iron ore. They made iron shields, weapons, an assortment of military metal equipment and agricultural implements like hoes and knives.

(iii) Salt Making

According to Ga-Adangme traditions, the salt industry was the staple in the economy of the peoples of the Accra Plains from the beginning of the earliest settlements along the coastal lagoons and rivers. A similar statement is expressed in Fante oral traditions. The Fante traditions are confirmed in European written records which state that the Etsi (the aborigines) people of Abramboe, Eguafo, Fetu, Asebu, Cabesterra and Akoti developed an industry in salt which was traded from the coast through middle Ghana to the middle of the Niger.

Apart from the coastal areas, salt was also available at Daboya in the Northern Region. Asante and the forest country in general did not produce salt and, therefore, bought large quantities of salt elsewhere. On the coast, practically every settlement had its salt works, but certain areas stood out as major centres of production. Among these were Ada, Anomabu, Mouree and Elmina.

Salt was so important in Ghana's inter-state trade that in 1715 the Dutch factor at Shama reported the arrival of about 10 Asante traders who bought nothing else because "they came to buy salt". In the early 18th century, Asante and other inland peoples visited Elmina and Eguafo on the coast to buy nothing but salt. Some traders from Eguafo also sent salt into the interior for sale. Some of the traders went to "*Serem*" (north), traders from Abrem went as far as Bonduku. These salt traders bought the salt at Elmina in exchange for farm products supplied by the people of Abrem who were mainly farmers.

Salt was either mined or extracted from lagoon and sea water. In both cases male and female slave labour was employed. Daboya salt was mined by the male slaves from rocks and the town remained the major source of rock salt in pre-colonial Ghana. The slaves dug out the salt-impregnated rock, crushed them into containers and mixed them with water. The mixture was then put on fire and boiled till the water evaporated, leaving salt crystals. The salt was extracted from the lagoon or sea water by both male and female slaves in several ways. The slaves dug pits to trap the sea water which was then exposed to evaporation. This process was practised at Ada. The dry season from December to March was the period for making salt through this process. Another method of salt extraction the slaves employed was to put the lagoon or sea water in salt pans and boil the water until it evaporated. This was the method employed at Sekondi, Takoradi, Elmina, Cape Coast, Winneba, Accra and Osu. The quality of the salt extracted from lagoon or sea water was very high. On all parts of the coast except at Accra, the salt was described as quite fine and very white, especially in Fante land. Salt from Daboya was not as white as lagoon or sea salt, but it kept its properties much longer than the lagoon or sea salt which under exposure to heat and dampness soon lost its freshness and savour. De Marees relates that the best salt was from Ahanta and the Songhor lagoon, west of Accra.

Marketing the salt was a very important business and some of the salt makers used their slaves to travel to the coastal markets with the salt for sale. Some professional traders with the help of their slaves, travelled to the salt manufacturing points to collect the salt for sale at the coastal markets. Others went inland, to Asante and the North to exchange salt for gold dust, ivory, cotton cloths and slaves.

(iv) Rubber Production

Rubber production, though late in comparison with the industries described above, also required both male and female slave labour.

Before the 1860s, a Basel Mission agent at Akropong exported some rubber, but this was an isolated event. After 1882 when attention was drawn to the possibilities of rubber production in Ghana by Alfred Moloney, a few Ghanaians on the coast and in the interior began to tap rubber. Up to 1885 rubber exports came mainly from Akyem Abuakwa, Akwapim, Krepe and Wassaw, with Wassaw producing the best rubber. In 1885 rubber stood second to palm oil in value in the list of Ghana's agricultural products. By 1887 rubber production had spread to Asante and the Brong Ahafo Regions. The exploitation of rubber in these regions more than doubled the volume of exports. In 1890 Ghana stood third among the rubber producing countries of the world.

Rubber production was peasant-related. Rubber production required hard work and slave labour was indispensable. Usually after the rainy season the latex dropped to the ground and this was collected by the slaves. Otherwise, the latex had to be tapped. The tapping, preparation, transportation and the actual trading of the product were mostly done by slaves.

There were three main types of traders in the rubber trade and the type of work the slave did depended on the kind of trader to whom he or she was attached. First, there were those who contracted with local collecting agents to obtain supplies, so that they collected the assembled loads without themselves visiting the bush. In this case, the slaves carried the loads of rubber from the centre of production to the export centre. Second, there were itinerant traders who visited bush settlements and collected rubber from the tappers. The slaves in this case travelled with their owners to these settlements and transported loads of rubber to the markets. Third, there were local tappers who carried their rubber to the coast for sale. The slaves in this case had to help in the rubber tapping, preparation and transportation to the coast. The District Commissioner of Axim reported on 10th August, 1899 that:

> I have heard from a fairly reliable source, that a considerable number of slaves are imported up to Ellubo and thence sent into the interior to work at timber and rubber.[9]

All the rubber producing areas established trading posts to facilitate contact between middlemen and small-scale producers and to expedite the 'bulking' of raw rubber to the coast. Some Asante traders went with their slaves to the Brong district to buy rubber, which was often exchanged for kola nuts or sometimes slaves. The notable trading posts were at Nkoranza, Berekum and Bantama.

With respect to the traders who moved from the interior to the coast to sell rubber produced with slave labour, there were also two main types of traders. There were occasional traders and professional traders. Occasional traders made only periodic trading journeys and the rubber they bought from the trading posts was carried by their wives, children and slaves. Professional traders dealt directly with the merchants on the coast. They bought the rubber from the trading posts and used hired labour *('bo paa')* and slave labour for porterage. These traders sold the rubber to a broker or a firm stationed on the coast and engaged in the import and export trade. The rubber was exchanged for textiles, tobacco, spirits and other European goods.

(v) The Art And Craft Industries

Many towns and villages in pre-colonial Ghana had art and craft industries and both male and female slave labour was used. There was pottery, basketry, cloth-weaving, wood carving, metal working, soap making, bead making and leather working. Pottery was one of Ghana's oldest crafts. Almost every region in Ghana had its own pottery industry but Brong, Asante, Kwahu, Akwapim and Ga-Adangme excelled in the industry. The basket industry covered many parts of southern and northern Ghana. Cloth weaving was also practised in almost every region in Ghana, the notable ones being the Northern, Asante, Brong Ahafo and Volta Regions. The Akan speaking areas were popular for the wood carving industry. Metal working was practised in the Northern, Brong, Asante, Volta and Central Regions. In Northern Ghana, the Puda and Navrongo areas were important producers of iron ware. In the Volta Region it was the Akpafu-Santrokofi area which was noted for iron working. In the Central Region the stretch of coast from Otuam to Fete had a high concentration of iron forges. Soap making was popular in the Akan speaking areas, while bead making was a noted craft on the Fante coast. Leather working was confined to Northern Ghana where cattle, sheep and goats thrived and where the hides of these animals were plentiful.

Pottery was traditionally the work of women and it was also hereditary. Pottery makers employed slave women to help in the moulding, baking and selling of the pots. In the basket industry, both male and female slaves aided their owners to produce baskets for the intra and inter-state trade. The early industries in cloth weaving originally produced a special bark cloth known as *kyenkyen* in Akan. Male slaves were made to remove the bark of the tree called *kyenkyen* in long narrow strips. The strips were softened in water and beaten with mallets. After it was treated and dried, it became like a piece of cloth. It was worn throughout Ghana and other West African states right down to the early years of the 20th century. It is believed that from the 18th century onwards cloth weaving was introduced into the Asante and Volta Regions. Asante became famous for its Kente and Adinkra cloths. Cloth weaving was hereditary, passed down from father to son. Male slave labour was employed whenever necessary. Cotton spinning was also associated with cloth weaving and women were mainly responsible for spinning thread. In the Northern, Brong Ahafo, Asante and Volta Regions, slave women helped their mistresses to spin thread. Adansi oral traditions recollect that the spinning of thread was taught to the women by the female slaves who were brought down from the North.

The Akan speaking areas were popular for the wood carving industry. This industry was male-dominated and it was passed down from father to son. Wood carvers employed male slave labour when necessary. The Akan skills of wood carving were already known when the earliest Portuguese made contact with Elmina. Indeed Fante oral traditions trace the use of the wooden stool as a symbol of office back to the pre-European period in Adansi and Brong Ahafo. Wood carvers produced religious work of art, drums, musical instruments, chief's state umbrella frames and tops and stools; household furniture; building materials like doors, architectural wooden panels, frames, posts, lintels as well as canoes.

The most important metals on which craft industries were based were iron, brass, bronze, silver and gold. Black smithing was a very important craft industry. Male slaves helped to produce arrows, spears, hoes, cutlasses and chisels. In the gold smithing industry, male slaves helped their owners to produce gold currency, gold ornaments and gold weights.

Soap making was usually the work of women. Female slaves helped their mistresses to cut the peelings of plantain and later cocoa. The peelings were dried and burnt to ashes and then soaked in water in a basket underlain with a fluffy plantain stuff ('Baha' in Akan). The end product which was collected in a tray was boiled in palm oil and other ingredients until the mixture thickened and settled.

Beads were manufactured from special clay or from granite stones. The male slaves dug the clay and the female slaves moulded it into the shapes they required. By means of a process known as "cire perdue" or "lost wax", the object was heated by fire and after it had cooled down, it was polished. When the Portuguese introduced Aggrey beads into Ghana, the indigenous bead-making industry declined. Slaves helped their owners to polish and clean the Aggrey beads.

With respect to the leather working industry, male slaves helped their masters to make hides from the skins of animals. The hides were used in making saddles for horses, leather clothing and adornment of chiefs' skins, bags, talismans and charms.

(D) SLAVES IN THE ADMINISTRATIVE SECTORS OF STATE

In practically all the centralised political states in pre-colonial Ghana, slaves were recruited into some of the administrative sectors of the state. These centralised political states included the Akan, Ga, Adangme, Ewe, Gonja, Dagomba, Mamprusi and Wala. Among the Akan of Asante the basic political structure consisted of the chief as the executive head assisted by the Queenmother. Next in the hierarchy were two senior Elders or sub-chiefs. Of the two the 'Krontihene' was in charge of the army assisted by the other, the 'Akwamuhene'. The next important officials were the clan chief ('Abusuahene'); chief of the Left wing division of the army ('Benkumhene'); chief of the Right wing division of the army ('Nifahene'); head of the Advance guard ('Twafohene'); head of the main body of the army ('Adontenhene'); head of the chief's bodyguard ('Ankobeahene') and the head of the Rearguard ('Kyidomhene'). The head of the household division (the 'Gyasehene') was the next in rank. Other senior officials were the linguists ('Akyeame').

The Head of the Household division (the 'Gyasehene') was usually a slave. Under him were various sub-divisions which were also manned by slaves. These were the stool carriers' sub-division; the drummers' and horn-blowers' sub-division (i.e. the music department); the umbrella carriers' sub-division; the sub-division of caretakers of the royal mausoleum; the bathroom attendants' sub-division; the 'soul-washers' sub-division (i.e. the religious department); the elephant-tail switchers' sub-division; the fan-bearers sub-division; the hammock carriers sub-division; the floor-polishers' sub-division; the minstrels' sub-division; the gunbearers' sub-division; the heralds', sword-bearers', shield-bearers' and assistant linguists' sub-division (i.e. the diplomatic corps); the financial sub-division and the kitchen department. Finally there were the eunuchs, the attendants and the executioners.

The Household Administrative division also had its female counterpart in the Queenmother's Palace organisation. Thus while male slaves dominated the royal Household division at the Chief's palace, female slaves were the predominant members of the Queenmother's palace administration.

The Head of the royal Household had onerous responsibilities. Apart from co-ordinating the work of the various sub-divisions and making sure the palace administration ran well, he was also in charge of the chief's personal bodyguard. The 'Gyasehene' also assisted in the running of the affairs of the state. He was additionally charged with the conduct of diplomatic and trade relations and the collection and disbursement of state revenue. Sometimes the Head of the Household had an assistant to help him, in the person of the 'Gyasewahene'. Slaves who excelled were given higher administrative positions and responsibilities. Indeed it was in the Household ('Gyase') division that one sees conspicuously the role slaves played in the political life of centralised states in pre-colonial Ghana. No wonder Lewin described slaves as politically indispensable to Ghanaian society. In 1927 De Graft Johnson, assistant secretary for Native Affairs remarked:

> The system of chief's rule is closely related to the domestic slaves system. In fact it subsists on it. A free people are always difficult to handle...it is quite possible that primitive communities like those in the Northern Territories might be disturbed by an investigation regarding the extent to which slavery still forms a part of the local domestic arrangement or political economy. It may break up compounds or weaken the authority of the local chiefs.[10]

The importance of slaves in the administration of the state is further borne out by the Okyenhene's outburst against the Basel Missionaries at Kyebi in 1870:

> Must I let my horn blowers, my drummers, my pipers, my sword bearers and executioners, my hammock carriers etc. become Christians? If I do, then I can no longer carry out my ceremonies, nor can I receive foreign embassies worthily. Whoever has an obligation to serve me will never be allowed to become a Christian.[11]

In November 1906, when it seemed that the British colonial administration was contemplating the abolition of the indigenous institution of slavery in Asante, the chiefs and elders of Adansi wrote to the British commissioner responsible for the southern district thus:

> The freedom of every slave we beg to say that is impossible for we Ashantis to do...What could the kings, chiefs, and headmen do, if these are set free? All our drums, blowing horns, swords, elephant's tails, basket carrying and farming are done by these, as we have no money like Europeans to do necessaries for us...and how can we kings and chiefs attend any calling by the government at Obuasi or Kumasi while we have nobody to carry us, beat our drums, blow our horns, carry our swords, and other necessary things.[12]

The chiefs and Elders were in no mood to risk the destruction of Asante's political, social and economic institutions which were inextricably linked to slavery.

(E)   SLAVES IN THE MILITARY

The centralised political states of pre-colonial Ghana enlisted male slaves into their armies. Tilleman said the king of Akwamu had the "best and most skilled slaves in the whole land for war". The Akan armies consisted generally of five major divisions – Advance guard, a Main body, Right and Left Wings and the Rear guard. In each of these divisions, male slaves could be found. Some slaves were actually given command positions in battle. This gave them the opportunity to display their valour which was invariably rewarded with honours from the king or chief. The Ananta stool, for example, was created by Asantehene Opoku Ware for Ofosu for boldly repulsing an attack by Apotwe, the chief of Assin.

Apart from actual fighting on the battlefield, slaves performed other tasks in times of war. They fetched firewood and water, food, clothing and other necessary items, and ran errands. All slaves in the Household division were automatically members of the royal bodyguard. They accompanied the king or chief to war whenever he went himself. When there was no war, they stayed with him, guarding him and keeping an eye on daily events at the court. Asantehene Osei Kwadwo instituted the Nkonsong and Hyiawu as special bodyguards from Banda male prisoners. In 1817 Asantehene Osei Bonsu possessed 'a guard of foreigners' (natives of Nkoranza).

Under Asantehene Kofi Karikari the Asante army was modernised The task of re-organising and modernising the army was entrusted to Prince Owusu Ansah. New regiments of professional soldiers were created and male slaves were conscripted into these regiments. In addition to slaves, free men from the northern Region of the country were recruited into the army. Wilks observes that:

> The tradition was already an old one, of incorporating into the army units of those loosely described as "Hausa", i.e. of those of foreign origins who tended to use the Hausa language as a lingua franca. Reindorf reported a tradition that the armies of Opoku Ware which invaded the Akyem country in 1742 included Hausa mercenaries...There was a Hausa component in the Asante army in 1874.[13]

Asantehene Mensah Bonsu, followed the precedent set by his predecessors and recruited soldiers, 'principally foreigners', into the modern regiments.

Many of the recruits to the Hausa regiments were unfree subjects of northern origins, belonging to Asante chiefs who reluctantly surrendered them to the central authority for enlistment.[14]

The 'Hausa' force of the modernised Asante army numbered between 300 and 400 men by early 1879. By 1881 it had increased to about 1,000 men. The senior posts in the army were given to Asantes. The 'Hausa' were deliberately excluded from positions of command "lest they became too powerful and identified themselves with the cause of the Muslims of Salaga". The modernised army was equipped with breech loading rifles, sniders and Martini-Henrys. These replaced the obsolete flintlocks which had remained the principal weapon of the Asante forces in 1874. Prince Owusu Ansah served as the Inspector General of the modern Asante army. With the aid of a British drill book, he evolved a basic training programme and secured the services as drill instructors of a West Indian and a Fante soldier. The quality of the training was such that the Bekwaihene Yaw Poku equipped 60 of his personal troops with sniders and sent them to Prince Owusu Ansah in Kumasi for training. The 'Hausa' army was given uniforms. They wore blue baft tunis and a red fez with blue tassel.

Service in the modern Asante army at the end of the 19th century was unpaid for slaves, all others were paid. New and raw recruits were paid twice monthly at the rate of either 18 shillings or 9 shillings per month of 42 days. The rates of pay enjoyed by the recruit depended on his status. Trained men were paid between 12 and 16 dollars a month.

The exact numbers of slaves recruited into the armies of centralised states in pre-colonial Ghana is difficult to tell. The documents are filled with comments like "slaves formed a sizeable proportion of the labour force and military strength in certain areas". With respect to slaves received as tribute by Asante from Dagomba, Mamprusi and Mossi "the majority were retained in Ashanti as fighting men, not sold to Europeans". In 1817, Bowdich attempted calculating the population of Asante from its military force. He estimated a population of one million and a force of 346,000. Of this force, Bowdich considered the greater proportion to consist of slaves.

In 1820 Dupuis remarked:

> The military resources of Ashanti are great indeed. The Bashaw Mohammed assured me that the armies of Ashanti that fought in Gyaman amounted to upwards of 80,000 men...The king of Dahomey can raise about 50,000 men. The king of Benin is by far the most powerful of the three monarchs, in regard to the number of his troops, for he can arm 200,000 upon an emergency.[15]

Some slaves belonged to 'Asafo' Companies in Asante, Fante and the Ga states. The Companies numbered between 500 and 1,000 men. The proportion of slaves in the Asafo Companies is difficult to tell because it is not documented. In Asante the Asafo Company was at the disposal of any of the generals of the main divisions of the army. In Elmina, out of 10 bands that formed the Asafo Company, one of them consisted purely of slaves and was called the 'Alatabanfo'. On the Ga coast, slaves comprised the 'Alata' quarter and became involved in Ga political, military and social life. One of the main duties of the Asafo Companies was to protect the inhabitants against any external attacks because they were regarded as soldiers of the state. The Asafo Companies also provided personal services to kings and chiefs, like the building and maintenance of their palaces, setting up of royal farms etc. It was usually the young and energetic who were engaged in these services.

(F)   SLAVES AND DOMESTIC CHORES

Male and female slaves were used extensively in the performance of domestic chores in the palaces, shrines and individual households in pre-colonial Ghana. The chores involved cooking, washing, fetching of water and firewood, sweeping, cleaning and running errands.

In the early 1600s De Marees remarked on the industry of Ghanaian women. He observed that after a hard day's work the women went into their barns and huts containing millet to pound the millet. According to him, those who had slaves left the pounding and winnowing of the millet to them. He added:

> Slaves cook and smoke food and help women in their household chores with such things as baking bread, collecting fire wood in the field and similar things... One does not find here any servants who serve people for payment or a salary; all of them are slaves or captives who have to spend their life in slavery.[16]

Three centuries later, De Graft Johnson made the following remarks with respect to the use of male and female slaves:

> those who stay in the same house perform such household duties as hired servants in European countries do. In return they are fed and clothed and are given all the privileges of children while staying with their masters.[17]

Pre-colonial Ghanaian society expected menial duties in the household and palaces to be carried out by slaves. Hence the Akan proverb: *"Atantanie nti na ye to odonko"* (We buy a slave because of filthy work). Slaves were generally required to work harder in the households and at any assignment given to them by their owners. Indeed slavery became synonymous with hard work.

One aspect of the work of both male and female slaves, particularly the females, was child care. In the royal households in particular, slaves served as "nannies" to the royal babies and children. It was in recognition of this role, that Asantehene Osei Yaw Akoto (1824-1838) created a special stool called *"mmagyegyefuo akonnwa"*. The occupant of this stool, usually a male slave, was the head of all the nannies at the Asantehene's court and responsible for the care and training of the royal children.

Oral traditions relate that sometimes a royal baby would be attended to by several nannies. One would be solely responsible for feeding the baby; another would be required to put the child to sleep; while some other slave would be given the duty of bathing and dressing up the baby. A different slave took charge of the training of the baby as it grew up. The ages of these nannies varied according to the work assigned to them. Some were small girls and boys; others were young men and women; while others were middle aged. An informant recalled that her grandmother, a member of the Akwapim royal family was carried to school and back by a female slave. Other slaves served her in other capacities.

A special song called 'kwadwom', originally sung only at the Asantehene's court, originated in the work of the nannies in the palace. It was a male slave in the royal household called Kwaw who originated these songs. Later it was taught to the nannies to sing to the royal children. It was also sung to the king in times of war, at meetings of state as well as on festive occasions. The songs are rich in appellations and genealogies, and honour men of valour who served the king and the Golden Stool.

(G)   SLAVES AND SACRIFICES

Both documentary and oral records affirm that almost every ethnic group in pre-colonial Ghana practised human sacrifice as part of its traditional belief system.

Traditional religion in Ghana was based on the belief in a Supreme God, the Creator. The Akan called him 'Nyame', the Ga 'Nyonmo', the Ewe and Adangme 'Mawu,' the Gonja 'Eboore', the Mamprusi 'Nwuni' and the Tallensi 'Nayiwum'. This God was so great and so far off that He needed to be worshipped through intermediaries – the lesser gods and the ancestors. Just as a king or chief could not be approached directly by their subjects except through office holders, so also God could not be approached directly except through intermediaries. The gods were deemed to inhabit rivers, trees, mountains etc. and usually manifested their presence in shrines headed by traditional priests. The gods were believed to be controlled by the Supreme God from whom they derived their powers. Reverence of the ancestors was a result of the belief that death was not the end of man. At death the soul was supposed to go to the land of spirits to join other departed souls. In this land of spirits the dead watched over the affairs of the living, punishing offenders and rewarding those who conformed to accepted ways and lived exemplary lives. In the spirit world, people were supposed to retain their earthly status and honour. Chiefs, therefore, needed their regalia and retinue. Among the Akan, Krobo, Tallensi and many northern societies, the Earth was also regarded as an object of worship. In Northern Ghana the Earth Priest, the 'tendana' was a powerful functionary of considerable authority. Land was deemed to belong to the living and the dead. For this reason land could not be alienated. It was merely held in trust by the living for the present and future generations. Land came to be invested with an element of sacredness. In addition, as the main provider of the means of sustenance, land became a source of wonder and reverence. The Akan believed that land was created on a Thursday, hence they called it "Asaase Yaa" and permitted no work to be done on that day.

It was the custom in pre-colonial Ghana to make offerings from time to time to the lesser gods and the ancestors deemed to possess power for good and evil. They were supposed to know people's thoughts and were credited with the capacity to expose and kill witches and those who plotted evil. The needs of men which the ancestors were assumed to know because they had lived in human society before included children, abundant harvest, more wealth, long life, solidarity and harmony among men; continuity of the cultural pattern; peace, plenty and the avoidance of disruptive quarrels. It was believed that these were also the needs and wishes of the gods, and that the ancestors did for the living what the living were also expected to do to maintain and nourish the ancestors. The offerings were accompanied by requests for protection and guidance, good health, fertility and prosperity.

For the common people the offerings usually consisted of eggs, fowl or sheep. For the king, chiefs and people of royal blood, the offerings consisted of the above mentioned items in addition to human beings. It was usually male and female slaves who suffered this fate. Reverence of the gods and ancestors was marked by the celebration of certain festivals, particularly Adae, Odwira, Appo, Akwambo, Aboakyir (among the Akan), Homowo (among the Ga), Ngmayini (among the Adangme), Hogbetsotso and Volo (among the Ewe), Kobena (Dagaare), Kadetofoo (Gonja), Galoga (Frafra), Buguru (Mamprusi) and Damba (Dagbani). These festivals were characterised by the offering of sacrifices. The 'washing of the stools' during such festivals required human blood and male and female slaves were sacrificed to "purify and feed" the stools. Oral traditions of the Effutu people relate how they sacrificed annually to the god Penkye Otu, who demanded nothing less than human blood. The Ningos also sacrificed a human being annually to their god called Angmu. In 1817, Bowdich reported that the Asante king's offering to the gods was usually 10 ounces of gold dust and 3 or 4 slaves. Bowdich also witnessed the sacrifice of 100 male and female slaves during the celebration of an important festival in Asante. In 1820 Dupuis observed that during the Adae Festival about 70 Gyaman male and female slaves were sacrificed in Asante.

During the celebration of royal funerals the public became agitated by the prospect of human sacrifice. In the early 1600s De Marees observed among the coastal states that:

> Anytime a king comes to die, much more mourning and sadness is shown about it than when another person dies. Any nobleman who may have served the king during his lifetime will present to him when he has died a slave to serve him.[18]

In 1858 and 1861 a number of runaway male slaves from Asante told British officials that they did so because they were going to be sacrificed.[19] In 1874 Chief Kwaku Amo of Akyem Abuakwa killed 3 slaves in connection with the celebration of the funeral of his brother Nifahene Duodu.[20] In the early 1880s, on the death of the mother of Opoku, one of the four greatest men in the Asante kingdom, many slaves were sacrificed in celebration of the funeral. When Asantehene Osei Kwamina died, about 200 male and female slaves were sacrificed within a space of three months.[21]

In 1882, 3 men from Adukrom in Akwapim went to Atebubu to trade. One of them called Kwabena Chati was left behind. In their absence, the king of Nsuta died and Kwabena Chati was killed as a sacrifice. When the king of Atebubu sent messengers to Nsuta to ask why this had been done, he was told that the late king's son bought Kwabena Chati for 2 pounds and 5 shillings and, therefore, he had the right to kill him. In the 1880s, sacrifices continued to be made. Rev. Hayfron informed Mr. Watts, the acting Colonial Secretary, that sacrifices were made by Ghanaians not merely for the sake of killing but because Ghanaians believed in a future state, a world of spirits, where the same social customs as prevailed among the living were strictly observed. He stressed that in the spirit world as on earth, royalty and headmen, chiefs and generals must have their stool bearers and slaves. To let them depart from this earth unattended to would be to inflict on them public and unending disgrace in the world beyond the grave.[22] In 1887, it was reported that at the death of Asantehene Kofi Karikari's uncle, 200 male and female slaves were sacrificed in Asante as part of the custom performed for chiefs who fell in battle during the war.[23]

Akan drum language confirms the custom of sacrificing slaves in celebration of the funeral of royalty and other dignitaries. One such message recorded by Emeritus Professor J.H. Kwabena Nketia declares:

> Abokyi Kwasiedu Berempong,
> Kwaadata a yede no ko ayie,
> odonko bi nan sisi mfikyire ha.

> Nobleman Abokyi Kwasiedu,
> One kept in hiding for the funeral,
> The foot marks of a slave are behind
> the house.[24]

In addition to sacrifice during festivals and funerals, certain day to day state dealings also called for human sacrifice. In the 1870s, the Christian missionaries Ramseyer and Kuhne witnessed several sacrifices in Kumasi in connection with day to day observance of custom. They reported, for example, that on one occasion, the Asantehene went to Bantama (a suburb of Kumasi) to see to the repair of the roof of the royal burial palace. Every ceremony connected with this building was accompanied by the shedding of human blood. The victims were slaves and criminals.

Apart from the ritual purposes outlined above for which slaves were sacrificed, there were also private reasons adduced by kings and chiefs for indulging in human sacrifice. Sometimes in memory of the dead, human sacrifices were made. In 1887, Ellis observed that years after a person's death, slaves and captives were sacrificed to his memory. The number of persons sacrificed depended upon the wealth and rank of the deceased, but the greatest 'slaughter' took place at the death of a king and in memory of a king.

Sometimes sacrifices were done out of sheer sadism. Reindorf records that in the 16th and 17th centuries, one of the kings of Agona (in modern Central Region) called Nyarko Ako, gave the heads of beheaded slaves to his son to play with. The king was reported to have said "These are thy toys, grow up and play with them". Ako continued this practice for a long time until Kwaw Ehura Aku, king of Gomoa Assin turned to King Oduro Tibo of Assinfufru to protect them and other neighbours from this outrageous practice of King Nyarko Ako. The united Assin forces marched against Ako and defeated him. This revelation by Reindorf is startling and one wonders how many more of such practices might have gone on in pre-colonial Ghana.

Under customary law, only kings and chiefs exercised the power of life and death over citizens. Human sacrifice was, therefore, by and large a royal prerogative. Kings and chiefs designated special officials known as the state executioners to perform this function. In Asante, execution of slaves and criminals was done at a place called 'Akyerekuro' (the village of the condemned).

These executions usually took place at the time of festivals – the Adae or Odwira, at the funerals of prominent citizens, during visits of embassies to the capital etc. The victims were deemed to have been despatched to 'Asaman' (the land of the dead) to attend to important personalities in the underworld.

(H)   SLAVES AND PROCREATION

During the pre-colonial period, people acquired slaves for varied personal reasons. A dominant reason was for procreation. In the table already cited at the beginning of this chapter, it is clear from oral data collected between 1990 and 2002 in all the current 10 regions of Ghana, that female slaves were used for procreation more than their male counterparts.

This data is confirmed by documentary records. Brodie Cruickshank, who lived in Ghana for 18 years noted that:

> The desire for offspring is particularly strong among the African women, barrenness being considered a great reproach. It is the cause of much discord between husband and wife, and frequently leads to separations. Among the higher classes, a slave girl is generally given by the bride's family to attend to her in her husband's house. The slave, in many instances, becomes the concubine of the husband; and her mistress, when she has no children of her own, regards the offspring of her maid as her own progeny.[25]

In Adansi, female slaves were often married to their owners, owner's children or owner's relations. In Apagya, whenever prisoners of war were brought home, the females among them were married by the victors. In Eyanmain, Eyan Denkyira and Eyan Abaasa, female slaves were married in order for them to produce more men to help in defending the state. People travelled to the northern part of Ghana to buy slaves whom they married when they were females or integrated into the family as brothers when they were male slaves.

In Armitage's report on the Gonja and Dagomba kingdoms dated 7th January 1898, he remarked:

> Many slaves are brought down yearly by the Moshis, and are sold to the Gonja people, who put them to work on their farms. The female slave as a rule, either marries her master or becomes his concubine.[26]

District Commissioner J.R.G. Syme of Bawku compiled a history of the Kusasis in June 1932 in which he noted that a very large proportion of the Kusasis were descendants of unions between Kusasis and imported slaves, male and female. Others were descendants of Mossi, Grussi and Bimoba immigrants.[27]

Recent scholarship on slavery emphasises that most slaves in sub-Saharan Africa were women. The European export markets purchased male slaves by a margin of at least two to one. The Muslim market of the Arab world absorbed primarily female slaves, and the internal African market absorbed mostly women and children. The major current debate over the function of female slaves centres on production and reproduction. Many scholars have rightly concluded that African women were preferred as slaves primarily because of their value in reproduction.[28]

Meillassoux puts this across strongly:

> In the domestic society a woman's reproductive capacity is what is most expected of her. Her submission as a laborer follows from her submission as a procreator.[29]

M.A. Klein has noted two types of slave systems in the Western Sudan: the Household mode of production, where slaves made up a small percentage of the population, lived within the household, and worked alongside the members of the household, and the Slave mode of production in which slaves lived in separate settlements and their labour was the source of sustenance for a ruling class that did not engage in physical labour and lived off the surplus produced by the slaves. He observes that reproduction was more important within the Household mode of production. Statistics of the slave population in pre-colonial Ghana is difficult to come by, let alone the female percentage. However, the detailed account given so far of the uses of both male and female slaves shows the importance of female slaves in production. Reproduction was also very crucial. According to the Table already referred to above, procreation ranked next to agriculture in terms of the major uses to which slaves were put. It is not a case of one being more important than the other. Both were important depending on individual needs and needs of the state. Obviously a female slave was priced higher than her male counterpart because of her productive as well as reproductive value. Support for this view is lent by a system of 'trial marriage' that developed in the past among the Manya Krobo whereby a wife was taken to live on a man's farm for a year or so to prove her worth as a labourer. The man would not commit himself to a binding marriage until he had convinced himself of the woman's abilities as a hard farm worker and a good market saleswoman.[137] Chiefs, nobles and members of royalty as well as commoners married slaves. Traditions assert that beautiful and neat female slaves found themselves as wives of chiefs, nobles and members of royalty, while others served as concubines. Conquerors, buyers, owners and owner's sons or relations also married female slaves.

It was not uncommon to find men with barren wives buying female slaves to marry for purposes of procreation. Wealthy women with no children of their own also bought female slaves and adopted them into their families. In traditional culture childbirth and plentiful children were regarded as a divine blessing. Childlessness was treated as a curse resulting from a possible breach of taboo. The acquisition of female slaves filled the vacuum created in a woman's life by childlessness.

Families threatened by extinction bought female slaves and incorporated them into the family by marrying them. Whole towns and villages were often repopulated with slaves. After a catastrophe like war, famine or small pox had decimated the population of settlements, female slaves were purchased to procreate in order to restore the lost numbers. According to oral tradition, when the attention of the king or chief was drawn to the decline in population, he ordered the purchase of slave women for purposes of reproduction. The female's role of procreation made her an indispensable member of the community. The data collected during field work referred to women as the bedrock of the family, and builders of the family on whom continuity of the lineage depended. It is this biological and physiological role of females that raised the premium on female slaves vis-à-vis their male counterparts. Children born out of such marriages or arrangements became free members of the lineage. Sometimes people bought both male and female slaves and married them. The children of such marriages became part of the household and 'replenished' the family.

Among the Akan personable male slaves were encouraged to have affairs with female members of royalty in order to produce children with unique physical features. Especially selected were the tall and handsome men from the north. Some traditions assert that male slaves used in this way were often killed later so as to hide their children's slave paternity.

Production and reproduction apart, slaves were sometimes acquired for prestige reasons as the number of slaves one had reflected one's wealth and position in society. Along with gold, money, wives and houses, slaves constituted primary indices of wealth and mobility.
De Graft Johnson remarks:

> To be sure the wealth and power of any family in the past were measured not by the amount of gold in its coffers, or the extent of its landed property or by sheer prestige, but by the number of domestic servants it would master to urge its private and political rights.[30]

An informant at Dormaa gave the following personal reasons for acquiring slaves:

It was sheer necessity that compelled us to own slaves. What the wise man did when he had money was to buy a slave. You might grow old that you would not be able to go to work on your farm and it was the slave who would work for you. Thus your whole life in old age was solely dependent on your slave.[31]

From the 15th to the 19th century, Ghana's economy was almost totally dependent on slave labour. Slaves farmed, collected fruits and nuts, reared livestock, hunted and fished for their owners. They acted as buyers and carriers in Ghana's trade both within and outside the country. They were a productive force in industry – gold mining, iron working, salt making and rubber production. In the art and craft industry, male slaves performed various roles. Slaves contributed their quota to the political, military, religious and social life of Ghana by serving in various administrative positions in the state and meeting the social and religious needs of individuals, families, states and chiefdoms.

SLAVES AND THE PRE-COLONIAL SOCIAL STRUCTURE

K inship formed the core of Ghana's pre-colonial social structure. In other words kinship was the basis for the organisation of groups and relationships around which the fabric of social life was built. Kinship ties were derived from consanguinity, marriage or adoption. In all the major ethnic groups studied in this book, the kinship system remained paramount and slaves were invariably integrated into the kin of their owners. By this process slaves also became part of their owner's family, lineage and clan.

Ghanaian clans were either patrilineal or matrilineal, depending on the ethnic group. Most Akans were matrilineal, while the Mole-Dagbani, Ewe and Ga-Adangme were patrilineal. The clan consisted of a group of people, male and female, believed to have descended through one line only, either male or female, from a common putative ancestor or ancestress. The clan was usually a large and inclusive group such that genealogical ties connecting all the members to the founder were not clearly known. The clans were either dispersed geographically or were found in the same settlement. Among the Akan and Anlo for example, the clans were dispersed, but among the Tallensi and the Ga-Adangme they were more localised. Among some of the ethnic groups such as the Akan, Tallensi and some northern Ewe groups, the clan was said to be exogamous. In others, including the Anlo, there were no restrictions. The number of clans differed from society to society. While the Akan had seven or eight, the Anlo had fifteen.

The lineage in pre-colonial Ghana, consisted of a segment of the clan found in one locality. It comprised a group of people, male and female, who were descended through one line only from a common ancestor or ancestress. The lineage was a corporate group and, therefore, exhibited one or more of the following characteristics: it had a leader; it owned property and its members met regularly to discuss matters of common interest.

The family was of great sociological significance in pre-colonial Ghana. It went beyond that of the nuclear family to include members of the extended family, servants and slaves. A typical household comprised the following: the head of the household, usually a male and a father; his wife or wives; unmarried children of both sexes; married sons and their wives and children; the head of the household's mother and his younger brothers and unmarried sisters; sons and daughters of the head of the household's married sisters; household pawns, slaves newly acquired, and descendants of other household slaves who by a kind of legal fiction were classed as belonging to the head of the household's clan.

The family consisted of the entire lineal descendants of a common ancestor. It was matrilineal, patrilineal or both as in the case of the Ga Mashi and Yeji. Among the ethnic groups which were matrilineal, every woman who married and had children originated a family. By customary law in pre-colonial Ghana, the stranger was a member of the family of the person with whom he lodged, or of the family of his landlord or of the family to which he voluntarily attached himself upon giving drink to the head and the elders of the family. If he was not attached to any particular family, he belonged to the family into which he married. It was by reason of this customary law that slaves became members of their owners' families. One process of integration of the slave into the family was through adoption. Another process was through marriage. In the course of time the adopted slave and his descendants so merged and intermarried with the owner's own kinsmen, that only a few would know their origin. For slaves, servants and strangers, their membership of families was attained through adoption or marriage. The other members of the families

The excavation of a female slave at Jenini on 3/06/04, Samory Toure's
slave camp which is forty-five minutes drive from Sampa.
In the picture are the author and
Dr. Yaw Bredwa-Mensah, the Archaeologist.

The Jenini Chief Nana Kwadwo Sebo and his elders in his palace on 2/06/04. About 30 houses in Jenini are situated on a mass grave of African slaves.

The author and her research team in the chief's palace at Jenini.

The village of Buko, ten minutes drive from Sampa. Oral history relates that the French and the British met here to carve out territories for themselves.

The British Flag (The Union Jack) which has been kept over 100 years on display. It affirmed Britain's sovereignty on the land in the late 1880's.

The ancient building in Bonduku near the palace kept as a memorial to show that the chief and his people were the earliest settlers of the town and therefore the royals.

The author in the house of Lt. Col. Blinger in Bonduku. He seized the area for the French government during the Scramble and Partition of Africa in the 1880s.

The chief of Bonduku (in cloth) with his elders and the author on 6/06/04.

The palace of Buhari Toure in Bonduku built in the 1800s. Oral traditions state that Samory Toure stayed in this palace when he was on his way to the Slave Market at Buna.

The Slave Market at Sampa where slaves were bought.
The white calico tied around the tree indicates
that the spirits of the slaves are embodied in the tree.

*The Slave Camp at Sampa where slaves were held in transit
to the slave market in Sampa.*

Sampa was an important Military Post in Ghana in the late 1800s. In the above picture is the British Colonial Government Military Cemetery in Sampa. Two British soldiers and one African soldier from the Gold Coast Constabulary are buried here.

owed their membership of the family to birth and, therefore, to blood ties. Circumstances of birth and blood ties were very important criteria for membership of royalty. It was these criteria which gave them political and social rights over commoners and slaves. In a matrilineal society, a slave belonging to a patrilineal society would be physiologically unconnected by the primary tie of blood to a mother's group. In a patrilineal society, the same would be true for a slave from a matrilineal society.

The acceptance of slaves into the families of their owners did not mean that the slaves were regarded as equal in social status with the rest of the family. The slaves continued to perform certain functions in the family associated with their condition. These functions differed from family to family and depended mostly on the motives for acquiring the slaves. If the motive was labour-related, the slave would do all work associated with agriculture, trade or industry. If the motive was military or political, the slave would be required to perform those functions at the palaces. A slave's status was always known to the members of the family. Even though in the course of time, slave descendants might appear to be completely integrated into a family, the head of the family and his Elders would never lose sight of the slaves' servile origins. Slaves and their descendants never forgot their original status. An Akan proverb states that *"Akoa ne ne wura ba edi agoro a, na n'akoa wo ne tirim"*. (A slave may play with his master's child, but never forgets his status as a slave).

Adoption of a slave into a family, lineage and clan did not involve any ceremony. It was a process which was accomplished over a long period of time. By the third and fourth generation, slave descendants would have become completely merged into a family, lineage and clan. Marriage to a slave, involved a simple public ceremony though the rites varied from family to family and from town to town. If a freeman wanted to marry a female slave, which was often the case, he provided a "small drink" to the slave's head of family. Others demanded drink and a little dowry for the head of the family. In some cases the freeman was required to buy drink for all the townspeople. In other cases, a bottle of gin was sent to the king or chief to inform him of the marriage. The ceremony was necessary firstly because it gave the marriage customary backing; secondly, it enabled the free spouse to collect a fine from anyone who seduced the slave because it would be publicly known that the slave was married; thirdly it symbolised integration of the slave into the family. Marriages between slaves did not involve any ceremony if the slaves belonged to the same owner, otherwise the usual customary drink was presented to the owner of the slave.

A male slave could enter into a marriage with a female slave owned by his own master/mistress, a female slave owned by another master/mistress or a free woman. A female slave could enter into a marriage with a male slave owned by her master/mistress, a male slave owned by another master/mistress or a free man. The children of marriages between slaves of the same owner, remained slaves although they were recognised as part of the owner's family. The children of marriages between a slave and a free man or woman who did not own him or her became half free because they were considered as belonging to the owner of the slave. They were called *okanifa* (half Akan) by the Akan. The children of a marriage between a slave and his or her owner or between the slave and a relative of his or her owner were recognised as free men or women. In matrilineal societies, the desire to marry female slaves was very strong partly because a man had undisputed right over his slave wife and her children. The female slave had no family in her new home and became permanently attached to the family of his owner. The bonds of marriage strengthened this link. In a patrilineal society there was no problem with a husband's rights over his wife and children, because the children customarily belonged to the man.

NAMING

As members of the family, either by adoption or marriage, slaves were often given new names by their owners. These names were supposed to be evidence or proof of integration and identity. The kind of name given to a slave depended on the circumstances under which he/she was acquired. If the slave was acquired with the sole aim of adoption into the family, the slave was given the family name of the owner or named after his/her relation. Other slaves assumed the family name as they became integrated into the family of their owner. If a slave arrived in the household at a time his/her owner was going through difficult times, the owner commemorated his/her situation by giving the slave a special name. For example, an Akan slave owner could call the slave: *Se ebewie* (how will the crisis end?); *Aka me ne wo* (you and I are without family); *Me na, meye wo deeben?* (mother, what harm/ offence did I cause you?); *Biako ye ya* (it is tragic to be lonesome). Sometimes the slaves were given *Bebudin* (proverbial names). Some of these names in Akan were: *Mesre Nyame* (I implore God); *Kra Nyame* (God of my soul); *Nso Nyame ye* (nothing is too hard for God); *Ade Nyinaa wo Nyame nsam* (everything is in the hands of God) and *Benyaade* (you came to gain). Other slaves were given *"Nyeso din"* (Answer or 'Response' Names). When the owner called the slave, he expected a specific response. For example, the owner would say in Akan *"Se ebe wie"* (how will the crisis end?), and the slave would reply *"Nyame na onim"* (only God knows). Sometimes slaves were given day names like Akosua, Adwoa, Kwabena, Kofi etc. commemorating the day the slave entered the household. Slaves who won the heart of their owners earned names of commendation such as *Barima ena* (heroes are difficult to find) or *Akoa pa ye na* (a faithful and good servant is a blessing). A few owners kept the slaves' "alien" names and this sometimes indicated that the slave had not been fully integrated into the family.

RESIDENTIAL PATTERN

There was no fixed residential pattern for slaves. Some slaves lived in the same house with their owners. Wealthy slave owners with more than one house, sometimes kept their slaves in a separate house. Among members of royalty and in the palaces, slaves were usually housed in separate quarters. Slaves resided in towns, villages and hamlets just as free men and women did, but they were more conspicuous in villages and hamlets primarily engaged in peasant farming and industry. Whether residences were patrilocal, virilocal or duo-local, slaves were usually resident in households, as a greater part of their duties were of a domestic nature.

STATUS

Oral and documentary records confirm that slaves formed the lowest social group in pre-colonial Ghana, their membership of their owners' family and household notwithstanding. Barbot mentioned five categories of people in pre-colonial Ghana. The first group comprised kings or captains; the second consisted of the chief governors or magistrates; the third was made up of those who either by inheritance or their own industry in trade had much money and slaves; the fourth comprised the common people and the fifth and last, slaves. Bosman reiterated Barbot's classification when he referred to five degrees of people in pre-colonial Ghana. His fifth degree consisted of slaves. In Akwamu, Bosman realised that only two categories of people were recognised: the king and his friends formed one category while slaves formed the second category. Pre-colonial Akyem Abuakwa society recognised three distinct groups of people. At the top of the social ladder were the occupants of stools – mpankanfo, Adikrofo and Mmusuapanin. Next came the free born commoners. On the lowest rung of the social ladder were slaves and pawns. In Asante, Lystad found three groups of people: members of royalty, commoners and slaves. Buah refers to "Ghanaian native Society" as consisting of three social classes. The first class consisted of the king and the queenmother; the second class comprised heads of lineages or the Elders; the third class were the commoners, comprising all other free born persons in the society. Outside these three classes were servants and slaves. Cruickshank asserted that Gold Coast Society was composed of only two classes – masters and slaves. During my field work two groups of people were often stressed to me, the freeborn and the slave. The freeborn included members of royalty.

In terms of social status, the position of slaves in pre-colonial Ghana was similar to that of slaves in ancient Mesopotamia, Persia, India, China, Classical Greece, Rome, the Islamic World, Japan, Mexico and Europe. They were the lowest rung of the social ladder. The difference, so far as Ghana is concerned, lay in the issue of kinship, the kind of treatment meted out to the slave and his rights.

TREATMENT

The treatment of slaves in pre-colonial Ghana, depended on the owner, the family and the household in which he/she resided. On the whole the records portray a picture of humane treatment. Slaves were well treated, especially if they were part of the owner's family, lineage and clan. They were even better treated when they were married into the owner's family. Dormaa oral tradition relates that slaves had to be kindly treated as part and parcel of one's own family, otherwise they might run away, when they went on errands or worked on the farms alone without their owners. Komenda oral tradition paints a picture of peaceful co-existence between masters and their slaves during pre-colonial times. Oral tradition of Kwamankese states that at Ayeldo, slaves were humanely treated; at Odompo, slaves were treated as relatives and at Katakyiase, slaves "were treated nicely". Dagomba traditions also talk about humane treatment of slaves. All the ethnic groups studied during this period of research have oral traditions that stress that on the whole slaves were well treated in pre-colonial Ghana.

Observers from outside Ghana expressed pleasant surprise at the humane treatment of slaves. Freeman, Klose, Dr. Madden, Beecham, Crowther and some British Commissioners were a few of such observers. Freeman remarked that slavery in Ghana was very different from that of Europe, North America and the West Indies. Klose felt that the slave in Ghana, was much better off than his/her counterpart in Europe and America. In the 1840s, Dr. Madden described the treatment of slaves as "mild". District Commissioner Crowther who worked in Ghana at the turn of the 20th century in his evidence before the Committee of West Africa Lands in London on 7th February, 1913, described slaves in Ghana as "more like adopted children".

The treatment of slaves in pre-colonial Ghana was regulated by customary rules and norms. The first rule was that a slave was generally deemed to be part of the family and household of the owner. The second rule was that a slave was entitled to food, clothing and shelter. The third rule enjoined every child to be polite and respectful to everyone, including slaves. The fourth rule obliged slave owners to make themselves accessible to their slaves. This was reflected in an Akan proverb which says *wo nkoa suro wo anim asem a, wonni nim mma wo* (if your slaves/servants fear to speak to you, they will not gain victories for you). The fifth rule required slave owners to be forthright with their slaves without being unnecessarily harsh. This was expressed in an Akan proverb *wofere wo afenaaa, wudi nnuan fi* (if you neglect to reprimand your female slave/servant, you eat unhealthy food). Slave owners needed wisdom and tact in dealing with their slaves because while indiscipline would make the slave lose the respect due to his/her owner, undue severity could make the slave obdurate. An Akan proverb states: *Akoa te se kyekyire; wode nsu kakra gu no so a, na ahono* (a slave/servant is like roasted corn flour, when a little water is sprinkled on it, it dissolves). In other words, a slave/servant was easily influenced by kind treatment and, therefore, slave owners needed to create a balance between good/kind treatment and harsh/severe discipline. Slaves could be punished if they did wrong, just as children of free parents. Traditions aver that slaves could be caned, kept indoors or starved for a few hours or a few days, depending on the severity of the offence. Bad behaviour by children and slaves was often seen as proof of indiscipline and poor training. This was again expressed in an Akan proverb, *Akoa ampow a, na efiri owura* (if a slave/servant is not well behaved, the cause can be traced to his/her owner). There appears, therefore, to have been a system of checks and balances in pre-colonial Ghana with respect to slave treatment. Though every owner was aware of the customary saying that "the slave's life is in the hands of his/her master/mistress" (in Akan: *Akoa nkwa ne ne wura)*, a slave whatever his/her offence could not be killed by his/her owner. It was only the king or chief who had the power of life and death over the slave and in fact over every citizen in the kingdom, chiefdom or state. The Akans say *Ohene nkoara na owo sikan* (it is only the chief who wields the sword). Anyone who maltreated the slave to the point of death or who mutilated the slave had to face the full rigours of the law. Bosman reported in the 17th century that in Akyem anyone who murdered a slave was usually fined six and thirty crowns. In Asante such a person was liable to pay a heavy fine.

In the event of his/her being cruelly treated by his/her owner, a slave in pre-colonial Ghana could have recourse to one of the following remedies. First, he/she could wait for an opportune time to run away. Second, he/she could seek protection by throwing himself/herself on the mercy of a god at the traditional grove or on an ancestral spirit at the royal mausoleum. Third, he/she could "swear an oath" on another person to adopt him/her, in which case that person paid compensation to the owner. In Accra, the traditional priests often asked runaway slaves to pay some money in order to be protected by the gods. Reindorf noted that the priests made "a good revenue" through this practice.

Slave owners demanded complete obedience from their slaves. Muller relates that newly purchased slaves were obliged to swear an oath of loyalty to their owners. In 1870, Gyasehene Amoako of Akyem Abuakwa told the Basel missionaries that his slaves were his "sons" and he would insist on their obedience to his orders. One of my informants in Salaga, told me that an insolent slave – one who did not want to go to the farm or contemplated escape – could suffer execution on the authority of the chief. A day would be fixed for his/her execution which was often done under a baobab tree at the "Buba Kasoa" (big market). The execution could be called off if he/she gave an undertaking that he/she would be obedient.

It is clear from the records that not all slave owners obeyed the traditional rules regarding the treatment of slaves. While the general consensus portrays slaves as being humanely treated, a few records indicate harsh treatment. The European records are not unanimous in their assessment of treatment of slaves

---

by their African owners. De Marees in the 17th century and Zimmerman in the middle of the 19th century take a more favourable view of treatment of slaves by their African masters. For example De Marees averred that slaves were not treated very differently from other members of the households to which they belonged though he remarked upon the cruel practice of branding and marking of slaves to facilitate their recovery if they should run away. Significantly only De Marees, of all the records consulted, makes this observation. The branding of slaves was not a common Ghanaian practice. De Marees might have mistaken the various tribal markings of slaves from various ethnic groups both within Ghana and outside Ghana as brands. Branding of slaves was a common European practice and the slaves owned by Europeans on the coast, which comprised personal servants and castle slaves, might in some cases have been branded. Among the Kusasis, the children of slaves they bought were absorbed into the tribe and known as Kusasis. By the third generation they would all bear Kusasi facial markings. Among some of the ethnic groups, the markings were a means of identity and not punishment or a sign of ill treatment. In the 1930s, a man called Agbeng Kusasi, who lived at Zabungu, four miles south of Bawku, bought a Busanga male called Akorli. This slave had many children by Kusasi women. The children were given Busanga markings but they called themselves Kusasis. The grandchildren who had Busanga markings called themselves Kusasis.[1]

Basel missionary, Zimmerman, noted that slaves were well treated by their owners and this was a normal situation. He commented as follows:

> With the normal situation where the master treats his slaves in a fatherly way, the slaves leave only in particularly tense situations or out of their own light-headedness or disobedience.[2]

Where slaves had been harshly treated, Zimmerman stated that they had run away. He realised that educated slave owners, the merchants on the coast, mulattos and the 'great princes among the Twis' often kept a distance from their slaves, but other people did not. With respect to harsh treatment of slaves by their African masters, Barbot writing at the turn of the 18th century remarked that slaves were severely and barbarously treated by their owners. These owners also fed them poorly and beat them cruelly, to the extent that there were "scabs and wounds" on the bodies of many of them when they were sold to them.[3] It is not clear from Barbot's report whether these were domestic slaves or war captives bought directly from the slave market.

Cruickshank, who lived in Ghana for eighteen years during the early part of the 19th century, had two opinions on the treatment of slaves. In the first opinion he stated that "the condition of slaves in Ghana was not one of unmitigated hardship". He attributed this to the customary law which enjoined owners to make slaves part of the family and the rights and privileges slaves enjoyed from this relationship. In the second opinion Cruickshank stated that as a magistrate, he had the opportunity of adjudicating numerous court cases in which slaves accused their owners of ill-treating them. When the nature of the master's right over the slave was investigated and found to be groundless, the slave was emancipated. When on the other hand the master's right was found to be valid, the slave was obliged to pay a redemption price for his/her freedom. Certificates of freedom were then issued by the magistrate. Cruickshank said that during his long period of magisterial duties in Ghana, he granted thousands of certificates of freedom.[4] As a Government official, Cruickshank's second opinion of the treatment of domestic slaves may well have been influenced by the Abolition Law passed by the British government in 1807. As for Boyle, he wrote in the year of inauguration of British colonial rule when the British government's face was set against indigenous slavery. Indeed the Proclamation Act defined the Queen's powers and jurisdiction to include among others "the extinction of human sacrifices," the "abolition of slave dealing" and the adoption of "measures with regard to domestic slavery and pawning".

In 1874 Boyle observed:

> As to the ill-treatment of slaves, it behoves a conscientious content

to speak cautiously. You will find very different reports. Captain Helden assured me he had traced and caused to be produced in court various implements of torture whereof runaway slaves complained.[5]

Like Cruickshank his statement as a colonial official does not make him an impartial observer.

Slave resistance, revolt, and rebellion can be useful indices of grievances and ill-treatment. An examination of the available records from the 15th to the 19th century, however, revealed only five recorded instances of revolt and rebellion. In neither of these cases was the cause of rebellion clearly stated. In the 1640s, a slave in Assin killed his master, an important person in the state, and subsequently disrupted the caravan trade between Assin and the districts to the north. During that same period, three female slaves from Elmina burnt down all the granaries of the Eguafohene.[6] The records are unfortunately silent on what kind of punishment was given to these slaves. On 21st November, 1770 at a Council meeting held at Cape Coast Castle, 12 slaves belonging to John Kabes, one of the principal men at Komenda, were arraigned on a charge of murdering him. Eight of the ring leaders in the presence of the linguists of Komenda and Elmina, the kings of Abramboe and Eguafo, as well as many important political personalities from Fante land and other parts of the country, were found guilty of murder, and unanimously sentenced to "death for their unparalleled audacity and villainous behaviour". The sentences were intended to preserve peace and tranquility among members of John Kabes' family and to deter other slaves "from behaving in this cruel and atrocious manner to their masters".[7]

In the 18th century, there were two rebellions in Asante. The first was the Bonduku slave rebellion in Kumasi. During the Asante campaign against Bonduku, some of the Bonduku slaves in Asante, rebelled and joined their tribesmen. These were slaves who had been enrolled in the army and were in possession of military weapons. The Asantehene Osei Bonsu, who made this disclosure to Mr. Hutchinson in 1819, did not indicate the cause of the rebellion or the nature of the punishment meted out to these rebellious slaves.[8] The fifteenth chief of the Juaben state in Asante called Asafo Adjei, was a slave who was asked to occupy the stool as a regent, during the minority of the lawful heir. He later rebelled and fled with his supporters to Kyebi. Eventually he founded the New Juaben state in Koforidua.[9]

The commonest form of resistance during the pre-colonial period was flight. Slaves whose masters and mistresses disobeyed the traditional rules and norms governing treatment of slaves ran away. Tradition tolerated such an eventuality. Among all the ethnic groups and in every time period, slaves availed themselves of such an opportunity whenever it arose. No matter the norms of a culture, there are people who diverge from them. There were some cruel masters/mistresses and there were some rebellious slaves.

RIGHTS AND PRIVILEGES

Slaves in pre-colonial Ghana enjoyed certain rights and privileges. They had the right to be fed, clothed, housed and granted the privileges of children while staying with their owners. They had the right to marry. They enjoyed the privilege of an independent income. This was very common among slaves who traded for their owners. Some slaves became wealthy merchants through their own trading efforts. Slaves who farmed for their owners often had portions of the family or community lands assigned to them to make their own farms, and appropriate income therefrom. The fact that pre-colonial Ghanaian society allowed slaves to amass private wealth was reflected in the Akan proverb *Akoa nim som a ofa ne ti ade di* (a loyal and faithful servant has debts to his/her master/mistress remitted). A slave who acquired sufficient wealth had the privilege and right to purchase a slave of his/her own. Basel missionary, Eisenschmid, reported in 1863 that a slave in Kyebi had ended up as a slave owner himself.[10] In his/her new capacity as a slave master/mistress he/she became entitled to the rights and privileges of slave owners and liable to the duties and obligations of slave owners. His/her slave master/mistress did not deal directly with slaves owned by him/her. In the interest of peace and harmony he/she gave orders to the latter indirectly through his/her slave.

Although slaves were supposed to "have no voice while their master lives," among some of the Akan people, the children of slaves and their descendants had a right to object to the succession of a new master. The new master could be a brother, a nephew, a cousin or a distant blood relation of the deceased master, or even one of the domestic servants, or a person who belonged to the same clan as the deceased. A little token of gold and money was usually given to such slaves to reconcile them each time a new master was designated. Slaves who had been completely integrated into the family had the privilege of attending family meetings, discussing family affairs and even inheriting. Slaves were eligible for summons as witnesses in traditional court cases. They were entitled to be in court together with children, wives, husbands and other 'blood' relations. As "children" of their owners, the slaves were entitled to have their personal debts paid by their masters. Their owners were also liable to pay compensation and restitution for every injury caused by them to other persons either wilfully or accidentally.

Slaves gained their freedom through informal or formal means. Although oral tradition of all the ethnic groups stated that a slave was a slave for life as were his/her descendants, slaves did achieve their freedom through acts of omission over a long period of time. Slaves in Akan societies were covered by the traditional and customary law that forbade the disclosure of anyone's origins. This was expressed in the popular Akan saying *obi nkyere obi ase*. On the occasion of a chief's enstoolment, the political officers of state often required him to make a number of vows as he swore the oath of allegiance. One of the first vows he usually made was that he would never disclose the origins of any person. Among the Akan, the Elders would say: *Ka_kyere no se, yempe asekyere*. This law also applied to every citizen in the traditional state. The result was that with the passage of generations the slave origins of a person became obscure. The formal way by which a slave achieved his/her freedom was through monetary payment. In Asante it was often the Asante-born slave who had the opportunity of recovering his/her lost status. Oral traditions refer to two stages by which Asantes were redeemed. The first stage involved the payment of the actual purchase price by the buyer, as well as an additional payment of money as a seal or stamping fee (this seal was symbolised by the saying *wato ati no trama*). The payment of the "seal money" known as "trama" made the sale absolute and irrevocable. In order to nullify or reverse the contract the "trama" had to be returned. The second stage by which Asantes were redeemed was through pawning. The slave had to go through several stages of liberation. First, he/she had to move from slavery to pawnship. The chief or queenmother was approached by the linguist on behalf of the slave and some amount of money called "trama" was paid by the slave and one sheep slaughtered. After the slave had moved from slavery into pawnship, two or three days were allowed to elapse before someone representing himself/herself as the debtor, went to the chief or queenmother again and declared publicly that he/she wanted to redeem his/her pawn. Another amount of money was paid and thereafter the pawn gained his/her freedom. He/she then went back to his/her original family and "re-entered" it without further formalities, except a ritual notification to the ancestral spirits. After this he/she became re-possessed of all his/her former rights, privileges and obligations.

Among the Fantes, all natives were considered to be free people and persons enslaved could always be redeemed by their families whenever they were traced. This was not the usual case with respect to non-Fante slaves who were supposed to be slaves for life. Fante slaves who acquired ample means were able to purchase not only their freedom but that of other slaves as well.

All slaves were entitled to legal protection when they became domiciled in another traditional state. Their status did not change. They were regarded as under the authority and jurisdiction of the chief and Elders of their new domicile. They could sue and be sued; they could swear the state oaths; they could act as witnesses in legal actions and "drink the gods" to prove their words.

Finally, there were avenues for social, political and economic mobility open to slaves. Slaves could rise to positions of authority in the family, society and the state. They could succeed to political offices on the death of their owners. They could act as regents when there were no suitable heirs to the skin or stool.

In the religious field, there is a recorded case of a slave who was made a traditional priest in Accra during the 18th century. Okaidsha, the chief of Accra having removed all the gods from the Asere quarter to Gbese and Sakumo from Lomotso Kumah, deposed its priest called Odoi Blem and replaced him with a slave whom he bought.[11]

Slaves and their descendants could inherit their owner's property as well as hold property of their own. These rights and privileges were based on the fact that the slaves and their descendants were part of their owner's families. Membership of a family involved certain legal rights and duties. The first was common ownership of property. The second was common liability to pay family debts and the third was the common right of members to sit or be represented on the family council. In pre-colonial customary law, a distinction was made between stool property, family property and personally acquired property or private property. A slave or his/her descendant could not inherit stool property but they could inherit family property under certain circumstances. Family property was in the custody of the head of the family. Upon the death of the head of the family, his successor inherited the family property. Slaves and their descendants who rose to become heads of families therefore had the privilege of inheriting the family property.

The commonest form of property slaves and their descendants inherited was personally acquired or private property. Some owners gave their properties to their slaves because of their meritorious services. Others did so because having no children of their own, they had adopted their slaves, or because customary laws of succession and inheritance enjoined that. In matrilineal societies inheritance descended through the maternal line from uncle to nephew. If the uncle had no direct heir in the person of a brother, the son of his own sister or a cousin's son in the female line was the next heir. This decision was usually taken by the unanimous consent of the family. If there was no other male person, a female was chosen. Issues of female slaves were often the last to be allowed to inherit property. If the deceased was a female, her moveable property went to her female children. If there were no females in the family at all to succeed, the males, if any, succeeded. If there was no genuine successor at all a female slave could succeed. In patrilineal societies, inheritance descended through the paternal line from father to sons. The same customary laws were applicable. Failing genuine successors, slaves and their descendants inherited the properties.

Sarbah lists four kinds of successors – Real, Proper, Ordinary and Extra-ordinary. In matrilineal societies, the real successor of a man was his mother. Proper successors were the uterine brothers and sisters of the deceased. Ordinary successors were persons descended from the maternal grandmother, such as a person's nephew or nieces or the issue of such aunts. Extraordinary successors were either an issue by a domestic slave with a male person of "heritable blood (Odehye)"; or a slave, clan or tribal relative. Sarbah was emphatic:

> Where there are freeborn in the house and slaves, the country law is that slaves cannot inherit as long as there are any of the blood surviving. They may inherit by will, or, where the blood is under age, one may be selected from the slaves to succeed. Those of the blood would be those coming out of the womb of the head.[12]

These laws of succession and inheritance were applied in the case of Ocran V Bandafoo held before Judicial Assessor Chalmers on 13th October, 1873 and in the case of Mansah and others V Dolphyne held before Judge Henry Stubbins on 11th May, 1883. In the Mansah V Dolphyne case one of the witnesses testified that the children of a man by his slave took property in preference to household slaves.[13] So even among the slaves there was discrimination in the selection process.

In pre-colonial customary law, a slave's personally acquired property could not be passed on to his children. The property reverted to the family into which he was adopted and more specifically to the owner. Such was the case even in matrilineal societies. A freeborn father could not pass on property to his children.

In 1732 Barbot remarked:

> The right of inheritance all over the Gold Coast except at Accra is very strangely settled, for the children born legitimate never inherit their parents [i.e. father's] effects. The brothers and sister's children are the lawful heirs. All that the son of the king or braffo or cabocciro has of right is his deceased father's office, his shield and cymiter, but no goods, chattels or money.[14]

Barbot was obviously looking at the matrilineal societies among the Akan states and the Ga patrilineal society. In pre-colonial Ghanaian matrilineal societies, perhaps it was easier for the slave and his descendants to accept and understand that the slave's personally acquired property did not pass on to his children. This was because in traditional matrilineal societies no freeborn father or even a father of royal children could pass on his personally acquired property to his own children. It went to his sister's son. In patrilineal societies, this must have been difficult for the slave and his descendants to accept, because a father's personally acquired property went to his sons. Oral data, archival material and court records make it very clear that a slave's property reverted to his owner when he died or to the owner's family. This customary law was affirmed in the cases of Kweku Kodieh V Nana Kwame Affram held before the West African Court of Appeal in Accra on 19th May, 1930; Kanjarga V Deteh held in the Asante Judicial Division of the High Court on 30th November, 1951 and Gyimah V Kumah held in the High Court Accra on 20th April, 1959.[15] Because of this Customary Law, Rattray contended that "a master encouraged his slave because ultimately everything the slave possessed went to his master".[16]

Sometimes the sharing of a deceased slave's personally acquired property became a bone of contention among the free born family members. This was so in the case Kodieh V Afram (1930) when both claimed they had the right to administer the estate of the deceased Kwaku Damptey. Afram based his claim on the fact that the deceased was his slave. The Circuit Court in Asante which first heard the case gave judgement in favour of Afram. Kodieh, unhappy about the judgement appealed to the West African Court. The court opined that at the time of the case, slavery had been abolished and, therefore, the claim based on slavery was "repugnant to justice, equity and good conscience". The judgement of the Circuit Court was set aside and letters of administration granted to Kwaku Kodieh.[17] In the case of Abena Buor V Kwame Gyankyi held in the Divisional Court of Kumasi on 9th July, 1945, the dispute centred on who was the deceased slave's successor under Native Law as the property involved was great. Kwame Gyankyi told Abena Buor that his late father called Bimpeh was his slave and, therefore, he was the rightful successor under Customary Law. The court found out during the proceedings that the late Bimpeh had named Gyankyi as his successor. It concluded:

> Bimpeh's origin is inconclusive and I make no finding on this point, but finding as I do that Bimpeh made defendant his successor and that plaintiff acknowledged him as such, I give judgement in this case in favour of the defendant.[18]

It was as if Bimpeh, aware of his servile origins and the Customary Law with respect to his status, affirmed the Law by naming Gyankyi as his successor instead of Akosua.

In the case of Opanin Kwasi Abebrese V Kwaku Anane held in the Divisional Court of Kumasi on 8th July, 1949, the question at stake was who was the true successor to the property of the deceased Kwaku Amaabre. In its judgement, the court said that it was not disputed that Amaabre's ancestor came to the family as a slave and had to all intents and purposes become a member of the family. The question was whether he became attached to any one section of the family or he was for whoever was the Head of the family. Opanin Abebrese maintained that the late Amaabre belonged to his particular section of the family. Other members of the family denied this and stated that Amaabre belonged to whoever was the Head of the family. The court was satisfied that Opanin Abebrese had a right to succeed to the property of Amaabre not because Amaabre belonged to his part of the family but because he was the Head of the family.[19] In a land dispute held at the District Court II at Abetifi on 5th May, 1961, involving Kwame Adomako V Opanin Yaw Anim and others, the land was used by a deceased slave called Badu for farming. The essence of the dispute was whether the land belonged to Badu personally or was stool land. If it was stool land, the land would customarily revert to the stool; if it was family land, it would revert to the family; but if it was personally acquired land, that is, land given to the slave as a gift or bought by the slave from his private income, then the land would be inherited by whoever was elected by the family to be the deceased slave's successor.[20]

Data from the questionnaires administered during field work in all the ten administrative regions of Ghana from 1990 to 2002, indicated a response by over 55% of the Respondents that slaves could inherit property in times past. Three major reasons were given. First was that it was customary for "good, faithful and loyal" slaves to be rewarded with inheritance of property. The second reason was failure of heirs. The third reason was that the slave's membership of the family entitled him/her to inherit property like any other family member. The Respondents who indicated that slaves could not inherit property also gave the following reasons. First, they said the slave was not a member of the family. Second, the slave was of inferior status and third, the slave was a stranger and not a native.

DISABILITIES

While it is true that the slave in pre-colonial Ghana was in "a state of servitude guarded by rights," it is also true that the slave suffered a number of disabilities. One of the first disabilities a slave faced was the possibility of being sacrificed in accordance with traditional customs and religious beliefs. Slaves formed a 'pool' for this purpose. A freeman or woman would scarcely be sacrificed. The second disability was that his/her status as a slave was never entirely forgotten, no matter how high he/she rose on the social scale. The third disability had to do with physical appearance. The slave was supposed to dress very modestly. Hence the Akan saying *Odonko nsiesie ne ho te se ne wura* (a slave is not free to dress like his/her master/mistress). Rattray asserts that in Asante a slave was not allowed to wear any gold ornaments. A slave generally wore a jerkin of blue and white material called "koboaka," drawers "kadana" and a metal or stone bangle on the right upper arm. Such dressing was however not compulsory. Barbot observed:

> The dress of the commoner sort, as fishermen or canoe men, sellers of wine and other handicrafts is various but very ordinary. The well to do men and women wear beautiful ornaments. The slaves are generally poor habitated and always bare-headed.[21]

Kea relates that slaves were distinguished from free commoners by the law that forbade them to wear headgear.

The fourth disability was linked to behaviour. The slave was supposed to be unassuming and he was not supposed to mix too freely with free men and women. Among the Akan, if the slave became too presumptuous he/she could be sacrificed. This was reflected in the saying *odonko po bebrebe a yede no ko ayie* (the over sophisticated slave risks being sacrificed for a funeral). Fifthly, slaves performed very much the same tasks as other free men and women but they were required to work harder. Hence the designation of certain types of work as *odonko adwuma* (slave work or hard work). Sixthly, a slave was not supposed to take any decision of his/her own, or to embark on any enterprise without permission or instruction from his/her owner. A slave's thinking was supposed to be subsumed under his/her masters: *Akoa nyansa wo ne wura tirim*. The seventh disability which was strongly felt in patrilineal societies, was that a slave's personally acquired property reverted to his/her owner or the family on his/her death.

Finally, slaves were modestly buried. They were not buried in the family cemetery but at a site reserved for those of his kind. The material is varied with respect to the mode of burial. Some assert that the slave was put on a board and dropped in a hole in the ground. Others contend that the slaves were never buried when they died but that their bodies were thrown away onto a plot of land to be eventually devoured by birds or beasts of prey.

In 1844 T.B. Freeman shockingly remarked:

> All slaves, except a few favoured ones, are considered not worth the trouble of a decent burial and are consequently taken, and thrown into the water which runs round the town where they are eaten by the thousands of fishes which this small river contains. No persons are allowed to touch these fishes.[22]

Oral data collected during field work talked about modest burial for slaves. A funeral custom was not held for a slave when he died. Those who were privileged to have funeral customs held for them were those who had risen to important positions in the society. A master or mistress who had lost a good, faithful, loyal and hardworking slave would definitely be sad at his/her passing away but he/she would not do anything elaborate for the deceased slave.

SLAVES AND SUCCESSION TO POLITICAL OFFICE

It has already been noted in chapter four that some slaves played important roles in the administration of traditional states in pre-colonial Ghana. In the Palaces they served in the Household division as well as in the Treasury and Trade Departments. They also served in the army not only as part of the rank and file but exceptional ones such as Ofosu, Amankwatia, Opoku Frefre and Adu Bofo of Asante were given command positions in battle. Some slaves were given the opportunity of becoming family Heads in the families into which they had been integrated. The pre-colonial Ghanaian social structure was transposed into the traditional political realm. By virtue of his membership in a family, lineage and clan, a slave could rise to occupy a position of authority. This chapter discusses the issue of political mobility in pre-colonial Ghana.

TRADITIONAL LAWS OF SUCCESSION

In Northern, Upper East and Upper West Regions, succession to a "skin" was traced patrilineally and it was the privilege of a number of royal branches. These royal branches claimed their right to the skin, and the privileges and responsibilities they enjoyed thereof, from the fact that their ancestors were the first or early settlers in the area. The genealogical tree of the royal branches was traced through the paternal line to the early ancestors. Among the Bawkus for example, their chiefship was traced to Ali, son of Na Atiabia of Mamprusi.

Their first rule of succession provided for the eldest surviving brother or cousin of a deceased chief to succeed to the skin. After brothers and cousins the right of succession passed to brothers' sons in order of seniority. Under no circumstance could a brother be passed over in favour of a son or nephew even if the son or nephew was older than the brother. The second rule provided for the supersession of the rightful heir on grounds of any of the following disabilities: blindness or loss of one eye, leprosy, madness, the loss of a finger or toe, deformity, bad character or incompetence, left-handedness and behaviour discreditable to a member of the chief's family e.g. continual drunkenness or excessive consorting with the common people.

In the event of such a disqualification, the skin was passed on to the next person in direct line of succession or to an outsider. It was this second rule which enabled slaves to occasionally succeed to a skin. Oral data collected in the Northern, Upper East and Upper West Regions indicated that it was not a normal practice for a slave to be enskinned, but in the event of a failure of heirs, a slave who had been integrated into the family and become part of the family could occupy the skin. Oral tradition also relates that slaves could not under any circumstances occupy the office of *Tendana* (the traditional priest and custodian of the land). The office of *Tendana* passed from father to son. To become a *Tendana* one had to be in possession of one's father's gods or the gods of his ancestors. Unfortunately, the chieftaincy reports, the archival material and the court records I studied in these regions did not provide specific examples of slaves who had been enskinned as a result of the second rule of succession.

In the Brong Ahafo Region, succession was traced matrilineally, except in the Mo traditional state which claimed succession patrilineally and the Yeji traditional state which claimed that succession was traced through both the matrilineal and patrilineal lines. Ahafo chieftaincy records indicate that pre-colonial traditional rule required that "any candidate to be enstooled on any stool should be the real royal of the said stool". The Queenmother and a senior member of the royal family were responsible for nominating a candidate to the stool. The Duayaw-Nkwanta records indicate that after a candidate had been nominated, the 'oman' (state) accepted him if he was deemed to be of an unblemished character and his pedigree was not challenged by any member of the Awompi or electoral body.

Stool royals were the only people eligible to occupy the stool, but if no eligible royal was available either by reason of extinction of the direct line or disqualification through physical deformity or any other reasonable cause, the "oman" in consultation with the Queenmother, could elect a member from a collateral family. In the absence of that, "a stool son or grandson," an euphemism for slaves and palace servants, could be appointed to occupy the stool. Any such appointed chief was required to renounce future claims to the stool by members of his family. It is clear from oral data collected in the Brong Ahafo Region that a good, faithful and loyal slave who was a member of his family could succeed to a stool. A palace slave could also succeed to the royal stool in lieu of legitimate or qualified heirs.

In the Eastern Region succession was both matrilineal and patrilineal depending on the ethnic group concerned. Among the Akwapim communities succession was patrilineal. Membership of royalty was stressed in succession matters. Nonetheless a slave could succeed to the stool if there was no suitable heir. In the Central Region where succession was traced matrilineally, the pattern was the same. The Greater Accra and Volta Region chieftaincy reports traced succession patrilineally and emphasised one's right to occupy a stool as a function of his membership of the royal family. A loyal, faithful and good slave could succeed to the stool, usually when there was no heir to the stool.

Of all the ten administrative regions studied, the Asante Region appeared to have been the most generous in allowing slaves to succeed to stools. Succession was traced matrilineally and slaves who had become members of families could succeed to stools. The commonest occasion again appeared to have been when there was no suitable heir. Adansi oral tradition relates that the offspring of a marriage between a free royal male and a female slave could be enstooled as a chief if there were no full-blooded royals available. Children of marriages between slaves could also be enstooled when there were no royals available. In certain cases they were made regents till such a time that a suitable royal was found. When a slave acted as regent of a stool, the regime was called *hweso* (look after). A black stool was not made for a slave chief when he died. Libation to a deceased chief of slave origins was always poured on the ground instead of on the stool. Denkyira oral traditions state that a slave who had been integrated into his owner's family could be enstooled as a chief when there were no royals available. In Asante, just as in all the other regions of Ghana, those entitled to political office were those of the royal family, *adehyee*. The royalty claimed their monopoly of office was justified by the fact that their maternal ancestors were the first to settle in the town or village. The word for royalty *ode hyee* literally means he who owns the boundary. A slave who was asked to occupy a stool was highly privileged. It was not a matter of course that succession should pass to a slave or non-royal if there was no mature member of royalty. With respect to the stools in the Kumasi Traditional area, the decision to appoint a successor or not depended on the will of the Asantehene, the Queenmother and Elders of the stool in question.

CASES IN WHICH SLAVES WERE DENIED ACCESS TO STOOLS

Some families insisted that they would not allow slaves in the family access to the stool because of their slave antecedents. In the Brong Ahafo Region, for example, the 'Safohene' at Akrodie in Goaso refused to allow the slaves in his family to succeed to the stool. He admitted that they were one family but their section of the family could not inherit the stool.[1] In the Eastern Region, the Oyoko stool at Apinamang, denied access to slaves in the family. In a succession dispute, a member of the royal family told one of the slaves *wobo ntete abusua, wo nana biara ntraa Ayokofoo akonnwa a ewo Apinamang so da* (you have no blood ties with the Oyoko clan, no ancestor of yours has ever sat on the Oyoko stool of Apinamang). In effect he was told that as a slave, he could not have prior claim to the stool.[2] In another case at Kyebi, Okyeame Nyankomago told one Yaw Okata that he was a native of Zabarima (i.e. from the Northern Region) and, therefore, he had no claim to the stool. He admitted though that "if a slave keeps longer in a house he becomes a member of a certain stool".[3] In the Greater Accra region, there was a succession dispute with respect to the Prampram and Otublohum stools. The families insisted that the slaves had no right of succession.[4] With respect to the Asante Region the families in charge of the Tuobodum and the Kaasi stools refused to allow slaves to occupy the stools. A similar incident happened in the case of the Tandoh stool of Wassaw Fiasi, Tarkwa, in the Western Region.[5]

CASES OF PROLONGATION OF VACANCIES TO PREVENT NON-ROYALS INHERITING

There were cases in which some families allowed the stools to be vacant for years instead of asking a slave or servant to take care of the stool. For example, when the Ahubrafoo stool became vacant after the death of its first chief during the reign of Asantehene Osei Tutu, the stool remained without a chief for over one hundred years until Asantehene Prempeh II appointed a new chief to the stool. In the case of the Kuntenase stool, when the fifteenth chief was destooled, the Queenmother administered the stool until 1924 when a new chief was appointed. After the death of the second chief of the Mamesene stool, the stool became vacant because there was no mature successor to the stool, until 1922 when a new chief was enstooled.[6] The stool Elders of the above mentioned stools preferred leaving them vacant to allowing a person of non-royal blood to succeed to them. Some of the reasons oral data gave with respect to some families not allowing slaves to occupy stools were that first, they were not members of the royal family. Second, they were of inferior status. Third, it was against their custom and tradition. This was linked with blood and the goodwill of the gods and the ancestors. It was feared that the gods and the ancestors would be offended if a person of non-royal blood occupied the stool. The three reasons outlined above were given in all the ten administrative regions of Ghana. A fourth reason given in Northern, Upper West, Upper East, Central, Eastern, Greater Accra and Volta Regions was that a slave was a stranger and not a native of the land and, therefore, had no right to occupy a stool, but it was intimated that when no heir was available, the slave, as a member of the household and family, could succeed to the stool. In an interview with two elderly men at Mamprobi in Accra on 29th March, 1993, they indicated that some slaves who occupied stools by reason of this concession were often tempted to 'lord it over' persons of royal blood. This led to the Ga saying *Ablekuma abakoma wo* (the strangers have overwhelmed us).

EXAMPLES OF SLAVES SUCCEEDING TO STOOLS

Central Region

In the 18th and 19th centuries, the Mankessim stool allowed a slave succession to the stool because there was no suitable heir. In Cape Coast, a slave called Bisoo, a Mossi by birth, was elevated to occupy a stool. He was described as shrewd and intelligent. A Krontihene of the Simpa Division was a slave.[7]

Greater Accra Region

In Accra, there was the remarkable example of Kodjo, a slave of the English Company in the 18th century, who rose to become chief of the whole of James Town comprising Sempe, Akanmadze and Alata. Kodjo was one of the slaves who had been brought from Nigeria. He and his descendants occupied this position because of some great qualities he exhibited as a linguist and messenger of the English Company. Initially, Kodjo was acknowledged by Chief Otu Blafo of the Otublohum quarter as the first chief of the Alata quarter of Accra town. Gradually Kodjo extended his power and influence over the whole of James Town. Kodjo's descendants 'forgot' their original status as slaves, and one of them called Kodjo IV claimed in 1907 that the head of the Sempe division, the original owners of the land, was his 'Mankralo' (divisional chief). This assertion by Kodjo IV so infuriated Noi, representative of Sempe, that in a commission of enquiry held by Crowther in 1907, he asked:

I am a Ga, did you come from Lagos and make me Mankralo here? Can you who say you are a stranger make me Mankralo?[8]

Volta, Eastern and Brong Ahafo Regions

In the 18th and 19th centuries the division of Penyi authorised that a stool 'son' should occupy the stool until the eligible candidate reached his majority. In Kyebi, a 'son' of the stool was allowed to occupy one of the sub-stools. The Asonson stool in Odumase was on a few occasions occupied by stool 'sons.' In Sunyani, a slave called Kra Kwesi, a "soul washer" of the Kyeremasuhene was privileged to succeed to the stool.[9]

Asante Region

A study of the histories of 212 Asante stools reveals that there were 36 royal stools which were occupied at one time or the other during pre-colonial times by slaves and servants. This constitutes about one fifth of the total number of Asante stools. There were fifty five recorded instances when slaves and servants succeeded to these royal stools. In the Asantehene's palace, the Mpaboahene, Gyebi and Banahene linguist stool, Dua Kyeame, Fontomfrom and Nsenie stools were occupied at certain points in time by slaves and servants of the stool. The sixth chiefs of the Mpaboahene, Dua Kyeame, Fontomfrom and Nsenie stools, namely Kwadwo Frimpong, Kwadwo Apau II, Asamang and Appiagyei succeeded to the stools because there was no mature royal to occupy the stool. In the case of the Gyebi and Banahene linguist stool, the fourth in succession, Opanin Kwabena Kwaku, succeeded to the stool because the Asantehene honoured him for being a faithful and industrious servant.[10]

In Kumasi and the towns and villages within fourteen and forty-eight miles radius of Kumasi, namely, Adum, Ofiri and Manso, Akyawkrom, Dadiesoaba, Debooso, Obuokurom, Nkawie Kumah, Jachie, Boaman, Twafuo, Ekyi, Asuboa, Sekyedomase, Asamang, Juaben and Ejisu, the royal stools witnessed succession by slaves and servants of the palaces and households. The thirteenth and sixteenth chiefs of the Adum stool, Akwasi Bafuor and Bafuor Asamoah Toto II respectively, are described in traditions as "sons of the stool". The ninth chief of the Ofiri and Manso stool called Kwasi Afriyie; the fourteenth chief of Akyawkrom called Kwasi Adom; the second, fourth, eleventh, twelfth and fifteenth chiefs of the Dadiesoaba stool called Nti Kumah, Oti Awere, Nti Takoro, Kwabena Sekyere and Kofi Nsiah respectively and the ninth chief of Abuokrom called Yaw Boakye were all appointed because there was no mature royal to occupy the vacant stools.[11]

The under listed stools were also occupied by slaves and servants at the palaces because there was no mature royal:- Jachie, the ninth in succession called Amoafo; Boaman, the sixth, eighth, tenth and thirteenth chiefs called Nana Burade, Nana Addo Boaman, Nana Akoku and Nana Kwaku Antwi; Twafuo, the seventh chief Bafuor Ekyi and Asuboa, the fifth chief Kwadwo Kwakye. The same reason is given for the enstoolment of Asafo Adjei as the fifteenth chief of Juaben and Kwabena Agyeman as the tenth chief of Asamang. The Debooso stool was occupied by Kwabena Asamoah because there was no suitable royal. For the same reason Mossi and Kofi Kyem were enstooled as the eighth and tenth chiefs respectively of the Debooso stool.[12]

The Nkawie Kumah stool was inherited by the second chief Marfo with the Queenmother's consent, and the Ejisu stool was occupied by the twenty-third chief Kwadwo Boateng because those who were eligible were too young. Boateng was asked to rule until the young royals were old enough to rule.[13]

The reason given for the appointment of the sixth chief Kwadwo Mensah to the Sekyedomase stool is that there was no qualified royal to occupy the stool. The Amoako stool was, however, occupied by Oti Kwatia because after the death of the second chief called Yankyira, there was a great family dispute among members of the royal house. The Asantehene thought it wise to appoint a non-royal who had no interest in the family dispute to occupy the stool. Oti Kwatia seemed to have ruled so well that the Asantehene ordered his stool to be blackened as a mark of great honour. Oti Kwatia's case is illustrative of the extent of political mobility in Asante.[14]

As part of a system of 'checks and balances,' slaves who were privileged to occupy such stools were first made to understand that they were only regents and would have to hand over the stool any time a mature successor was found. Second, they were made to know in no uncertain terms that the stool was not to be passed on to members of their families. Third, they were not buried at the Royal Mausoleum if they died on the stool. Fourth, their stools were not blackened if they died on the stool. In 50 out of the 55 instances found where slaves succeeded to stools in pre-colonial Asante, the stools were not blackened. It was Asante custom to blacken stools of deceased chiefs who ruled successfully as a sign of great honour. The stool was varnished with a mixture of soot and the yolk of egg and kept in a special room. Because of the polish it acquired it was described as a black stool, "Akonnwa tuntum". In pre-colonial Asante, it was also customary for any lineage of consequence to have a stool, because the stool served as the symbol of authority of the chosen head of the lineage. If the lineage head was also a chief, or an elder to the chief, then his own personal stool was preserved in his memory when he died. Subsequent lineage heads all had their black stools kept in the same room – the stool room. Some lineages kept only the stool of the founder or only those of stool Elders who rendered special service to their lineages. The black stool was believed to be inhabited by the spirit or "sunsum" of the head of the lineage for whom it was consecrated, and, therefore, it possessed the magical quality of being able to protect the living members of the lineage. Sacrifices were, therefore, offered to it and prayers made at appointed times. The black stool was in fact a substitute for the physical body, "mogya", of the dead person. The Golden Stool of Asante enshrined the soul of the whole Ashanti nation. It was the greatest of all the royal stools in Asante and the most pre-eminent of all the black stools. It was customary in pre-colonial Asante to offer food and drink to the black stools twice a week and on festive occasions. The Asantes believed that if a person was not a true royal and he became fortunate to inherit a stool of which he was not a true descendant, his stool should not be blackened because the spirit of the original stool ancestor would not usually respond to libation poured on sacred days. This is why the issue of true, real or pure blood was stressed in chieftaincy cases.

Research has established that there are only four instances where slaves and servants had their stools blackened. The first instance was that of the second chief of Dadiesoaba stool called Nti Kumah. In addition to having his stool blackened, his descendants were given formal recognition as royals of the stool. As such they became eligible to contest the stool whenever it became vacant. Nti Kumah must have ruled extremely well to have received this high honour, in fact the highest honour in the land. The second instance was that of the Kona stool whose eleventh occupant, Kwaku Banahene, had his stool blackened. He was, however, made to swear before the Stool Elders that his descendants would be permanently excluded from occupying the stool. The third instance was the Amoako stool occupied by Oti Kwatia. He was the third chief and was appointed to the stool in the midst of a serious family dispute among the members of the stool house. He is said to have ruled so well that the Asantehene was highly impressed, and honoured him. The fourth instance was that of the Gyasewa stool. All the slaves who had their stools blackened attained the highest political status in Asante.[15]

In all the fifty five recorded instances of slaves and servants succeeding to royal stools in Asante, those chosen were people connected with the day to day running of the palaces who had proved themselves faithful, wise and sagacious. In addition to some slaves succeeding to royal stools, other slaves also had the singular honour of having special stools created for them. Again, Asante was the most generous in this regard. In all the ten administrative regions in Ghana studied, only Asante and the Central Regions had examples of such stools. In the Central Region the name of the stool and the slave are not given but it is reported by J.C. de Graft Johnson, Assistant Secretary for Native Affairs in the 1920s.

THE "ESOM DWA" (SERVICE STOOL)

31 out of 212 pre-colonial Asante stools studied were Service Stools, "Esom Dwa". These stools were created solely for non-royal slaves, servants and

dependants at the palaces for faithful, loyal and dedicated service to the state. About one sixth, therefore, of the pre-colonial Asante stools were created for the slaves and servants of the palaces. The Service Stool, "Esom Dwa", had certain characteristics. First, it was a patrilineal stool. This was unusual in a matrilineal society. Family stools, ancestral stools and some created stools in Asante were matrilineal stools. It was only the "Esom Dwa" and the "Mmamma Dwa" (stools for the sons and grandsons of the Asantehene) which were patrilineal stools. The second characteristic was that although the "Esom Dwa" was patrilineal, succession did not always have to pass from father to son. The stools were for slaves and servants at the palaces and, therefore, appointment to the stools was by the prerogative of the Asantehene. Any stool dependant at the Asantehene's palace could be appointed to occupy the stool when it became vacant. The third characteristic of the "Esom Dwa" was that the stool did not belong to any clan as was the case with all other pre-colonial Asante stools. The stool belonged to the administrative and military divisions of the state. The fourth characteristic of the "Esom Dwa" was that virtually all the occupants of the stool swore the oath of allegiance on taking office to the Asantehene with the "Ahwihwibaa" sword. This was a sword of less significance compared to the "Mponponsuo" sword used by paramount chiefs and senior chiefs of the Asante union. The final characteristic was that the "Esom Dwa" was not blackened after the death of its occupant.

The first of such "Service Stools" to be created in Asante was the Kyiniye-kyimfuo stool. It was created by the second Kumasihene Oti Akenten (1630-1660) for a loyal slave called Antwi Panin. The occupant of the stool was responsible for the safe keeping of the king's traditional umbrellas and for the supervision of all umbrella holders of the king. The umbrella holders were part of the "Gyase" (Household) division of the palace. Antwi Panin was succeeded by the following stool dependants: Antwi Kumah, Kwabena Yinka, Bogya-bi-ye-dom, Kwabena Sarkodie, Akwasi Owusu and Kofi Abebrese.[16]

Obiri Yeboah (1660-1697) the third Kumasihene created four "Service Stools," namely, Suma, Atomfuo, Enon and Soadoro. The duties of the Sumahene were first, to provide drink to the king when he was taking traditional meals in the afternoon at 2 o'clock and in the evening at 6 o'clock; and second, to provide water and to see to the cleaning of the king's hands after meals. Third, the Sumahene provided the king with a chewing stick (the traditional toothbrush) after meals. The stool has been occupied by six men, all stool dependants. The Atomfuohene was the chief of the King's blacksmiths. The first occupant, Esumin, was said to have discharged his duties at the King's court with skill and dexterity. The King made him responsible for all activities connected with this industry. The chief of the blacksmiths swore the oath of allegiance to the King with the *Gyapatia* sword, a sword of less significance than the *Ahwihwibaa* sword. It was of inferior quality and used by the *Adikrofo* (sub-chiefs) who preceded the *Abremponfoo* (Senior chiefs). The swearing-in ceremony was not held at the open court of the king as those involving the use of the *Mponponsuo* and *Ahwihwibaa*. The Enonhene was one of the eight chiefs who served at the King's mausoleum. He was responsible for all customary rites performed at the mausoleum on Mondays and Thursdays and also the rites connected with the celebration of the "Akwasidae" and "Awukudae" festivals. He was also charged with the duty of performing all rituals connected with the skeleton of King Opoku Fofie. The Soadoro stool was created for a hunter and servant of the Oyoko people called Kwadwo Tene. He was put in charge of the King's silver regalia, namely the silver stool, silver pipe, silver calabash and a pair of silver sandals.[17]

Osei Tutu, fourth Kumasihene and first Asantehene of the Asante union (c1697-1717), created nine "Service Stools". The Asokwa, Nkonnwasoafo, Mmentia, Baamu, Abenase, Prempeh Drum, Pekyi No. 2, Ahensan and Akropong stools. Asokwa was a town five miles from Kumasi. It was under the Gyase administrative division. The occupant of the stool was put in charge of the Asantehene's horns. He also assisted the Batahene to trade for the Asantehene. He was made responsible for the weeding and fencing of the palace and cutting of firewood. The Nkonnwasoafohene belonged to the Gyase division and was chief of all the Asantehene's stool carriers. He was given the privilege of going directly to the Asantehene without passing through the

Gyasehene. The Mmentiahene also belonged to the Gyase division and was responsible for the Asantehene's short horns. All short horn blowers who exhibited qualities of faithfulness and competence were entitled to occupy the stool. Bampanase-Baamu was the sacred place where the blackened stools of the heroic Asante kings were kept. In Asante tradition it was the first place of residence of Osei Tutu. The duty of the chief was to guard and keep this sacred place. The Abenase stool belonged to the Gyase division. The occupant was in charge of the Asantehene's clothing, head of the kente weavers and "dresser" of the Asantehene's bed. The Prempeh drum was made for Osei Tutu, probably by Okomfo Anokye to head the king's procession. The Pekyi No. 2 stool was regarded as a military one because it was created for the gallant servants of the king. It was part of the Kronti military division. The first chief was called Ankuma Pekyi. Pekyi No. 2 was a village eleven miles from Kumasi. The occupant of the Ahensan stool was one of the twelve accredited linguists of the Asantehene. Ahensan was a village three miles from Kumasi. The stool of Akropong, ten miles from Kumasi, was originally created for the sons and grandsons of the Asantehene. Ansere, a faithful slave who had served Asantehene Osei Tutu in Denkyira, Akwamu and Kumasi was honoured by the king with the occupancy of the stool.[18]

Opoku Ware, the fifth Kumasihene and second Asantehene of the Asante Union (1717-1750) created five "Service Stools"– Ananta, Gyasewa, Nnibi, Bohyen and Derma. The Ananta stool was created for Ofosu, in recognition of the spirit of initiative and valour he displayed when he repulsed an attack by Apotwe, the chief of Assin. The troops of Ofosu were made part of the king's personal bodyguard. The Anantahene went to the *Krafie* on ceremonial occasions to keep guard whilst the Asantehene performed certain rituals. He was made equal in status to the Bantamahene in military affairs. He was charged with the responsibility of challenging the Bantamahene if he was trying to bring trouble or seize power in the state. He had seven chiefs under him, including the chief of the medicine men. In the administrative division he belonged to the Gyase group. The Nnibihene belonged to the Gyase division and was directly under the Sanahene. He, therefore, performed the role of assistant state treasurer. The Bohyehene was one of the traditional priests attached to the king's mausoleum at Bremang. He had the responsibility of pouring libation to the ancestral gods on Mondays, Thursdays and after the celebration of the Awukudae and Akwasidae festivals. He was also responsible for the 'outdooring' and 'indooring' ceremonies of the skeleton of Asantehene Kwaku Dua I. The Derma stool was created for Ntiamoah, a faithful servant and hunter. His duty was to supply meat regularly to the Asantehene. [19]

Asantehene Osei Kwadwo (1764-1777) created the Nkonsong and Hyiawu military stools initially for two of his brothers who had rendered faithful service to him. After the Banda war, however, he decided to educate the male captives to serve as his special bodyguard. The stools, therefore, acquired a new character. [20]

Four "Service Stools" were created during the reign of the famous nineteenth Century Asantehene Osei Tutu Kwame Asibey Bonsu (1801-1824). These were the Atene Akuapong, Danpoomu, Akyiniyekyinfuo and the Sepe Owusu Ansah stools. [21] The Atene Akuapong stool was created after the Gyaman war (1820). The occupant was given the duty of guarding the Golden Stool. All successors to the stools have been stool dependants at the palace. Asantehene Prempeh II changed the status of the stool into a hereditary stool of matrilineal descent. Currently the stool belongs to a group known as Werehuduoefo. Only descendants of this group have a legal claim to the stool. The Danpoomu stool was also created after the Gyaman war. The first chief Denim was a Gyaman captive. The chief of the stool was responsible for the safe keeping of the valuable property of the Asantehene. This included state swords, golden guns, golden bottles and fans. All the successors to this stool have been servants of the palace. The Akyiniyekyinfuo stool was captured from the Gyamans during the Gyaman war and made a "Service Stool". The duties of the occupant were firstly, to safe-guard the keys to the room where the various umbrellas of the Asantehene were kept and secondly, to see to the day to day administration of the various umbrellas of the Asantehene. The Sepe Owusu Ansah stool was also created after the Gyaman war. It became part of the Ankobea division of the court. Sepe Owusu Ansah was a suburb about three miles from Kumasi. Traditionally this stool was also known as the Gyedu stool. Gyedu, a prominent citizen of Gyaman, and his relatives were captured during the Gyaman war. Asantehene Osei Bonsu ruled that Gyedu should serve him through the Anaminakohene. The horns attached to the stool blow *Hwan na oye wo! Osei Bonsu na oye wo!* (Who created you? It is Osei Bonsu who created you).

Asantehene Osei Yaw Akoto (1824-1838) created the Mmagyegyefuo stool. The occupant of this stool was made the head of all the nannies at the Asantehene's court. He was responsible for caring for and training the royal children. The stool was designed for any of the king's household servants/ slaves who excelled at caring for the royal children.[22]

The Omanti stool was created by Asantehene Prempeh I (1888-1931) for Kwaku Fi, a slave at the court. It became a stool for household servants who proved themselves industrious, energetic and faithful. The Omantihene was made part of the Manwere division. He was also made a 'nanny' to the Asantehene.[23] All the slaves who occupied the "Service Stools" regarded themselves as highly privileged.

THE BANTAMA AND GYASEWA STOOLS

Two other stools which deserve special mention in this chapter are the *Bantama* and *Gyasewa* stools. Although they fall under the category of "Service Stools" they are in a class of their own in terms of status. They are classic examples of the attainment of the highest political mobility in pre-colonial Ghana.

The Bantama stool is described in traditions as non-ancestral, non-royal, non-hereditary and of patrilineal descent.[24] The stool was created by Asantehene Osei Tutu for Amankwatia Panin, a stool carrier of Denkyirahene Boa Amponsem who had followed him to Kumasi. He was made Krontihene (commander in chief of the Asante army) during the Dormaa war. This was a great honour because it meant that Amankwatia Panin was one of the highest officials in the Asante military unit. He had under him the Akwamuhene (second in command), the Benkum and Nifahene (left and right wing chiefs), the Adontenhene (Head of the main body), Ankobeahene (Head of the Body guard), Kyidomhene (Head of the Rearguard) and the Gyasehene (Head of the Palace Household). In the civilian administrative set up in the Asantehene's palace, Amankwatia Panin became one of the important administrators. So far as the whole Asante Nation is concerned, Amankwatia Panin became part of Bowdich's Aristocracy. Bowdich talked about three estates of government, the King, Aristocracy and the Assembly of Captains. The Aristocracy dealt with foreign issues, supervised domestic affairs and exercised judicial authority.

When Amankwatia Panin died, he was succeeded by his son Amankwatia. It was Amankwa Abinowa alias Amankwatia VI that Bowdich met on his visit to Kumasi in 1817. The Aristocracy then consisted of four officials – the Bantamahene Amankwatia, Asafohene Kwakye Kofi, Gyasewahene Opoku Frefre and Adumhene Adum Ata. Wilks describes the Aristocracy as the Privy or Inner Council and the Assembly of Captains as the Asantemanhyiamu. Membership in the Asantemanhyiamu was on territorial basis. It comprised all the Amanhene (Paramount Chiefs), some senior Kumasi chiefs and a few provincial rulers.

In pre-colonial days the Bantamahene had seven warrior chiefs under him to strengthen the Kronti division. These were the Bantama-Baamuhene, the Essuowinhene, Afarihene, Akwaboahene, Twafuo Baah, Kurawumahene and Amakye Barihene.

The importance of the Bantama stool is still reflected in contemporary times.

The Gyasewa stool was created by Asantehene Opoku Ware for his son Adusei Atwiniwa. When Adusei died, he was succeeded by his uncle Ntim Panin, but he was soon destooled for mismanagement. Asantehene Osei Bonsu gave the stool to Opoku Frefre, a stool servant, for faithful and long service in the palace.[25] Opoku Frefre was the son of slave parents. After spending his child-hood with his father at Anyatiase near Lake Bosumtwe, he was taken as a servant by Oyokohene Buapon of Kumasi. He accompanied Oyokohene Buapon to the court of Asantehene Osei Kwadwo. The Asantehene was much impressed by Opoku's talents and nicknamed him "Frefre" (Tia Frede-frede) which means nimble. On the death of the Oyokohene, Opoku Frefre was taken as part of the death duties ("Awunyadie") to the Asantehene's palace. He became one of the most favoured of the young palace servants because of his alertness. Asantehene Osei Kwadwo noted his talents and gave him to Gyasewahene Ntim Panin for training in the Treasury Department. Opoku served under the Sanahene Yaw Dadie (State Treasurer) and the Fotosanfohene Esom Adu (Chief Cashier). He soon rose to become the Fotosanfohene. During the reign of Asantehene Osei Bonsu, he was appointed Gyasewahene (Head of the Exchequer). Opoku was elevated to the highest political office so far as the Asante financial administration was concerned. Under him were the Sanahene (State Treasurer), the Fotosanfo (cashiers), Towgyefo and Nsumagyefo (collectors of tributes and taxes) and the Batafo (traders).

In the Asante national political hierarchy, Opoku Frefre was part of Bowdich's Aristocracy or Wilks' Privy/Inner Council. The Aristocracy played an important role in the central and provincial administration of the Asante kingdom. Opoku Frefre was among three officials who were put in charge of the conquered provinces. He was in charge of the provinces of Akyem and Akwamu. Opoku and the other officials delegated officers of their own choice to take care of these provinces, while they themselves concentrated on the affairs of the central administration. Opoku Frefre was also a great warrior. In 1802, he held a military command in the expeditionary force sent to the north western provinces. Five years later he led the forces which invaded Fante land and fought Anomabu. In 1811 he was appointed by Asantehene Osei Bonsu to command an expedition against Winneba and Bereku, to prevent their attacks upon Accra. He campaigned in Akyem, Akwapim, Shai, Ada, Krobo etc. Between 1818 and 1819 he held a senior military command in the Gyaman expeditionary force which captured the Imam of Bonduku. In the early 1820s, Opoku Frefre was regarded as the best and most powerful of the Asante generals. In 1826 he commanded an Asante division in the south-eastern provinces. Due to his military prowess, Dupuis heard a song being sung in his honour during his mission to Kumasi in 1820. It was as follows:

> Where shall we find such a warrior as strong and beautiful Apacoo Kudjo whose eyes are like the panther in fight? O great slave of the King, how you are beloved! Your victories delight his ears. Who fought the Gyamans and killed their cabocer Adouai? Apacoo Kudjo.[26]

Opoku Frefre's ruthlessness in warfare earned him the title *obu abasa* (the breaker of arms). The Gyasewa stool also came to be known as the *Obuabasa stool* and the stools under the Gyasewa division also came to be known by that name.

In October 1817, Opoku Frefre displayed his wealth publicly before the Asantehene and the citizens of Kumasi. It was a mark of the highest honour in the land. On that occasion Asantehene Osei Bonsu declared the Gyasewa stool hereditary for Opoku Frefre's family. As part of the Asante mechanism of checks and balances, the occupant of the Gyasewa stool was prohibited from using the title Nana. The approved title was Opanin. When Opoku Frefre died, the Asantehene had his stool blackened.

Opoku Frefre was followed in succession by four of his sons – Adu Damte (1826-39), Adu Nantwiri (who ruled briefly), Adu Boahen (1840-67) and Adu Bofo (1867-1876). Of all the sons, the youngest, Adu Bofo became the most famous in Asante history because like his father, he also played a prominent role in Asante political and military life. Adu Bofo's mother was a slave. Adu Bofo is remembered in Asante traditions for undertaking the Krepe campaign of 1868. It was in this campaign that the Ramseyers and Kuhne, missionaries at Anum, and Bonnat, the trader at Ho, were taken captives to Kumasi. In June 1869, Adu Bofo faced the forces of Dompreh, the leader of Akyem Kotoku's resistance to Asante. Around 1870, after fifteen engagements against

Dompreh, Dompreh was finally killed in battle at Abutia. The following year, Adu Bofo returned to Kumasi where he was publicly honoured by Asantehene Kofi Karikari. He was presented with many gifts including slaves.

In 1872, Adu Bofo was sent on an invasion of the British protected territories. He was elevated to commander of the army for the south west, while the actual commander of the Asante army, Bantamahene Amankwatia, was appointed commander in chief for the invasion of the south. Adu Bofo's success in the Krepe campaign and other campaigns raised him to a position of great importance. According to tradition, when Adu Bofo died, the Kronkohene Kwadwo Apan made a bid for the stool, but he did not succeed. By the decree of the Asantehene that was not possible. Kofi Poku, son of Adu Bofo's brother Adu Boahen, succeeded to the Gyasewa stool. Since then succession has indeed passed through the descendants of Opoku Frefre. The only person who sat on the stool and was not descended from Opoku Frefre was one Kwame Tuah (1900-6). He was appointed by the British government after the Yaa Asantewaa war. After Tua, Kwabena Asubonten (1906-22), a son of Adu Bofo succeeded.

Traditional laws of succession in pre-colonial Ghana were traced patrilineally, matrilineally or both, depending on the ethnic group. Priority was given to members of royalty. In the absence of suitable or mature heirs, slaves and servants were allowed to succeed to the skin/stool. Some families did not adhere to these rules and refused to allow slaves and servants succession to the skin/stool. In some cases the stool was vacant for many years, awaiting the rightful successor. Examples of slaves succeeding to stools can be found in the Central, Greater Accra, Volta, Eastern, Brong Ahafo and Asante Regions. The Asante Region was perhaps the most generous in allowing slaves to succeed to stools. In all, 31 special Service Stools ("Esom Dwa") were created for slaves, servants and dependants at the palaces for faithful, loyal and dedicated service to the state. The succession to stools and the creation of special service stools for slaves in pre-colonial Ghana was not a casual gesture. It was a mark of great honour and an eloquent proof of the highest political mobility.

THE ABOLITION OF INDIGENOUS SLAVERY

T he abolition of the indigenous institution of slavery was a long and gradual process spanning a period of about one hundred years. After the promulgation of the law that abolished the Atlantic slave trade in 1807, the concern and efforts of British officials in Ghana were focused on the implementation of the law. All attention was immediately focused on the Atlantic slave trade leaving the indigenous institution of slavery to continue to thrive. From the governorship of Macarthy in 1821 to the governorship of R. Pine in 1873, British governors and officials contended with this institution. The attitudes, efforts and frustrations of the British officials with respect to abolition of slavery, are best discussed in four phases. The first phase is from 1807-1873; the second phase deals with the 1874 proclamation abolishing indigenous slavery in the Protectorate and its effects; the third phase covers 1896-1908 when the British government began to administer Asante and the Northern Territories; the fourth phase deals with the period 1908-1928 when the British officials continue to effect changes with respect to abolition and take stock of their efforts. Since the fourth phase falls outside the scope of this book, a summary has been provided in the Appendix.

1807-1873: THE FIRST PHASE OF ABOLITION

The year 1807 was not only significant in Ghana because of the abolition of the Atlantic slave trade. It also marked the beginning of the British government's direct dealings with the British settlements on the coast. From the time that the

The Donko Nsuo in Assin Manso.

The tomb stones of Crystal, a Jamaican woman who fought against racism and Samuel Carson, an African American naval officer. They were buried at Assin Manso in August 1998.

The sign post to the slave cemetery in Assin Praso.

On the right is the gate to the mass African slave grave.

This is the mass grave of African slaves.

Sign post and gate leading to the European Colonial Officers' Cemetery in Assin Praso.

The European Colonial Officers' Cemetery at Assin Praso.

The Pra river.

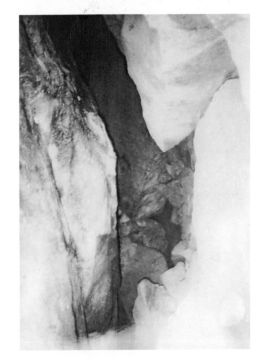

*This cave was a hiding place
against slave raiders
in the Shai area of the
Greater Accra Region.*

Fort Apollonia, Benyin in the Western Region.
The British built this fort in the late 1700s.

Princestown, the only German fort in Africa was built
in the 1680s in Ahanta, Western Region.

Fort Orange, Sekondi was built by the Dutch in the 1670s.

Fort Sebastian, Shama was built by the Portuguese around 1520-26.

Elmina Castle in the Central Region built by the Portuguese in 1482.

Cape Coast Castle built as a Trade Lodge in 1555 by the Portuguese and named 'Cabo Corso'. Developed into a Permanent Fort in 1653 by the Swedes and called 'Carolusberg'. Taken over by the British in 1655 and extended into a big Castle.

Fort Good Hope, Senya Bereku built by the Dutch in 1705.

The tunnel in Fort Good Hope connecting the mainland to the sea. Slaves and trade goods passed through this tunnel.

An outer view of the Christianborg Castle, Accra built by the Danes in the 17th century.

The renovated Christiansborg Castle. It is the present seat of Government.

Fort Patience, Apam built by the Dutch in 1697.

Fort Fredensborg, Old Ningo built by the Danes in the late 18th century.

Ruins of Kongenssteen the Danish Fort at Ada.

At the back of Fort Kongeenssteen is the German missionary cemetery.

Fort Prinzenstein built by the Danes in 1784 in Keta, Volta Region.

The side view of the fort.

British Parliament decreed the ending of the Atlantic slave trade, the issue of "African civilisation" became an indispensable element in Britain's plans.

From 1807 to 1821 the British Company of merchants was saddled with the responsibility of ensuring that abolition was carried out to its fullest extent. The documents show an overwhelming pre-occupation with the Atlantic slave trade. The result was that indigenous slavery was conveniently ignored. When Sir Charles Macarthy took over the reins of government on the coast in 1821, the issue of slavery, both Atlantic and indigenous, engaged his attention. Macarthy found it easier to declare the Atlantic Slave Trade Abolition Law than to apply it. He was the first governor to meet the slavery problem squarely. The question of slavery, both Atlantic and indigenous, was also of concern to his successor George Maclean. Maclean made it clear during his administration that the exportation of slaves was strictly prohibited by the laws of England, but he kept silent on the indigenous institution. In spite of his pronouncements, the Atlantic slave trade continued to exist. He was criticised for tolerating slavery and in 1837 he appeared before the Committee of Merchants on charges of recognising slavery. Maclean told the committee that indigenous slavery had been in existence in Ghana from time immemorial and his government could not be held answerable for the continuation of the practice. The British government appointed Dr. R.R. Madden in 1840 to examine the whole question of slavery. He discovered that indigenous slavery prevailed on every part of the coast. The slaves were happy and were used mainly for domestic service. He remarked in surprise:

> I was not aware, however, that slavery existed in any part of the British empire or of its settlements except in India, Ceylon and St. Helena, which were specifically exempted from the operation of the general *Act of Emancipation* of 1834, till I visited the Gold Coast. There I found English subjects holding slaves and pawns, buying, selling and disposing of them as property at their deaths, and the official sanction of the authorities even given to this system. I called on Capt. Maclean to take steps to put it down.[1]

Following Madden's report a Select Committee was appointed to deal in depth with the issues raised. Sir John Jeremie, Governor-General based in Sierra Leone issued the following proclamation on 4th March, 1841:

> Now, therefore, be it known that by several acts of Parliament... commonly called the Slave Trade Abolition Act and the Slave Emancipation Act, it is unlawful for any person to hold slaves in any country whatever, except India, Saint Helena and Ceylon; and that in all such cases the holders are liable to severe punishment and the persons thus unlawfully held in slavery to seizure and confiscation.[2]

In correspondence with Lord Russell, Maclean expressed difficulties he encountered trying to implement this proclamation. He did not have a problem with the European residents but the Ghanaians themselves were unwilling to co-operate, especially when to them there appeared to be a very thin line between Atlantic slavery and indigenous slavery. Maclean emphasised that indigenous slavery had always existed in Ghana and throughout his administration he had pointed this out to the African Committee of Merchants. Lord Russell encouraged Maclean to enforce the Slavery Abolition Act "against any person holding another in slavery or in pawn within the dominions of the British Crown". In spite of what appeared to have been the failure of Maclean in dealing effectively with slavery, the Select Committee on West African Forts of 1842, commended his efforts in administering the settlements with a miserable pittance of between £3,500 and £4,000 a year from four ill-provided forts of Dixcove, Cape Coast, Anomabu and British Accra manned by a few ill-paid black soldiers. Maclean stated boldly at the end of his administration that from 1830-1842 he had tried as much as possible to deal effectively with the Atlantic slave trade. He had done his best under the prevailing circumstances and had reduced the exportation of slaves. With respect to indigenous slavery he stated:

> I have invariably prevented, upon my own responsibility, the transmission of domestic slaves from the settlements to the interior,

by native owners, for the purposes of sale. And I have even, as far as in me lay, prohibited the transfer of domestic slaves under any circumstances from one person to another. And in many instances where it has been proved before me and my brother magistrates that a slave has been treated with undue severity by his master, I have enfranchised him. In short, while as President of the Council I had no authority to interfere with the system of domestic slavery which I found in existence when I entered upon my duties, I uniformly did everything in my power to modify and mitigate it, and in point of fact, domestic slavery when I left the coast, existed in little more than name.[3]

Throughout the 1840s, Sir John Jeremie's proclamation of 4th March 1841 was the guide for British officials. The colonial office position was that this proclamation was an affirmation of a principle of law which declared it unlawful for any person to hold slaves in a British Territory. There did not seem to be any distinction between slaves for Atlantic usage and slaves for indigenous purposes. Slaves were slaves. Another guiding principle for the officials was for them to distinguish between the laws of Great Britain and the laws of other lands. The laws of Great Britain were binding only within the British Dominions except in a few peculiar cases where the municipal law still applied to a British subject even in a foreign land.

The Colonial Office further stated:

This distinction is of a great importance in reference to the British Forts on the Gold Coast. Her Majesty's dominion on that coast is, as I understand, of very narrow local range... it extends only to the forts themselves. Whatever influence Great Britain may exercise beyond those precincts, my supposition is that beyond the very walls of the forts there is no sovereignty properly speaking vested in the British Crown but that the whole adjacent country is subject to the dominion of the native powers.[4]

This distinction meant that two different laws co-existed in Ghana. English law was applicable only within the territorial limits of Her Majesty's jurisdiction. In essence this also meant that the rest of the country could legitimately engage in indigenous slavery as the traditional laws had not abolished the institution but rather upheld it. In fact Lord Russell stated "it follows that within the fort of Cape Coast Castle a different rule of law regarding slavery may prevail" and that "with regard to persons living in the vicinity not within the British dominion the same rule does not apply". His reasons were that if the laws or usages of those countries tolerated slavery, they had no right to set aside those laws or usages except by persuasion, negotiation and other peaceful means.

As proof of the adherence to the laws and principles given by the Colonial Office with respect to slavery, one of the British officials informed Lord Stanley of the Colonial Office that in the 1840s the system of slavery existing among the "Native Population" of any class was not interfered with. What they did was to give every protection and redress to slaves who were ill-treated and emancipate them on the spot, although they had not received any instructions to do so. If this was the attitude of British officials to slavery, one wonders why Maclean was subjected to trial for tolerating indigenous slavery. Other officials asserted that the Atlantic slave trade had been entirely suppressed and notwithstanding the difficulty of dealing with the habits and prejudices of the "Natives" beyond the jurisdiction of the forts, they believed much had been done to ameliorate the condition of the slave population. They admitted that a lot more work needed to be done with respect to indigenous slavery and cautioned that "sudden and direct attempts to alter or abolish native customs and prejudices should be avoided". Another official on board a ship off Whydah on 15th May 1843 commented that the slave trade was a "vast disease of the continent of Africa". Presumably this official was patrolling the "Slave Coast" which stretched from the Volta Region in Ghana to the Cameroons.

On 20th May 1843, Maclean lamented to Lord Stanley that the "Slave Coast" had experienced more exportation of slaves during the last thirty years than any other portion of the coast of similar extent. Three cruisers had been dispatched to the coast to keep watch and not withstanding their vigilance, cargoes of slaves were still being exported without detection. The "Slave Coast" was a problem for all the officials manning the "Gold Coast". Some slaves from Ghana, especially from Asante and the Northern Territories, were sent through the Volta Region to the "Slave Coast". The Atlantic slave trade had not been totally suppressed and the question of indigenous slavery loomed large in British officials' thinking.

Between 1842 and 1845 the British Crown modified the judicial system on the coast upon the recommendations of the Select Committee's Report of 1842. A judicial officer was appointed to exercise jurisdiction outside the forts and Maclean was appointed to this new office. Maclean now took second place to a new Lieutenant-governor appointed in 1843 as a sequel to the British Settlements Act and the Foreign Jurisdiction Act of 1843. These Acts made it lawful for Her Majesty to establish all such laws, institutions and ordinances, and to constitute such courts and officers as may be necessary for the peace, order and good government of Her Majesty's subjects. The Foreign Jurisdiction Act made it lawful for Her Majesty to hold, exercise and enjoy any power or jurisdiction which Her Majesty has or may have at any time within any country or place out of Her Majesty's dominions. On the recommendations of the Select Committee of 1842, the chiefs on the coast were persuaded to signify their recognition of British jurisdiction by signing the famous Bond of 6th March, 1844. Before Governor Hill signed this Bond with the chiefs, he found it necessary to refute a rumour which was being circulated to the effect that it was the intention of Her Majesty's government to grant freedom to all slaves within the limits over which jurisdiction had been exercised. Governor Hill assured the chiefs that it was an idle report and that the export slave trade was all that was prohibited. They were, however, not at liberty to ill-use their domestic slaves, and if a person inherited a slave, that person was not at liberty to sell the slave again, but such a slave was to be considered a member of the family. The chiefs were delighted on hearing this and quickly appended their signatures to the "Bond". The Colonial Office interpreted this move as giving Her Majesty's government immediate control of the Protectorate. One hundred years later, one of Ghana's famous politicians called Obetsebi Lamptey described this Bond of friendship and protection as fateful. He stated as follows:

> Our fathers recognised British power and jurisdiction on these shores, little did they realise that they were signing away not only their independence and sovereignty, but were also clapping their neck into a noose of another slavery more insidious, more far reaching in its interests, more devastating in its effects than the physical slavery that preceded it".[5]

In 1847, the report on the "Slave Coast" was still not encouraging. It noted that the African slave trade had not declined on that part of the coast. The means used for its suppression was inadequate. The greater portion of the slaves shipped from the coast were not as of old taken away in the regular slave trading vessels but were shipped in foreign vessels - American, Hamburg, Bremen, French, Sardian and Greek. The report noticed vast numbers of swift canoes that could transport slaves along the shore quicker than a cruiser stationed on the coast between the River Volta and the mouth of the Benin River. So long as the Volta River and the Volta Region were a part of the "Slave Coast" the British government had an onerous task to deal with.

In 1850, Earl Grey of the Colonial Office decided to separate the "Gold Coast" from Sierra Leone as the area of jurisdiction had increased. "The vast district extending from Assini to Prampram and back to Ashanti" was all under the jurisdiction of the British Authorities. The official policy in this area with respect to slavery remained the same as in the 1840s. The Atlantic slave trade was prohibited by law; indigenous slavery was not to be practised by British subjects; and ill-treated slaves from any part of the country were to be set free. In the 1850s the Judicial Assessor was told that his office did not confer upon him the power of altering or abrogating the practice of English Law among the people of the Gold Coast. His post was to enable him control the native chiefs, to punish them for an undue severity in the exercise of their powers, to abolish such practices as were repugnant to humanity and to introduce improvements in the administration of justice. The Judicial Assessor informed the Colonial Office that with respect to the institution of slavery as it existed on the Gold Coast, he had only been able to make it a punishable offence for the owner of a slave to sell or transport slaves out of the Protectorate. He had also been able to protect slaves from ill-treatment, to ameliorate their condition by improving the laws applicable to master and slaves; to afford greater facilities for their manumission; and to support them in their resistance of all doubtful and ill defined claims upon them for servitude. With the transfer of a slave from one master to another within the Territories under British Protection he had not interfered unless it appeared that such transfer was made by compulsion and for the purpose of punishment.

In a case of slave dealing preferred against one John Marmon, a British merchant in British Accra which came before the Judicial Assessor's court on 24th November 1851, it came to light that Marmon and his Ghanaian wife had domestic slaves. English Law could not be applied to her as she was not a British subject. She could not consequently be sent for trial for felony with Marmon and had to be dealt with by the Judicial Assessor's Court which sentenced her to two years imprisonment for the offence of cruelly maltreating her slave and transporting her for sale to a district of the country where she might be less under the protecting care of the government.[6]

The slave trade continued in earnest on the "Slave Coast" throughout the 1850s. Some of the British officials noticed on a visit to Dahomey that some Ghanaians sent slaves to Popo for exportation. Such slaves either passed along the coast from Accra or at some distance from the coast through the interior. One official had drawn the attention of Governor Winniett to this practice, but he had not done anything about it. The chief of Lagos called Kosoko was described by a missionary as a tool in the hands of Brazilian slave dealers and an "agent in bribing the kings of Dahomey and Ashanti and other chiefs". The anti-slavery squadrons had been doing their best to put an end to the slave trade and considered that "Only two offenders are left, the king of Dahomey and the chief of Lagos who still refuse to yield to persuasion".

These two continued to thwart and frustrate the measures of Her Majesty's government.

Governor Hill, faced with dealing with the Atlantic slave trade on the "Slave Coast" and indigenous slavery, issued another Proclamation on slavery in 1851. Reports reaching the governor indicated that there was great excitement in the towns and the Proclamation was torn from the walls. At a Legislative Council meeting held at the Cape Coast Castle on 12th December 1851 to discuss the reactions, Magistrate Swanzy remarked that a portion of the Proclamation was highly objectionable and illegal because no Proclamation could make a law; they were only intended to enforce existing laws. The clause he objected to read:

> yet be it known, that from and after this date, the purchase of slaves for domestic service by educated natives is strictly prohibited.[7]

Swanzy opined that it would be illegal for any Magistrate or Judicial Assessor's Court to enforce one law with regard to the educated and a different law with regard to the uneducated. Magistrate Cruickshank remarked that the Proclamation was merely a declaration on the part of the government and was no law. The office of the Assessor was made for the purpose of endeavouring to introduce gradually better laws and customs in the country and they were gradually undergoing modification. This Proclamation, he went on, did not manumit the slaves of the people; it even recognised slavery among them - only declared that the government would not recognise the right of the educated natives - those who were on a footing with Europeans in their advantage - to hold slaves. If their slaves served them, they might, but the government would not recognise in its courts a slave of the educated natives.

On 15th December 1851, the educated natives complained to the governor about the Proclamation. They were sorry that King Kofi Amissah, the chiefs and the people of Cape Coast had been told that the Proclamation had no reference to them but to the educated ones. This action on the part of the government would affect the course of education. They stated that since the

Slave Trade Abolition Act of 1807 was passed, a period before some of them were born, they learnt that it applied solely to the exportation of slaves. It did not interfere with the possession of domestic slaves within the Gold Coast. They were not aware that any law had been introduced into the country and received by the people, which made it a felony for a certain class of natives of the land to be found to be holding domestic slaves. This social system had, for some time, been recognised by the local authority and among the native population, educated or uneducated, without discrimination. About ten years ago the magistrates and other European Residents put it beyond doubt that domestic slavery was not to be interfered with. To support their case, they enclosed a copy of a protest letter sent to Sir John Jeremie, the late Governor-General of Sierra Leone in 1841 and also copies of replies to certain queries furnished to Dr. Madden the Commissioner of Enquiry by Capt. Maclean. The Protestors went on to state that there was no law in the country that criminalised domestic slavery. They had been distinctly made to understand publicly in the Assessor's Court that the English Law was not to be applied to areas outside the Castle. They knew that the local government recognised the right of holding domestic slaves in the areas outside the Castle and this was not limited to any class of people. If the English Law operated in the areas outside the Castle then the Assessor could not be justified in purchasing from their respective owners (a few days after His Excellency's arrival) seven slaves whose full value was such that he paid 14 oz. of gold dust. Those slaves ran into the castle to be enlisted as soldiers and since English Law certainly prevailed within the walls of the Castle, they should have been unconditionally manumitted. The protestors dwelt on the suspicion that the Proclamation was made to injure their character and set their Correspondents in England against them. They expressed regret that His Excellency told the king, chiefs and people of Cape Coast that the Proclamation did not affect them (i.e. the native rulers and people) but was solely intended against the educated natives. The Protestors asked the government to consider compensating them if they insisted that they should give up their slaves. The names of the Protestors were Henry Barnes, Joseph Smith, Thomas Hughes, De Graft, Isaac Robertson, James Thompson, William Hooper, John Carr, Josiah Javia, John Hagan and

J.C. Grant. The Protestors also enclosed a copy of a meeting held by the British Resident Merchants at Cape Coast on 24th March 1841 on the Proclamation of Sir John Jeremie, and a copy of a memorandum written by Magistrate Cruickshank at Cape Coast on 26th August 1851. Cruickshank's memorandum accepted the existence of domestic slavery in Ghana and related that slavery had to continue to exist until ages of civilising influence had prepared the minds of men for its abolition. Cruickshank did not think the slaves themselves in their present ignorant and helpless condition would be able to make use of their freedom even if it were accorded them. There had not been in the history of the world an instance of what he called "Constitutional Slavery" i.e. slavery growing out of the natural formation of society – being suddenly and violently abolished. It had always been the work of time, of gradual progress and of the advancement of a people in knowledge and wealth. Cruickshank further stated:

> The abolition of slavery by the English in the West Indies is a very different thing from its abolition in a country where it forms the groundwork of the social system. There the slaves were strangers, had no country, were the property of Europeans to whom their liberation upon compensation was nothing different from the sale of any other property... Here domestic slavery is the root and foundation of the whole social system and can only give way to a very slow and gradual process.[8]

Cruickshank submitted ten proposals aimed at improving the condition of slaves. The records are unfortunately silent on whether the governor gave the Protestors compensation on freeing their slaves or whether the Protestors were allowed to keep their slaves but to treat them well. I am inclined to believe the latter option from the silence of the documents and from the several complaints the British officials often sent to the Colonial Office about their administrative handicaps, including finance, inadequate troops, staff and logistics.

The official policy and suggestions regarding slavery, however, began to yield some results as one J.P. Brown decided to free all of his domestic slaves in November 1852. According to him a recent visit he paid to England had "opened my eyes to the odium and error of keeping domestic slaves". He realised slavery was offensive to every right-minded person and although by birthright he was the eldest son in possession of some domestic slaves he was willing to give them up. "I beg to assure you that my motives are purely of a philanthropic nature," he stated.[9]

In March 1853 the Aborigines Protection Society of London wrote to the secretary of the Anti-Slavery Society to inform him of the existence of domestic slavery on the "Gold Coast". The Colonial Office reply was to assure the Anti-Slavery Society that the governor of the "Gold Coast" was fully alive to the existence of this "evil and he is using his best exertions to put an effectual stop to it". This assurance was put to the test a year later when there was a rebellion from the former Danish subjects. The rebellion was mainly against the imposition of the Poll Tax by Britain, but initially the British officials attributed the rebellion to "our stringent rules respecting the sale or transfer of slaves for transportation". This rebellion began in January 1854 and when all seemed quiet it resurfaced in October 1854. This time the hostilities were so bad that the governor sent a force to punish them for insulting the British flag. A number of casualties resulted from this exercise. In January 1855 however, the Acting Governor confidently informed the Colonial Office that

> never in the history of the Slave Districts of Negro Africa has there been for the people generally so happy a state of things as the present.[10]

The people in the Protectorate were under strong British protection against external and internal oppressors and pretenders. The chiefs had been deprived of the power of killing, kidnapping, plundering and selling into foreign countries their fellow creatures. But the Acting Governor believed that even the chiefs felt generally happy.

The Colonial Office Despatches of 1856 indicate that although the Gold Coast government was happy with the progress it had made with respect to slavery, it had only succeeded in ameliorating the condition of slaves as it still had to tolerate and recognise indigenous slavery. One of the major constraints was finance. The settlements were still being maintained on £4,000 a year, as was the case during Captain Maclean's administration.

By April 1857, the British protected Territories had further expanded in size and covered the line of coast from Apollonia in the west to Keta in the East, a distance of about 350 miles. The government divided the area into two - the Windward or Western districts and the Leeward or Eastern districts. In these areas indigenous slavery was regarded by the government as an issue of great difficulty because although they did not recognise the system, they were compelled to tolerate it as they did not have the means of suppressing it. In October 1857, the governor of Sierra Leone was so disappointed that their Protectorate over the "Gold Coast" necessarily involved the recognition of slavery and pawning that he suggested a withdrawal by the British government. If Her Majesty's government thought it right to retain the Protectorate, then the Protectorate should also be subject to English Law, so that slavery would not be tolerated. The Protectorate should be an asylum and no slave who took refuge within it should on any account be returned to his master. He concluded:

> A few free colonies on the coast would do more to abolish slavery and spread true civilisation than the largest Protectorate we could exercise, tolerating and sanctioning the barbarous institutions of the people. Slave owners would be far more careful not to ill-treat their slaves when they know that they could run into our colonies to be free... except in extreme cases their slaves will either be returned to them by us or be paid for.[11]

The governor of Sierra Leone would have been disappointed to learn that in the same month and year that he offered these suggestions, a merchant ship belonging to the U.S.A. called "The Thomas Watson" was seized off Keta on a charge of slave trading. In January 1858 another vessel equipped for the slave trade was seized on the roadstead of Prampram. Meanwhile the people of Apollonia had contracted a "Free Emigration System" with the French colonies of Martinique, Cayenne, Guadeloupe etc. This was slavery in disguise as the king of Apollonia called Amaki confessed later that 100 prisoners captured in September 1857 by the French as a result of the Apollonian attack against them had been transported by the French to Goree. "The Frenchmen have sold many of the people to Goree," he lamented. There was still quite a lot of slave trading and the "Slave Coast" of West Africa was a major contributor. Most of the slaves were taken to Cuba described in 1858 as the last remaining mart for the real slave merchant.[12]

The British government remained undaunted. In the late 1850's, when Sir B.C.C. Pine was appointed governor of the "Gold Coast" the memorandum prepared for him indicated that by the laws of Great Britain, slavery had been pronounced to be contrary to the principles of Justice and Humanity. This was the view not only of Britain but of all "civilised nations". Though internal slavery was viewed by many as devoid of many of the horrors inseparably linked with external slavery, it was a matter of vital importance that its continued existence in the settlements of the Gold Coast should still not be countenanced by Great Britain.

Following this memorandum was another memorandum for the guidance of the courts with respect to cases involving slavery and pawning. No Judicial Assessor, Commandant or Justice of Peace was on any account whatever to compel or order a slave or pawn to return to his master; in cases where it was proved that the master had been decidedly guilty of cruelty towards his slave, the slave might be emancipated and protected; in all other cases the courts should decline to adjudicate; any British subject who directly or indirectly was found implicated in slavery or pawning would be guilty of felony; and the officers must emancipate any slaves or pawns belonging to the offender, and take prompt steps to have him brought to justice under statutes 5 Geo. 4th Cap 113 & 6 & 7 Vic: Cap. 98.

The beginning of 1860 started on a rather sour note. There was evidence of the slave trade at Ada, Keta, Whydah and Lagos and it was necessary to put down the "iniquitous slave trade". The government at Cape Coast suggested the appointment of a naval force and a proper garrison of the fort of Keta. Apparently since the British government took over Keta and the Eastern districts from the Danes in 1850, the fort had not been effectually garrisoned. The logistics to do this remained a problem throughout the 1860's. Consequently the slave trade continued to thrive from Keta to Lagos. The Naval officers of the Anti-Slavery Squadron also noticed a brisk trade in slaves between Keta and Brazil. There were a number of known Portuguese slave dealers and one name which came up was Geraldo de Lima. Among the local people one John Tay was suspected of the same offence. Apart from the "Slave Coast" of West Africa, slave trading was also rife in the Congo. All the trading houses, except the English and Dutch, were engaged in the slave trade. In May 1863 the governor at Cape Coast reported to the Duke of Newcastle that he agreed with the opinion of the late Sir Winniett that Keta being in the neighbourhood of the slave marts in the upper part of the Bight of Benin was one of the chief strongholds for the slave trade on that part of the coast. Keta was useful as a rendezvous for those engaged in the traffic and collection of slaves and it was absolutely necessary for the government to reoccupy the fort on a much larger scale than had hitherto been done.

The attitude of governor Pine to slavery in 1863 was that it needed to be gradually eroded till full emancipation was achieved. Until this was done, the "Gold Coast" would never rise from degradation. A year later Pine had a meeting with the chiefs of the Protectorate and one of their grievances was the issue of slavery. Pine endeavoured to do his best to argue against the policy, propriety or advantage direct or indirect of slavery of whatever kind. He also explained to the chiefs that the British government did not at that present time instruct her officers to interfere with the unfortunate though mild system of indigenous slavery as it existed in the Protectorate. British officers were strictly enjoined to discourage and to refuse to recognise slavery in all their dealings judicial or otherwise. They were also obliged to offer protection to all slaves who so desired. Pine tried to convince the chiefs that it

would be economical, judicious and pleasing to all civilized nations if all owners would emancipate their slaves. The chiefs replied by asserting that the
U.S.A. had increased in wealth and prosperity because slavery was continuing
there and that Portugal had fallen since it relinquished slavery. The chiefs further complained that the neighbouring Dutch settlements were refusing to
give up their runaway slaves but they were formerly doing so. Pine informed
the chiefs that his government did not permit him to give up runaway slaves
and he totally agreed with the Dutch government. The policy was not to give
them up but to encourage them to return to their owners when no circumstances of ill usage or cruelty were alleged. The chiefs left the meeting disappointed that their grievances had not been met although they approached the
governor, "as their father and protector". They felt degraded in the eyes of
their people, because, to them, the government was not according them the
proper respect. Pine was applying a Proclamation issued by governor Ross
on 28 August 1862 that runaway slaves and pawns should not be given up.
Criminal slaves or pawns who had run away would be given up as well as
slaves and pawns who actually contracted debts.

Justice with respect to cases on slavery continued to be dealt with by the
courts throughout the 1860's. In September 1866 the Chief Justice reported
an interesting case in which 5 people suspected to be slaves were brought to
Cape Coast in a Dutch vessel in 1864. On enquiry he learnt that they were
brought by a "native" trader called Dawson and left in charge of his wife at
Cape Coast. Dawson claimed that he redeemed these people from slavery and
death at Whydah and gave them to his wife as domestic servants. The Chief
Justice planned to charge Dawson with importation of people into the
Protectorate, a violation of the Act 5 Geo. iv C113, but he was faced with the
dilemma of applying this law for British subjects to a native of the Protectorate.
If he applied the English Law, he might appear harsh. He, therefore, decided
to free the 5 people and ask Dawson to appear in court within 12 months. He
concluded that although the British government did not interfere with domestic
servitude because it was a deeply rooted institution of the country, he knew
the government would approve of his decision to punish any one who at-

tempted to purchase and import slaves from places beyond the sea.[13]

In the early 1870's the issue of slave trading from the Volta to Lagos continued to haunt British officials. Geraldo de Lima, the great slave trader in the Volta region, continued to be mentioned in despatches. Another dimension to the already seemingly unsolvable problem was the report that large numbers of slaves had been introduced into the Protectorate from across the River Pra for the purpose of being sold. The governor issued a proclamation on 1st November 1871 stating in very clear terms that all importation of persons into the Protectorate was contrary to the law and in direct contravention of the provision of the Act 5 Geo. 4th C113 for the suppression of the slave trade. Any person convicted of this offence was liable to punishment as a felon. A little investigation by one of the officials revealed that the people in Asante and the Northern Territories who were unaffected by all the laws and efforts being made against slavery in the Protectorate, found nothing illegal according to their native law and custom in selling as slaves captives who had been taken in war. The position of the Colonial Office on the sale of slaves in the Protectorate was that it was impossible to compromise on this issue as a pacesetter in Atlantic abolition. The government was trying as much as possible to influence people who were not British subjects in the Protectorate. They had to do this cautiously through encouragement to induce the people to desist from unwholesome practices and not through direct legislation. The best course of action in these circumstances was to endeavour to come to an understanding with the chiefs of the protected tribes to forbid the slave trade within their several districts. Any slave imported into what was strictly British Territory would have to be set free at once. In December 1872 a query was sent to the Commandants of the forts of Sekondi and Axim about an allegation of slave trading in their areas following a report that some slaves who had landed in Cuba were probably from that portion of the Gold Coast. The Commandant at Sekondi replied that no slaves had been exported from his district within the last three years. The Commandant at Axim reported the same and his enquiries at Apollonia revealed the same. The governor forwarded the reports from the Commandants to the Colonial Office on 16th

July 1873. It is interesting that the Commandants could only speak confidently about the past three years and not earlier. The probability that slave trading was going on in the extreme west part of the coast was high.

On 16th December 1873, the Colonial Office issued a memorandum on slavery. The position of the British government with respect to slavery and other traditional practices was described as embarrassing. The memorandum traced British attitude and efforts on slavery, both Atlantic and indigenous, from 1841 to 1873. The Abolition Law was very clear in British Territory but not so clear in the "Protected Territory". British territory seemed to comprise all the forts and castles dotted along the coastline from Apollonia in the west to Keta in the east. Those in the territory were regarded as British subjects. By 14th April 1874 the position of the British government towards slavery remained the same. The chief magistrate of the Gold Coast requested definite instructions on how slaves and slavery were to be dealt with. The governor advised the Colonial Office to consider carefully the government's position on indigenous slavery in the light of the governor's desire to establish a permanent political and social relationship with the "Protected Tribes".

JULY 1874 AND AFTER: THE SECOND PHASE OF ABOLITION

On 24th July 1874 the Gold Coast settlements were annexed by Britain and united with Lagos under a single government. The Gold Coast Colony and Protectorate was formally established. The new Secretary for Colonies, the Earl of Carnavon, made it clear that the Colony and Protectorate could no longer tolerate the recognition of indigenous slavery. Indigenous slavery was described as "utterly repugnant to all our principles". It had to be extinguished as soon as possible because "it has proved a source of difficulty on more than one occasion". On 14th October 1874 the Colonial Office minuted to governor Strahan of the Gold Coast that emancipation of slaves was being considered. On 3rd November 1874 the governor held a meeting with the kings and chiefs of the Western Districts and announced that the buying, selling and pawning of persons was prohibited and that the relations between master and servant as existing in England could alone be recognised or permitted. The kings and chiefs consulted among themselves for a short time and accepted the Proclamation by stating "we will give up buying slaves. We cannot do otherwise than as the Queen tells us". The governor also told the kings and chiefs that no forcible disruption of domestic arrangements was intended and that slaves and pawns had the option to remain with their masters or to leave. If they made them happy in their families there will not be any need for them to leave. On 7th November, the governor held a similar meeting in Accra with the kings and chiefs of the Eastern Districts and after they conferred amongst themselves for about 30 minutes they informed the governor that they were ready to obey the proclamation. The governor informed the Earl of Carnavon that the question of slavery was thus settled, and all that was now required was to pass the necessary ordinances and to punish promptly and firmly any attempt in individual cases to enforce servitude.

Two ordinances were proclaimed on 17th December 1874. The first abolished all forms of slave dealing, the second provided for the "abolition of slavery in the Protected Territories". Other related forms of involuntary servitude were also officially abolished. In January 1875 some of the kings and chiefs in the Protectorate presented three petitions to the Colonial Office complaining that the old and well established custom of slavery should not have been overthrown so suddenly; that they would be ruined without their slaves; that there would be a shortage of labour; that the freed slaves would become vagabonds and criminals and that trade would suffer. They claimed compensation for the slaves they had bought. One wonders why they accepted the Proclamation a month earlier, only to complain later. When the Earl of Carnavon received this petition on 6th February 1875 he opined to his staff that governor Strahan had been somewhat precipitate in carrying out the entire and unconditional abolition of slavery and that much inconvenience and disturbance of social relations would be caused by it. He concluded:

We may doubtless expect to receive many complaints and remonstrances. However as we have now put our hand to the plough, there can be no looking back and we must trust Captain Strahan's judgement to keep clear, while pursuing a vigorous policy of difficulties and embodiments.[14]

The first "scapegoat" of the Proclamation was Ennimil Quow, king of Wassaw. He was convicted on 26th April 1876 for breaching the Slave Dealing Abolition Ordinance by purchasing slaves and sentenced by the Judicial Assessor's Court to a fine of 100 ounces of gold dust and three years imprisonment, or in default of payment of the fine to a further term of two years imprisonment. On being informed by members of the king's family about this sentence, the Colonial Office considered the sentence unnecessarily severe and suggested a reduction in the length of imprisonment. Governor Strahan was to be strongly cautioned not to assume the right of dealing in a summary and too severe a manner with cases involving question of policy without prior consultation with Her Majesty's government. On 17th February 1877, Ennimil Quow requested the Colonial Office to send him to Lagos to complete his sentence and this was granted. By January 1887, Ennimil Quow had finished serving his sentence but was still at Lagos because he had not been able to pay the fine of 100 ounces of gold dust and £400. He would only be allowed to return to the "Gold Coast" by paying the fine and giving security in £1,000 to be of good behaviour and remain in the place of residence allotted to him. In 1889 he was re-installed king of Wassaw by request from his people.[15]

The second "scapegoat" of the 1874 Proclamation was King Amoako Atta of Akyem. On 17th March 1880, he was charged with conniving at slavery, the purchase, sale and pawning of human beings and misgovernment. In May, after investigations, nine cases were established against the Okyenhene, including the importation and purchase of slaves from countries outside the Protectorate. He, however, was convicted not on a charge of slave dealing but arson and sentenced to a minimum of five years penal servitude. The governor complained to the Secretary of State that several principal chiefs were also involved in the breach of the slavery laws.[16]

Meanwhile the Colonial Office received reports of slave dealing and trading in the Volta Region. In 1881 a ship called "The Spade" was prohibited from trading at the British ports because it was suspected of slave trading. The vessel had no Manifest or Bills of Lading and was from the Port of Bahia. There was still a lot of work to be done on slavery and slave trading.[17]

THE EFFECTS OF THE PROCLAMATION OF 3RD NOVEMBER 1874 AND THE ORDINANCES OF 17TH DECEMBER 1874

An examination of the documents from 1875 to about 1900 shows that two major effects resulted from the Proclamation of 3rd November 1874 and its subsequent ordinances. First, some slaves opted to remain with their former owners; second, some slaves took advantage of the Emancipation Ordinance to assert their liberty.

The Option Of Remaining With Their Former Owners

The documents suggest that the majority of freed slaves chose to remain with their former owners. Several factors accounted for this. First, slaves who were well treated by their owners and were, therefore, quite happy did not see the need to leave. Second, slaves who had helped their owners on farms and had been given some land themselves to farm were content to remain on the land. Basel missionary Dieterle reported in June 1875 from his station at Aburi that in Tutu, Obosomase, Ahwerase, Aburi and many farming villages, individual slaves who left their owners were few. Some of these, however, having got themselves Certificates of Freedom from the court in Accra, returned to their owner's villages to farm the land given to them by their owners. In the Guan villages (of which Larteh and Adukrom were the largest), where it was customary for slaves who married into families and behaved well to become heirs and family heads, most slaves preferred to remain with their owners. Other slaves remained out of fear and insecurity. Not all slaves were bold enough to venture out to begin new lives. Dieterle lamented that the slaves did not understand the meaning of true freedom. They only knew the proverb "if you have no master, you are lost".

In January 1875, Basel missionary, Eisenschmid, reported that in Akwapim the Emancipation had had effects in only a few cases. People talked about 50 cases, which were too few among so many slaves. In Kyebi many slaves left but in the other Akyem villages like Asiakwa, Asuom, Begoro etc. the chiefs had the Proclamation read out and erstwhile slaves were given the rights of citizenship. The majority, therefore, remained and worked out new conditions of service with their former owners.[19]

The Basel Mission report on Accra dated 30 June 1875 stated:

> The effects of the Emancipation have so far been small - only a few slaves have made use of it, and most masters have only lost one or two.[20]

Slaves in Accra remained because of the kind treatment they received; their work load was not too heavy; in addition it was more advantageous to stay on their owners' land than to break free and face the uncertainties which settling in a strange place involved. Others remained because they enjoyed their owners' protection and support and were members of their owners' families. Hermann Rottman observed:

> The full effect of the Emancipation will probably thus be felt only by degrees, for every slave now knows that it is legally forbidden to sell or buy slaves and that he can at any time obtain his full freedom.[21]

The story was the same for the Ga-Adangme area. A few slaves left but the majority remained. In the Ada farming villages the Proclamation was not even known. In the Ga-Adangme area the following was the report on the Emancipation:

The slaves remaining are treated as members of the family, receiving from their master no wages, only food, clothes and permission every now and again to earn something for themselves. The trusted emancipated slaves are even conducting business for their masters still.[22]

In Krobo Odumase, with only one or two exceptions, no slaves left their owners. At Abokobi, the effect of the Emancipation was described as limited. In any case, Abokobi had for some years past acquired a reputation as a place of refuge for runaway slaves. It was strange that with the passing of the Emancipation Law, fewer slaves ran to Abokobi.

In 1880, when Governor Usher of the Gold Coast and Mr. Hemming of the Colonial Office in London, took stock of the Emancipation Act from 1874 they were angry and disappointed at its effects. They concluded that the 1874 Emancipation had been too precipitate. In the 1890s, the Humanitarians in Britain were dissatisfied with the effects of the Emancipation. Slave trading was still going on in some parts of the Colony and Protectorate. Apparently the pressure to abolish slavery in 1874 in what was formally recognised as British Territory had come from a strong abolitionist lobby in England and not from the Colonial Office itself. The Colonial Office was definitely concerned with the issue of slavery, but Secretary of State, Lord Carnavon wanted to ensure that abolition was implemented in such a way that it would yield positive and not negative results. Governor Strahan had been too quick to act on the matter.

In September 1895, Basel Missionary Muller expressed regret at the effect of Emancipation in the following words:

> Once the laws over slavery were vigorously pursued by the regime, but for about the last 10 years the Colonial Office has left the people in peace and administered the slavery law in a very superficial way. Because the legal sanctions against slavery had fallen

into disuse, the Christians have become involved in slavery and pawning once again, and represents a great danger to the employees of the mission and the Gemeinde elders.[23]

Slaves Who Asserted Their Liberty

The Basel Mission records indicate that at Tutu, 13 slaves left out of a village population of 1,000 and in Ahwerase 19 left out of a village population of 700. On the entire Akwapim Ridge only 200 slaves left. The number of Akan slaves who left Aburi was negligible, those who left comprised mainly slaves from the Volta region, especially those from Peki, who had taken refuge at Aburi during the 1869 Asante invasion of their country. The numbers are not given. The interior of the Protectorate which was seriously affected by the Emancipation Act was Akyem Abuakwa. Basel missionary, Widman, reported in July 1875 that

> the Slave Emancipation is causing a lot of dust to rise... in Kibi it is said the young king is mishandling the slaves who no longer want to remain in his service, and the government must intervene there, if the Emancipation is to be anything more than a Paper Law.[24]

In Kyebi, most of the slaves were said to have come from surrounding Akyem villages and many of them returned to their homes. Those from further afield set off to farm any vacant land which was made available to them. The king of Akyem Abuakwa was reported to have lost "several hundreds of slaves". In Kyebi 100 slaves left their masters. People from the surrounding Akyem villages came to Kyebi to claim their ex-slave relatives. The sister and aunt of the Okyenhene lost almost all their slaves. The Okyenhene tried to bring back the slaves by force, but the Basel Mission protected them. At Begoro there was a wholesale migration of slaves. Missionary Mohr estimated that as many as 2,000 individuals claimed their freedom in Akyem Abuakwa.

The Fante coastal towns also witnessed a large exodus of slaves, especially from the houses of educated slave owners, the merchants, the mulattos and the "great princes". This exodus of slaves from Akyem and Fante land seemed to indicate harsh treatment of slaves. Some of the slaves of the Kyebi royal house "confessed" to the Basel missionaries that if the Okyenhene had publicly proclaimed the Emancipation and guaranteed them humane treatment in the future, they would have remained in his service.

The slaves who left their owners either went to the Basel Mission Stations or went to the coast to look for employment. All the mission stations in Akwapim, Akyem and Ga-Adangme, were places of refuge for the freed slaves. Kukurantumi and Anyinam mission stations were a favourite hide out for runaway slaves from Akyem, Kwahu and Asante. The missionaries had been protecting slaves years before the Emancipation Act was proclaimed. In Akyem Abuakwa Christianity was closely associated with slavery from the start. When Missionary Buck first went to Kyebi, the Akyems "despised the Christians as ex-slaves". In the 1850s, 1860s and early 1870s, the Basel Missionaries bought people out of slavery or freed slaves and rescued pawns from bondage by the payment of their debts. The Basel Mission had a Slave Emancipation Fund which was used to redeem slaves. They took care of abandoned slaves and offered refuge for escaped slaves whose lives were in danger. In 1865 for example, the Basel Missionaries in the Akyem district freed 3 slaves belonging to one Jonathan Palmer. One was a 40 year old woman from the North whom he had bought for $46 in 1856. Another was an Awuna boy of about 18 years of age called Asem Nyame who had been bought for $45 in 1859. The last was a woman of about 58 years old from Krepe called Nyame Ye Adom bought in early 1864. At the mission station some of the slaves were trained as skilled artisans, while others worked for the Mission Trading Society. A few earned their living by hunting, making palm oil, farming and trading.

The Basel Mission Boarding Schools were dominated by slave children after the Proclamation. In 1875 for example, there were 30 boys in the Kyebi school, all of them ex-slaves and ex-pawns. The mission wanted Basel to give an approval for 20 more of such boys. In 1877 the Kyebi Boarding School continued to be dominated by ex-slaves, but a few parents brought their children to the school. The missionaries expressed great relief at this development because the task of recruiting pupils for the school in the early stages was a hard one. Pupils from the school came from Kyebi, Asiakwa, Asante and Kwahu. Missionary Asante reported that the Boarding School was a real haven for the ex-slaves. No one dared touch them and they sat next to boys from royal families in the classroom. Once he overheard an ex-slave boy telling a boy of royalty "Go and fetch water, we are all alike now".[25]

In the early 1890s, the Basel Mission established slave villages in the Colony and Protectorate. Schopf estimated about a dozen of such villages inland from Accra. He mentioned a few like Apenkwa, Abokobi, Anye and Legon (Christian Village). There were about 1,000 slaves in Abokobi and Apenkwa, most of them were of Northern extraction and they were farmers. Those in Anye and Legon (Christian Village) farmed the land that belonged to King Tackie. Not all the missionaries in the Colony and Protectorate favoured the establishment of these villages and there was a whole lot of correspondence on the issue. The slaves who went to the coast in search of employment found work as porters, boatmen, warehousemen, messengers, domestic servants or general odd job men; others became petty traders. A number of them joined the police or the Gold Coast Constabulary.[26]

Before the Emancipation Act of 1874 the government had been enlisting slaves and pawns into the Gold Coast Constabulary. In 1873 the governor offered compensation to slave owners whose slaves had run away for enlistment. He authorised the payment of £5 per head for every recruit claimed by his owner. After 1874 the Constabulary was short of men. By 1879 several of the freed men who had joined the Constabulary deserted the force. Desertions averaged 15-20 a month for a force of about 600 men. Some deserted to become instructors with the Asante army at double pay, plus ration. In 1880 a Senior Native Officer of the Constabulary by name Abdul Karimu, who was going to Salaga on leave was authorised to recruit up to 150 men. Recruiting expeditions continued in 1882 and 1887. The irony of it was that these men were recruited from Salaga, well known at that time for slave trading. In the 1880s Governor Hill enlisted 300 slaves and agreed to remit a portion of their pay to their owners until the sum of £8, the price of their redemption, had been paid. It is against the background of the manpower needs of the Constabulary that one must appreciate the eagerness of the British government to welcome the freed slaves as well as runaway slaves from areas outside the Colony.[27]

There were also some slaves who left their owners and wandered about aimlessly. A few joined bands of robbers in the Ada district. Others became idle and disorderly. In the Akwapim area the Basel Missionaries reported that the freed slaves had not turned to criminal activities but that there had been a gang of robbers in the Accra area for a long time. It was possible some freed slaves joined them. In the Akyem area there was no incidence of robbery or violence by freed slaves, because there was vast land for farming and many slaves made use of this opportunity.[28]

The records do not indicate the numbers in terms of gender of those slaves who left their owners. The nature of work open to freed slaves suggests that most of them were men. Most of the females must have been married to their owners or owners' relations. Basel Missionary records indicate that some of the male slaves left their slave wives and children in the interior to seek employment on the coast. This happened, for example, in the Adangme area where the freed male slaves left for the Ga and Fante areas to seek employment.

The Persistence Of The Slave Trade

In spite of the Proclamation Ordinances and the efforts of the British officials to abolish slavery and the slave trade, the slave trade persisted. In January 1888, the governor asked the District Commissioner of the Volta River district to investigate reports that the slave trade was still going on in parts of the Colony and the Protectorate. The District Commissioner was urged to travel inland and find out all he could about the caravan routes passing through the interior. Slave trading and slave dealing were rife in Kwahu, Asante and the Northern Territories. So long as these areas continued to deal in slaves, the Colony and Protectorate could not be completely free from slavery. Throughout the 1880s, the Ada people brought down the Volta every season, canoe-loads of slaves, many of whom were sold at Ada itself. The children among them were sent to their numerous fishing and trading villages along the river to be assimilated. Large numbers of adult slaves were sent to the palm oil plantations of Krobo and Akwapim.[29]

In the early 1890s, Firminger reported that slavery was still in existence in the Colony. The evidence was so overwhelming that one official confessed:

> I have no doubt slavery still exists in many parts of the British Protectorate, but at all events it is carefully concealed.[30]

An official in London was scared of public outcry from the anti-slavery party in London that "the accursed thing exists and is tolerated in territory under British control". He therefore, found relief in another person's remark that Firminger's comments had been greatly exaggerated. Slavery was still going on in the German Protectorate of Togo land, the official stated. Herr Richter had called attention in the Reichstag to the fact that Togo land was a "hot bed of slave trading".

The governor of the Gold Coast unhappy about this state of affairs sent a letter to all the District Commissioners of the Colony to react to Firminger's allegations. The responses were mixed. The District Commissioner at Accra reported that "slave dealing exists to an alarming degree in the Colony". Dr. Cole, a Sierra Leonean at Ada, opined that "domestic slavery" still existed and it would be difficult to stop it because "it is carried on by nearly every class of natives of the Gold Coast". The District Commissioner at Axim, stated that his three years stay in the Colony did not make him believe Firminger's allegations. He stated that "the feeling with which old slaves remain with their masters is that of relations and not that of slaves". The District Commissioner at Dixcove and Shama thought that the slaves Firminger was alluding to were men and women slaves who had been living in the Protectorate before 1874 and were still living there. With respect to the Keta District, the report was that there were still large numbers of slaves in the Awuna District but that a very great number of these did not desire to change their condition and were quite aware of their right under British Law. The Report added that there were many parts of the Volta District which had not been visited by British officials and "it is probable that a primitive state of affairs exists there". Slave dealing was going on near Daboya market. Major Ewart of the Constabulary, writing on this same district, believed there was a lot of slave dealing going on but it was almost impossible to stop it. There was even a slave market at Bey Beach. The District Commissioner at Prampram was not aware of slave trading in his district but he was aware of two villages composed of former slaves who were now involved with "legitimate trade". The District Commissioner at Saltpond was not aware of the extent to which slave dealing existed but he was aware it did exist. His fears were that legislation aimed at the total repression of slave dealing in the out districts would be fruitless unless the government was prepared to police the Protectorate, a step which seemed impossible.[31]

In the Winneba and Tarkwa Districts reports indicated that slave dealing and slave trading were carried on to a large extent just outside the Protectorate, but the officials were not aware of any case in which a British subject had purchased slaves inside or outside the Protectorate. 19 cases of pawning and slave dealing had, however, been dealt with by the Winneba court. Some of the District Commissioners and private informers suggested to the government to offer handsome rewards to informers about the slave trade; to establish a system of registration of aliens and to make the provision of the Slave Dealing Ordinance more widely known. Sixteen years after the passing of the Slave Emancipation Act, the British government had not succeeded in putting a complete end to the slave trade and slavery. Ironically, Firminger who had made these serious allegations bought a slave girl at Salaga for £6.10. This information was given to the governor by an officer in the Constabulary called Ali. Surprisingly an official in London remarked in January 1891 as follows:

it should not be forgotten that barely a generation has passed away since the formal abolition of slavery on the Gold Coast, and it cannot be supposed that the habits and institutions of centuries, generally harmless as they have been rendered in their practical and domestic operation, can be thoroughly eradicated by anything but the process of time.[32]

Two months later, the quarter's report from the Ada District gave overwhelming evidence of slave dealing and slave trading in the Adangme area. Some of the slave dealers had even been interrogated and they revealed that most of the slaves were from the Salaga market. They bartered rum, gin or salt for a slave man or woman, boy or girl.

The Aborigines Rights Society in London became aware of the existence of slave trading and slave dealing in the Colony and Protectorate in the early 1890's and exerted pressure on the colonial officials. The officials tried to exonerate themselves by complaining that there was no staff available to carry out, any careful enquiry into the domestic state of the people even in the towns upon the coast. There was no local municipal police force at any of those towns and a great aversion existed to furnishing government officials with information. The civil police were very often strangers to the place and helpless for duties of the nature in question.

In the 1890s there were reports of slave trading in Kpandu, Buem and several parts of the Volta District. Basel missionary, Clerk, intimated that most slaves entering the Volta area were Mossis or Grushies, taken in the slave raids of Gazare. In 1892 some were brought to Worawora and sold. The richest man in Buem was called Nketia and he had a whole village full of slaves. Clerk advised the government to raise the price of gun powder, define who lives in the area of which colonial power, have both colonial powers (i.e. Britain and Germany) clearly outlaw slavery and station someone in the Kpandu-Krakye area to see to it that the trade really ceased. If such a person was a "Gold Coast man" he must be changed frequently in order to make sure that he did not allow himself to be bribed. Basel missionaries Muller and Rosler also gave some reports of slave trading in the Volta District in 1893. They mentioned Buem, Nkonya and all the land southwards to Anum. The slaves were mostly from the River Niger area. Muller asked Basel to make representations to Berlin on the matter of the slave trade in the Volta Region.[33]

According to Rosler the slave trade south of Salaga was almost exclusively in children of the ages 7-12 years. There appeared to have been more slaves in the British Protectorate than in the area immediately to the north. These slaves were brought south by Ada and Accra traders. Their new owners integrated them into their families and sometimes married them within the families. Some of the children from these marriages were enrolled in the Basel Mission Schools at Vakpo, Kpandu and Worawora.[34]

In 1894 and 1895 the Kete market in the Volta Region was actively involved in slave trading. Cattle, cloth and foodstuffs were openly on sale but the slaves were not sold publicly. Some of them were kept in the Krakye village and others were kept in traditional priests' shrines. A few slaves were aware of the British Emancipation Act and tried to run away. Those who were caught were often badly beaten. What was happening in Kete and other inland areas spilt over to the Colony and Protectorate. In 1894 Governor Hodgson sent a confidential report on the slave trade to the Colonial Office. He stated that it was an undoubted fact that there were no slave markets within the Protectorate and certainly no raids upon native villages. But he feared that slaves may be, and were brought into, the Protectorate. They were however never sold openly, for fear of the government and of the punishment which they knew awaited the buyers and sellers.

The late 1890s saw a repeat of what happened in the Colony and Protectorate in the early 1890s when Firminger made his allegations on slave trading. In 1897 and 1898 the governor made enquiries about slave trading from all the District Commissioners and the Commissioner of Police. He received three responses. First, there were those who responded positively that slavery and slave trading persisted. Second, there were those who were equivocal and third, there were those who responded negatively. The reports from Dixcove and Shama indicated that after the abolition of domestic slavery "the demand for slaves was heavy and that demand not having been satisfied still continues to be heavy". The Elmina District Commissioner stated that as far as he could gather, there "is and always has been a demand for slave children on the coast. The difficulty is to catch the delinquents".[35]

The District Commissioner was able to lay hands on two children who had been bought from Anomabu. He was informed that the slaves had been brought from Cape Coast where there were some links with the interior markets. The District Commissioner at Cape Coast reported that 13 cases of slave dealing were heard in the court of the Chief Commissioner between September 1896 and September 1897. Between 1893 and 1897 nine children were rescued from slavery and sent to the Roman Catholic Mission. The people of Cape Coast who wanted children went to Gyaman "where there is perpetual slave raiding". The children so bought were not treated as slaves but as adopted children. He ended his report by saying that there were over 200 slaves from Gyaman and Asante who, if asked, would indignantly deny that they were slaves because they were well treated.[36]

From Keta, the District Commissioner reported that what was called "domestic slavery" existed, but the so called slaves were never sold. They were usually blood relatives of the proprietor. They could not be called slaves because they could marry, trade on their own account and "as they are aware what the law is, are free to leave their masters if they choose". In Apollonia there were many slaves who had come mostly from the interior, especially from Samory Toure's camp at Bonduku. The slaves were taken to the coast by a route running from Grand Bassam to Herboland and then taken across the boundary to the Volta District. A large number of slaves were taken to the Volta by the Adas. Most of the canoes on the river which traded with the upper reaches were worked by slaves for Ada owners. The unfortunate part was that these people would "deny being slaves. They knew that should their owners be convicted for slave dealing, they would have no employment". Since these slaves had come from the interior, fending for themselves would be a great problem. They were aware that they could claim their freedom if they entered the Colony.[37]

In the Saltpond District there was some demand for slaves for domestic purposes "but to what extent the practice is carried out is very hard to say". The District Commissioner found many male carriers bringing down rubber to the coast. Upon interrogation they denied that they were slaves. There were slaves in Beyin who were used by Chief Bigdom and Mensah to bring rubber and other goods to the coast. Slaves were bought in Sefwi in exchange for goods and sold in the bush behind Beyin. Slave trading was also going on at Half Assini and Enchi. The District Commissioner for Axim cautioned the chiefs of Half Assini, Beyin and Attuabu to report any cases that came to their notice.[38]

Among those who were equivocal about the existence of slavery and slave trading was the Commissioner at Winneba. He intercepted and questioned between 60 and 70 rubber carriers from the interior he suspected were slaves, but they denied that they were slaves. Others he suspected of being slaves appeared to be well nourished. It was possible they had been purchased from their infancy. It was difficult to obtain any reliable information from them. The District Commissioner at Prampram was unable to get any information about the existence of slave trading. He was, therefore, not sure whether slavery and slave trading existed. The Tarkwa District Commissioner indicated that there was not much slavery in his district and very few slaves passed through his district to the coast. The District Commissioner of Akuse reported that it was possible slave children were still being brought down from the interior. It could not be proved conclusively that they were slaves except by their facial marks. They were often kept on the plantations until they had learnt the Adangme language and were fed and well treated so that they would not complain or wish to leave their owners.[39]

Among those who responded negatively to the existence of slavery and slave trading were the District Commissioner and the Commissioner of Police in Accra. The District Commissioner reported that there had not been an influx of either male or female slaves into the district. He had also not traced any slave dealing. The Commissioner of Police in Accra, indicated to the governor that he sent a circular to all Police Stations in the Colony requesting to be informed about the demand for slaves in the coast towns of the Colony. The District Commissioners informed him that they had forwarded their reports to the Governor. Only 3 cases of slave dealing came up in Accra. In Axim, the District Commissioner reported that there were practically no slaves in the town itself.[40]

In summary, ten districts indicated positively in 1896 and 1897 that slavery and slave trading existed. These districts were Dixcove, Shama, Elmina, Cape Coast, Keta, Apollonia, Ada, Saltpond, Beyin and Half Assini. Four districts were equivocal about the existence of slavery and slave dealing, namely, Winneba, Prampram, Tarkwa and Akuse. Only two districts, Accra and Axim, responded negatively to the existence of slavery and slave trading. It is clear from these reports that slavery and slave trading had not been completely eradicated. It is not surprising that after these extensive reports the Colonial Office on 1st March 1898 set itself the task of stopping slave dealing through first, the prevention of the slave trade; second, the closing of the slave markets and third, the prevention of dealing in slaves in the administrative districts. However, the Secretary of State shockingly remarked on 8th March 1898 that his impression from the reports was that there was little slave dealing and that the only risk of serious abuse was in the case of children. He wished the District Commissioners to exercise the greatest vigilance and endeavour to ascertain in any suspected cases of slavery how and where the slaves were obtained. He also wished the District Commissioners to find out whether the slaves were aware of their rights, or were being held against their will. This was perhaps a typical example of the British officials' difficulty in explaining their toleration of slavery to a very critical public in London or their inability to completely eradicate the institution. The Secretary of State had as it were "to save his face".

1896-1908: THE THIRD PHASE OF ABOLITION; ASANTE AND THE NORTHERN TERRITORIES

Between 1896 and 1908 the British government concerned itself with direct political dealings with Asante and the Northern Territories. "The Ashanti Issue" featured in correspondence between the Colonial Office and the governor throughout the 1890s. Slavery had been a major issue in Anglo-Asante diplomacy throughout the 19th century. In 1859 for example, Asantehene Kwaku Dua III entered into agreement with the Queen of Great Britain to stop all slave raiding, permit no slave market to be held in his dominions and ameliorate the condition of slaves in his jurisdiction. Nothing concrete happened. In 1894 the *Asantemanhyiamu* (Asante Council) accepted the appointment of a British Resident in Kumasi on condition that he would have restricted and clearly defined advisory functions. The *Asantemanhyiamu*, however, rejected the British offer of Protectorate status. Apparently one of the major reasons for this refusal was the fear that the establishment of British protection would result in the manumission of slaves. The people of Asante were aware of all the slavery laws in the Colony and Protectorate. The Colonial Office correspondence does indeed indicate that one of their objectives in their quest to settle the "Ashanti issue once and for all" was to "rescue thousands from abject misery and slavery". On 13th June 1895, the Colonial Office issued instructions to Governor Maxwell on the question of slavery in Asante. He was required to assure the Asantehene that the Ordinances abolishing slavery in the Gold Coast Colony and Protectorate would not be applied to Asante; that there was no desire to interfere with the institution of "domestic slavery" so long as it was not carried on in a manner repugnant to humanity. The traffic in slaves and the buying and selling of slaves could not, however, be allowed. If a slave escaped and took refuge in the British Residency he/she would be under the protection of the British flag and would not be given up. But the Resident would be instructed not to give any encouragement to slaves to seek an asylum with him.

The "Scramble for Africa" partly influenced Britain's attitude to slavery in

Asante. The British were careful not to take any action that might drive Asante into the arms of a rival colonial power. The chiefs and people of Asante as well as those in the Northern Territories were needed as Allies. A.W.L. Hemming of the Colonial Office remarked on 22 October 1895:

> It would be a mistake to frighten the king of Kumasi and the Ashanti generally on the question of slavery. We cannot sweep away their customs and institutions all at once. Domestic slavery should not be troubled at present. We can talk of these things when definite treaty or negotiations take place. This is assuming we have peace: If we have war we can impose any terms we like on Kumasi. Then we might probably apply laws of protection and proclaim the pardon of all slaves.[41]

Four days later, Hemming expressed fears that if the British officials made it known in Asante that Britain had entered a crusade against slavery, they would not have any Allies, "so we should move very wisely and carefully in this matter". He believed that abolition of domestic slavery would mean a "social revolution of the greatest character. All in Ashanti who have any thing to lose would gravely resist this act".

As Anglo-French struggle for the Ghanaian hinterland intensified, Governor Maxwell was granted permission by the Colonial Office in December 1895 to sign treaties with Nkoranza, Juaben, Mampong, Agogo and Nsuta. In early January 1896 the king of Bekwai asked for British protection. Treaty-making became easy for these states as well as the British because Asante was going through a complicated and confused domestic situation. Several states in the Northern, Brong Ahafo and Asante regions rebelled and joined hands with the British government.

On 17th January 1896 British Forces entered Kumasi without opposition. Asantehene Prempeh I, Asantehemaa Yaa Akyaa and a number of senior officials were arrested and deported. Asante was declared a Protectorate and

Lt. Col. B. Piggot appointed its first Resident. Britain was now in direct control of the internal affairs of Asante. The Asantes were informed that they could retain all slaves in their possession prior to the 1896 invasion but all slave dealing would henceforth cease. The open buying and selling of slaves was forbidden and made punishable. Slaves who wanted to redeem themselves could make the necessary arrangements with their owners.

After the Yaa Asantewaa War of 1900, slaves who had been bought or captured before the war were asked by the British government to remain with their owners. They could, however, redeem themselves with the consent of their owners. From 1896 to 1902 the British administration in Asante adopted an attitude of tolerance towards the institution of indigenous slavery and sought to eliminate its most glaring abuses. Slaves who ran away from their owners were returned to their owners if there was no proof of cruelty.

From Asante the British government turned to the Northern Territories. On 20th July 1896 Treaties were concluded with Bechem-Ahafo, Bornmfu, Wam and Asunafo-Ahafo. This was followed by a tour in August and September of the modern Brong Ahafo Region by Lt. Col. B. Piggot. The Brong people were encouraged to assist the British government to suppress the slave trade in the slave markets, especially in Atebubu and Kete Krachi. From the Brong-Ahafo region, Piggot visited the northern towns of Grumansi and Konkonson. At Konkonson, he intercepted two slave caravans. The slaves were all Dagartis from the Wa country and were mostly women and very small children. Piggot sent 59 of them to Rev. Ramseyer of the Basel Mission in Kumasi. It was during this tour that Piggot became fully aware of the activities of Samory Toure. Samory was waging constant warfare in the Northern Territories for the purpose of obtaining slaves. Piggot wished that Samory's activities could be suppressed. As a first step he suggested the stationing of a patrol consisting of one non-commissioned officer and 6 men at Guere and another patrol or a detached post on the Volta, as near as possible to Kete Krachi. Between December 1896 and August 1897, Samory's slave raiding activities continued to be a source of concern to the British government. Banda, which had signed a treaty of friendship and trade with Britain on 5th December 1894 became the base of Samory's Sofas. Bole, which had also signed a similar treaty on 13th June 1892, had been taken by Samory. The men had been killed and the women and children made slaves. Bona and Wa had also been raided by the Sofas, who had established posts at Banda, Bole, Buipe, Boniape and Debie. In the light of the activities of the Sofas and the fear of German penetration, Britain took steps to sign more treaties in the Northern Territories. On 9th January 1897, a treaty was signed with Wa and the British flag hoisted. It was then that some British officials became fully aware of the activities of another slave raider by name Babatu. On 16th March 1897 another treaty was signed with Bona and the British flag hoisted in Dokita. By this move the British secured "the three most important places in our hinterland outside the Neutral Zone". These were Bona (including Lobi), Wa and Mamprusi. In 1897 a treaty was signed with the king of Salaga by which he promised to abolish slavery and the slave trade. On 7th March 1898 more treaties were signed with Issa, Buse, Wagu and Nadawale after the French had attempted to make similar moves in the area. By September 1898, treaty signing and actual conquest of parts of the Northern Territories by Britain had been completed.

Alpin, the first British Resident for the Salaga District was specifically instructed:

> You will be most careful to allow no interference by men of the Gold Coast Constabulary under your command with the slaves or domestic servants of the towns and villages at which you stay. Nothing is more likely to cause trouble, and even a breach of the peace and to create an impression opposite to that which is the desire of the British government to foster, than an unauthorised and injudicious interference of the kind alluded to.[42]

Between 1898 and 1902 the British policy on slavery in the Northern Territories was similar to that of Asante, indigenous slavery was tolerated and slaves protected from ill-treatment, but the open buying and selling of slaves was prohibited. They also aimed at stamping out slave raiding completely. The reason for this policy was explained as follows by Northcott:

The institution is entwined with the national existence in these countries so closely that an attack upon it would dissolve the rude fabric of society as it exists and would lead to endless trouble and hostility. There is no hardship inherent in the lot of a slave, and I doubt if he would understand the advantage of being liberated from a light control and cast upon his own resources.[43]

Reading through the documents the impression one gets was that British policy of tolerance towards the indigenous institution of slavery was a function of the inadequacy of staff and logistics for the suppression of the institution. In 1899, for example, the Gold Coast military force was weak and its hold on Asante and the Northern Territories insufficiently strong. Communication between the Colony and the Northern Territories was also poor and needed to be improved. In the event the British were inclined to wait "until the civilising influence of a settled form of administration had made its mark in the country". The Reports of the Commandant at Gambaga on the Northern Territories for the year 1899 recommended that more officers be placed at the disposal of the Administrator to ensure success in the local administration. He stressed the need for a European officer to visit every part of the Hinterland at least twice a year. In his view the large districts of Dagarti and Dagomba required the constant presence of the white man, as nothing else would have any effect in checking slave dealing which regrettably persisted in those two countries.

In the 1880s and early 1890s slaves were sold openly in the Northern Territories. From 1896 onwards the fear that "the white man had come to suppress the slave trade" caused the merchants to keep their slaves in merchant houses and in closed courtyards. The slaves from Salaga passed unhindered to German Togo land, Hausa traders going on from Salaga to Kintampo to buy kola nuts also took with them slaves to sell. Hausa caravans did the same with respect to the Atebubu market. Armitage's report of 7th January 1898 on the Gonja and Dagomba states noted the continued reliance of Gonja farmers on regular supply of slaves.

Many slaves are brought down yearly by the Moshis, and are sold to the Gonja people, who put them to work on their farms. They are kindly treated, and more like members of the family than slaves to it. The female slave, as a rule, either marries her master or becomes his concubine. The price paid for a slave is from £2.10.0 to £4. The Gonja has never been a trader and prefers to farm and remains in his village. The Gonja are a tribe of farmers. Every village, however small, has it plantations.[44]

Between 26th September 1901 and 1st January 1902, an Order in Council was issued by Her Majesty annexing Asante and the Northern Territories to the Crown, defining the boundaries of the new Dependencies, and providing for its administration by a Chief Commissioner under the direct control of the Governor of the Gold Coast Colony. This Order in Council marked an important phase in the British government's attitude to indigenous slavery in Asante and the Northern Territories. Henceforth the government set itself the task of taking concrete steps to abolish the indigenous institution. This was the moment Lt. Col. Northcott had been waiting for with respect to the Northern Territories when he intimated in 1898 that every possible effort would be made to stamp out slave raiding, and it should be possible to do so soon after the settlement of the boundaries of the Northern Territories.

Between 1902 and 1905 the Chief Commissioners and District Commissioners of Asante and the Northern Territories held several meetings and discussions on the best steps to take to abolish the indigenous institution of slavery. The District Commissioners also held consultations with the principal chiefs and Elders of these regions as a result of which Chief Commissioner Fuller sent two proposals to the Governor. First, every child of a domestic slave born after a fixed date (say January 1913) was to be automatically free. Second, the value of every domestic slave and the debt of every pawn was to be ascertained and recorded and some deduction from such value or debt made for every subsequent year's service. In both cases the deductions were, if possible, to be so arranged as to ensure the freedom of the person concerned within a period of (say) seven years. In December 1905, the Governor signalled his approval of the proposals.

The British Administration in Asante and the Northern Territories spent the whole of 1906 formulating laws that would effectively end the institution. The proposed laws were discussed not only among the officials and the governor but also among the chiefs and Elders. Towards the end of 1906 the chiefs and Elders of Adansi wrote to the Commissioner responsible for the southern District of Asante, protesting against the British Administration's proposed laws to abolish indigenous slavery. They stated:

> The freedom of every slave we beg to say that it is impossible for we Ashantis to do...what could the kings, chiefs and headmen do, if these are set free? All our drums, blowing horns, swords, elephant's tails, basket carrying and farming are done by them, as we have no money like Europeans to do necessaries for us...and how can we kings and chiefs attend any calling by the government at Obuasi or Kumasi while we have nobody to carry us, beat our drums, blow our horns, carry our swords, and other necessary things.[45]

District Commissioner Soden followed up the above protest and advised the Chief Commissioner not to be too hasty in demanding complete abolition of indigenous slavery because the chiefs and Headmen in Asante would be in great difficulty. This was because the slaves were not only attendants at court but did all the menial work for the state. Soden suggested that abolition be carried out gradually, over a period of two decades or more. He believed that if civilisation continued to advance, indigenous slavery would gradually flicker out. In any case slaves were so well treated, he almost did not see the need for their emancipation.

Throughout 1907 the British Administration in Asante and the Northern Territories continued to liaise between the governor and the chiefs on acceptable laws to end the institution. The Asante in particular were very unhappy about the Administration's "new" attitude towards indigenous slavery and there were reports of protests throughout Asante. Consequently Chief Commissioner Fuller advised Colonial Secretary Bryan to allow the present conditions to continue and that the time had not yet come for any drastic measures to be introduced. Unwilling slaves could leave their owners and they would not be asked to return. The Colonial Secretary responded and asked the Chief Commissioner to defer taking action on the question of indigenous slavery until the question of Native Jurisdiction in Asante and the Northern Territories had been settled. The only guiding principle was that government would not assist in arresting fugitive slaves.

On 22nd June 1908, Chief Commissioner Fuller issued what he called "final" instructions with respect to pawns and slaves. These were, first, that slave families were not to be separated without their consent. Second, that the payment of a fixed amount (to be determined in consultation with the chiefs) should guarantee redemption and that a master could not refuse to free a slave on payment of the redemption fee. Third, that cruelty would, *ipso facto,* redeem a slave. Fourth, that the bearing of a child by a female slave to her master would convert her into a free woman. Fifth, every child of every domestic slave, born after a fixed date, (say 1st January 1913) was to be *ipso facto* free.

Abolition in Asante and the Northern Territories was carried out gradually and cautiously by the British government, because it coincided with the 'Scramble for Africa.' After Asante and the Northern Territories had been conquered by Britain, the Colonial government tolerated slavery for several years. Finally after years of consultation with the traditional rulers, laws emancipating slaves were passed in 1908.

PUBLIC REACTIONS TO THE 22ND JUNE 1908 FINAL INSTRUCTIONS WITH RESPECT TO PAWNS AND SLAVES

The immediate reaction to the 22nd June 1908 final instructions with respect to pawns and slaves was open protests in Kumasi and other districts in Asante. The British Administration remained undaunted and ignored the protests. Freed slaves who could readily trace their relatives and families who knew the whereabouts of their enslaved relatives appealed to the District Commissioners' court for redemption after payment of a fee. Asante in particular witnessed a spate of court cases dealing with redemption of relatives. Some freed slaves opted to stay with their former owners. Unfortunately the records do not indicate the number of slaves who left and those who remained. Two interesting cases of slaves who remained with their former owners are cited below. On 12th July 1909, the chief of Nkoranza wanted to redeem some Nkoranzas who had been sent to Kumasi as captives and had been sold to the Sefwis. Chief Commissioner Fuller wrote to the Colonial Secretary advocating complete freedom for the Nkoranzas in Sefwi. The District Commissioner resident at Dunkwa informed the Commissioner for the Western Province on 16th March 1910 that he had personally interviewed the Nkoranzas living in Sefwi and found that there were 13 of them – 1 man and 12 women. All refused to return home with the exception of 1 old woman. On 15th May 1916, the chief of Effiduase Nana Yaw Kra wrote to the District Commissioner at Ejura to help him bring back to Effiduase 17 of his people living in Sefwi. They did not seem willing to return to Effiduase in spite of repeated requests from the chief.[46]

Some freed slaves roamed aimlessly about while others tried to look for new owners. The British Administration advised all freed slaves who did not want to stay with their former owners to leave the district in which they had been residing at once for fear that their presence would irritate their former owners. Departing slaves were not to lay claim to any plantations or property they had been granted temporary use of by their owner.[47] Some freed slaves found new homes in the Basel Mission Stations. The stations in Kumasi and Agogo were specially noted as safe havens for fugitive slaves and abolition witnessed an exodus of freed slaves to those stations. European missionaries in Ghana were advised by their societies at home to exercise the greatest care and watchfulness as far as indigenous slavery was concerned. The Gospel was to be preached with mildness, constancy and firmness so as to make it appear that slavery in every form was opposed to the spirit and precepts of Christianity. They were also to inculcate the great principle of all souls being equal in the sight of God, and to protect slaves, as far as it lay in their power, from injurious treatment. The missionaries exerted a lot of pressure on the British Administration to abolish the indigenous institution of slavery. Ramseyer was especially vocal, having arrived in Kumasi in 1896 to found a Basel Mission station. He was totally against the British toleration of indigenous slavery during 1896 to 1908 and he wrote several letters to the governor condemning the official policy. He realised that the chiefs and elders were quite happy with this policy. Ramseyer in all his condemnation admitted that by 1905 the open buying and selling of slaves in Asante had ceased after the British Administration had kept their word to the letter to punish all offenders. He also admitted that the slaves were generally well treated and lived under good conditions. Nevertheless the institution needed to be abolished. Christian missionary work during this period had not yet started in the Northern Territories so the British officials sent slaves they had freed on their way to the markets or from slave dealers to the mission station in Kumasi. In the late 1890s the Basel missionaries contemplated building a "slave home" either in Atebubu or Nkoranza with the British government support.

The abolition process was a very tedious one for the British officials in Ghana. Initially they had to contend with both the Atlantic system and the indigenous institution. After concentrating their efforts on the Atlantic system for several decades, they attempted to deal with indigenous slavery. They first had the Forts, the Protected Territories and the Colony to deal with. Years later, they turned their attention to Asante and the Northern Territories. It was difficult for the age old institution to die out completely in spite of the enactment of laws and punishment for offenders. The problem of logistical support to carry out complete abolition was often a set back so far as the officials were concerned. A number of them used the fine excuse of the kind treatment of indigenous slaves to justify their "soft" positions. Eventually laws were passed abolishing indigenous slavery and emancipating slaves. The British Colonial government seemed to be primarily interested in freeing slaves. It did not define or give guidelines as to the kind of relationship that should henceforth exist between the owners and the freed slaves, the majority of whom opted to stay. Consequently, affected families defined for themselves the freed slave's new rights, privileges, obligations and social status. The result of this was that between 1908 and 1928 some families still regarded the legally freed slaves as slaves, while others got involved in some cases of slave dealing. This prompted the British government to pass "The Abolition of Slavery Declaration Ordinance" in 1928 to deal with the legal status of slavery.

It is intriguing to note that even after this Ordinance was passed, cases dealing with one's servile origins came up time and again in the Traditional and Regular Courts throughout the colonial period. The Post-colonial period has not been spared either. The issue of slavery continues to be raised periodically in the Traditional and Regular Courts with respect to chieftaincy disputes, social status, inheritance and land tenure.

EPILOGUE

This book has examined indigenous slavery in Ghana from its earliest beginnings to its gradual abolition. It has shown that the origins of the institution date back to the Neolithic and Iron Age period. It became institutionalised with the formation and expansion of states from the 1st to the 18th Century A.D. and reached its climax in the 19th century.

An examination of the various definitions, classifications and perceptions of slavery brought out the following main characteristics of slavery; namely, the slave as a commodity, the slave as a chattel, the slave as an inheritable being whose progeny inherit slave status; the slave as property; the slave as a "kinless", marginalised outsider. Not all of the characteristics were applicable to the Ghanaian situation. Even where there appeared to be similarities, one could still notice differences in the Ghanaian context. In Ghana the slave was a commodity and a property in the Ghanaian sense of the word; he/she was inheritable; and his/her progeny inherited slave status. The slave was, however, not a chattel and an outsider. Although he/she was sometimes a commodity to be exchanged for other goods, and the property of his/her owner, the slave in Ghana enjoyed certain rights and privileges. The fact that a slave could become a part of his/her owner's family and kin was a special feature of slavery in Ghana. Indeed the rights and privileges the slave enjoyed emanated mainly from his/her being a member of his/her owner's kin.

Pre-colonial Ghanaian society recognised five categories of voluntary and involuntary subordination of one person to another. There was the servant, the pawn, the slave, the war captive, and the slave under sentence of death. In looking at slavery in Ghana, one has to understand these categories as well as appreciate the similarities and differences between slavery in Ghana and those of other parts.

It was suggested that the earliest evidence of slavery might be found in the Neolithic period of Ghana's history. This was the period that marked the beginnings of sedentary habitation, agriculture and iron working. Slaves were probably used for labour on farms. As urbanisation and state building progressed, slave owning and slave dealing became part of the various states' political and social organisation. During the 16th, 17th and 18th Centuries A.D. Ghana witnessed greater political changes and developments in the form of the building of formidable states and kingdoms. Wars of conquest and expansion enabled the states to acquire prisoners of war who were invariably enslaved. The Portuguese brought slaves from different parts of West Africa particularly Nigeria, to Ghana. Some were employed as labourers by the European companies resident on the coast, while others were bought by the state and individuals for purposes of labour. The introduction of the Atlantic slave trade into Ghana from the 16th to the early part of the 19th century turned Ghana into a major supplier of slaves.

The major sources of slave supply for domestic use from the 15th to the 19th century were warfare, direct purchase from the markets, pawning, raiding, kidnapping and tribute. Minor sources included gifts, convicts and personal transactions. Prisoners of war constituted a large proportion of the total slave output. Many of the wars originated in sheer aggression and a desire for retribution. The 18th century wars were not unconnected with the prevailing high supply of firearms. Indeed the period marked the peak of the Atlantic slave trade. Prisoners of war satisfied the domestic as well as the external need for labour. Numerous markets scattered across the length and breadth of Ghana, provided venues for the direct purchase of slaves. Almost every region in Ghana had slave markets. In modern Upper East, Upper West and Northern Regions, I identified 4 of such markets. In modern Brong Ahafo and Asante Regions, I found 5 markets, in the Volta Region at least 5 markets. The Greater Accra and Eastern Regions had 7, the Central Region 5, the Western Region at least 3. The most famous market in the country was the Salaga market in the north. Slave trading and kidnapping became an established occupation among the Akwamu, Akyem, Kwahu, Fante, Krepe and Mole-Dagbani.

From oral and documentary data collected, I was able to identify nine (9) main slave routes in Ghana from the 15th to the 19th century (see Map III). These routes were also trade routes and they appeared to radiate from Kumasi northwards and southwards. Route I linked Kumasi to Sampa. Route II radiated from Kumasi to Wa and Bole. Route III connected Kumasi to Kintampo, Buipe, Daboya. Route IV linked Kumasi to Atebubu, Salaga and Yendi. Route V connected Kumasi to Accra. Route VI led southwards from Kumasi to Assin Fosu, Assin Manso, Anomabu and Cape Coast. Route VII was the route which connected Kumasi to Elmina, Takoradi and Axim. Route VIII linked Kumasi with Assini and Beyin. Route IX connected Kete Krachi to Akwamu, Ada and Keta. Along these routes plied private and official traders. No one was debarred from participating in the indigenous slave trade nor the Atlantic trade.

Domestic slaves were put to several uses during the period under study. First, they provided labour for agriculture, trade and industry. Agriculture involved farming for subsistence and for export. Male and female slaves traded for individuals, kings and chiefs in Ghana's intra-state trade, inter-state trade and long distance trade. Some served as carriers, while others transacted business on behalf of their owners. Slave labour was also required in the industries such as gold mining, iron-working, salt making, rubber production and the art and craft industries such as pottery, basketry, cloth-weaving and wood-working. Second, slaves were recruited into the administrative sectors of the state. Slaves usually headed and manned the Household division of the palaces as well as the sub-divisions within the Household.

Third, some slaves were enrolled in the military. They served in the various divisions of the army, such as the Advance Guard, the Right and Left Wings, the Main Body and the Rear Guard. Trusted slaves who displayed acts of valour were sometimes given command positions on the battle field. Others performed 'odd jobs' during military operations such as carrying food and clothing; fetching firewood and water. Apart from fighting on the battle field, slaves were also recruited as personal body guards of kings and chiefs and as members of some of the 'Asafo' companies.

Fourth, slaves performed domestic chores in the palaces, shrines and individual households. The chores involved cooking, washing, fetching water and firewood, sweeping, cleaning, going on errands and taking care of children. Fifth, some slaves were sacrificed from time to time in accordance with traditional beliefs and practices. On festive occasions and during the celebration of funerals of kings, chiefs and people of royalty, slaves were offered as sacrifices to the gods in supplication for protection, guidance, help and advice. Slaves were also sacrificed in day to day rituals of the state and sometimes at the personal whims of kings and chiefs. Human sacrifice was the prerogative of kings and chiefs who had the right of life and death over every citizen in their state.

Finally slaves were acquired by individuals for personal reasons, including procreation, prestige, wealth and power.

Kinship formed the core of Ghana's pre-colonial social structure and more often than not slaves were integrated into the kin of their owners. They thus became part of their owners' family, lineage and clan. The clan was patrilineal or matrilineal, depending on the ethnic group to which the slave became attached. Slaves became part of their owner's kin through adoption or marriage. The adoption of slaves into their owner's families was a gradual process and it did not necessarily confer equality of status with their owners or members of the family. Adopted slaves were still required to perform certain servile duties. Members of the family who owed their position in the family to birth rather than adoption guarded their birthright jealously. Slaves were given new names by their owners as a sign of integration and a new identity. They lived in the same houses with their owners, except in cases where the owner was wealthy enough to own more than one house. Among members of royalty, slaves were usually housed in separate quarters.

Social stratification of pre-colonial Ghana, placed slaves at the bottom of the social ladder though oral and documentary data affirm humane treatment of slaves. Traditional rules and norms governing slave treatment accounted for this kind of humane picture. These rules and norms required both the owners and the owned to play their part in order to ensure peaceful co-existence. Documentary records point out that some of the owners occasionally flouted the traditional rules and treated their slaves harshly but these were exceptions rather than the norm. Such owners were often made to face the full rigors of traditional law. That slaves were on the whole treated humanely is borne out by the fact that only 5 recorded instances of slave revolt or rebellion are mentioned in the records from the 15th to the 19th century.

Slaves enjoyed certain rights and privileges but also suffered from disabilities. They had the right to be fed, clothed and housed; to marry, earn independent income, have portions of the family or community land assigned to them; to purchase slaves of their own if they acquired sufficient wealth, to object to the succession of a new master on the death of their former owner; to be witnesses in court; to have their debts paid by their owners. They were entitled to protection and had opportunities for social, political and economic advancement. They could inherit their owner's property as well as hold property of their own, and had a good chance of being freed.

But slaves also suffered several disabilities. First, was their liability to be sacrificed. Second, their status as slaves imposed on them a permanent stigma. Third, their physical appearance was supposed to reflect their status. They were required to dress modestly. Some families preferred clothing their slaves in a particular way to reflect their low status. Four, they were sometimes not welcome in the company of freemen and women. Five, the slaves were required to work harder than the free or common man/woman. Six, slaves were not supposed to take any decisions of their own. Seven, slaves' personally acquired properties reverted to their owners or the family of their owners when they died. Eight, slaves were modestly buried.

Pre-colonial Ghanaian society provided ample opportunities for political mobility for slaves. Traditional laws of succession among the major ethnic groups made allowance for slaves to succeed to the stool or skin, if there was a failure of heirs. Such slaves were usually those who lived in the palaces and possessed experience in the day to day administration of the state. Hard work, loyalty and faithfulness were traits Elders of the state looked out for in the slaves. A slave who had been integrated into his/her owner's family qualified to be a candidate for the stool or skin when suitable heirs were not available. The offspring of a free royal male and a female slave was usually favoured in such circumstances. Slaves who ascended stools/skins acted in caretaker positions until suitable heirs were found to replace them. This could mean occupying the stool/skin for years.

Among the major ethnic groups in Ghana, the Asantes were perhaps the most generous in allowing slaves to succeed to stools. A study of 212 Asante stools revealed that 36 of these were occupied at one time or other by slaves from the 15th to the 19th century. There were 55 recorded instances when slaves succeeded to stools. To prevent the slaves from passing on the stool to their sons or to a member of their immediate family, certain conditions were laid down. First, they were made to understand that they were only caretakers and as such were not entitled to pass on the stool to members of their immediate families. Second, they were not buried at the Royal Mausoleum if they died on the stool, and their stools were not 'blackened'.

Asante also created special stools called "Esom Dwa" (Service Stools) for slaves and servants at the palaces. Of the 212 Asante stools I studied, 31 of these stools fell under this category. The 31 stools did not belong to any clan as was the case with all other Asante stools, but to the administrative and military departments of the state. The stools also had other characteristics which made them different from the royal stools. For example, though they were patrilineal rather than matrilineal, succession did not always pass from father to son. It was the Asantehene's prerogative to always appoint a successor to the stool whenever it became vacant. The occupants of the stool swore the oath of allegiance on taking office to the Asantehene with the "Ahwihwibaa" sword, while Paramount and Senior Chiefs swore with the "Mponponsuo" sword. The creation of these special Service Stools dates from the reign of

Oti Akenten (1630-1660) to the reign of Asantehene Prempeh I (1888-1931). The abolition of Indigenous Slavery was a hard and painful task. It proved difficult to uproot in one stroke, a system which had been embedded into the political, social and economic life of the state and family for centuries. The abolition story covers stages: 1807-1873; 1874-1896; 1896-1908 and 1908-1928. In the first stage the British Administration concentrated on the abolition of the Atlantic slave trade. Indigenous slavery was tolerated and sometimes ignored. British subjects who resided mainly in the forts and castles along the coast were not permitted to engage in domestic slavery. In 1873 the British Colonial office described its position with respect to indigenous slavery as "embarrassing" and issued a memorandum outlining its attitude to, and efforts at dealing with, slavery, both Atlantic and Indigenous from 1841-1873. The abolition laws were clear in British Territory and among British subjects but not in the Protectorate. The second stage was marked by the issue of a proclamation on 3rd November 1874 prohibiting the buying, selling and pawning of people. This was followed by the issue of two ordinances on 17th December 1874 abolishing all forms of slave dealing. Notwithstanding the Proclamation and the Ordinances, a majority of slaves in the Protectorate opted to remain with their owners. Others asserted their liberty and left to begin new lives. Unfortunately slave trading, both Atlantic and Indigenous, persisted.

During the third stage (1896-1908), abolition moved to Asante and the Northern Territories. From 1896 to 1902 the British Administration tolerated the institution in Asante but forbade the open buying and selling of slaves. Slaves who ran away from their owners were returned if it was proved that they had not been cruelly treated. In the Northern Territories the British administration tried to suppress the slave trade in the markets and contend with the slave raiding activities of Samory Toure and Babatu. After Asante and the Northern Territories had been annexed to the British Crown between 1901 and 1902, the Administration took more decisive and concrete steps to abolish indigenous slavery. On 22nd June 1908 "final" instructions were issued with respect to pawns and slaves. Immediately there were protests especially in Asante. When it became clear that the British Administration was determined, some slaves opted to leave their owners to begin new lives. Others chose to remain with their owners. The Basel Mission Stations became havens for freed slaves.

Freed slaves who remained with their respective kings and chiefs continued to serve in the Household ('Gyase') division of the palaces. They continued to play important roles in the political life of the various traditional states. They served as stool carriers, umbrella carriers, hammock-carriers; drummers and horn-blowers, minstrels, linguists; bathroom attendants, 'soul-washers,' caretakers of the royal mausoleum; elephant-tail switchers, fan-bearers, floor-polishers, cooks; eunuchs, gun-bearers, heralds, sword-bearers, shield-bearers; treasurers, assistant treasurers and attendants. Others were not assigned specific roles but were required to perform miscellaneous duties. Some remained in the military department serving under the various segments i.e. in the Right and Left Wings, the Advance Guard, the Main Body and the Rear Guard. Others continued to play their roles as special Bodyguards to the kings and chiefs. Before abolition, slaves who served in the above divisions of the palaces were not paid. They were housed, clothed and fed. After abolition they continued to be housed, clothed and fed but in addition, given some allowances. Those in the army were paid wages. This innovation by the traditional states became a new phenomenon in Ghana's traditional political life.

In the economic life of pre-colonial Ghana, slaves provided the bulk of the labour force in agriculture, trade and industry. After abolition, those who opted to stay with their former owners worked out personal arrangements with them. It is interesting to observe that Ghana did not face an economic crisis following abolition. This is borne out by the fact that Ghana's economy grew steadily after abolition. The records suggest that a majority of slaves remained with their former owners and continued to perform their labour duties under new kinds of arrangements. Perhaps the fact that abolition was carried out in stages helped to prevent any economic catastrophe.

The final stage of abolition, which falls outside the scope of this book (1908-

1928), was a period of 'stock-taking'. While trying to consolidate their gains, the British government dealt ruthlessly with cases which were brought before it on slave dealing in the Colony, Asante and the Northern Territories. In spite of all their efforts at abolition, vestiges of the indigenous institution persisted by the end of 1927, mainly because the British colonial government was obsessed with simply liberating slaves. It did not provide guidelines for the new kind of social relationships envisaged for former owners and their freed slaves who opted to remain with their adoptive families; nor did it review the traditional rules and norms governing the treatment of slaves. Consequently, it was left to the discretion of individual families to determine the freed slaves' relationship, rights, privileges, obligations and social status. In 1928 the British government felt the need to pass "The Abolition of Slavery Declaration Ordinance" to deal with the legal status of slavery.

Throughout the colonial period the Traditional and Regular Courts were called upon now and again to deal with cases questioning ex-slaves status in matters concerning succession to chiefly office, inheritance, land tenure and social rank. In post-colonial Ghana the rights of ex-slaves with regard to the above mentioned matters continue to be brought up in the Traditional and Regular Courts for affirmation or disavowal. Indigenous slavery and all that it stood for have left permanent marks on Ghana's traditional, social and political institutions. This state of affairs makes the study of indigenous slavery very relevant in contemporary Ghana.

1908-1928: THE FOURTH PHASE OF ABOLITION

From 1908 to 1928 some cases of slave dealing were brought to the attention of the British administration in the Colony, Asante and the Northern Territories. In 1908 for example, it was reported in Asante that one Efatoo Safow had bought a woman called Efua from the chief of Offinso. In 1911 there were reports of slave dealing in Cape Coast and other coastal towns. Most of the offenders were sentenced to imprisonment for a period of 7 years. In 1921 an Asante man from Nkawie called Yaw Boakye was sold to the head linguist of Bantama. Between 1924 and 1928 cases of slave dealing continued to be reported in the Colony, Asante and the Northern Territories. In January 1928 the Chief Commissioner of the Northern Territories admitted that some form of slave dealing existed but the worst offenders were the Krachi and Ada Districts.

Reports from the Colony, Asante and the Northern Territories for this period also indicate that the institution of indigenous slavery had not been completely eliminated. On 2 April 1918 for example, one Amma Brewaa appealed to the Chief Commissioner in Asante to be allowed to return to her country. She had been brought to Asante after the Krepe war of 1869 and was living with a chief called Asubonten. The chief was unwilling to let her return because he feared all the slaves in Asante would follow suit. This incident shows that abolition had not been thoroughly completed.

The Chief Commissioner, quite offended and embarrassed by this chief's reaction remarked:

I never heard such nonsense and Esubantin knows fully well that slavery has not been recognised in Ashanti for years past. All the woman has to do is to leave when and how she likes.[1]

In that same year the Asante Mamponghene Nana Osei Bonsu complained to the District Commissioner at Ejura that some of his horn blowers were deserting their duties and had joined the Basel Mission congregation as Christians. The District Commissioner asked the horn blowers to go back but Rev. S. Kwafo of the mission at Mampong asked the District Commissioner to reconsider his decision because horn blowing "supports the heinous institution of heathenism, slave dealing". He was obviously referring to the fact that the freed slaves who had remained in the palaces were still performing their traditional roles. In fact in 1927 de Graft Johnson, Assistant Secretary for Native Affairs related that a few years past, one of the easiest ways by which slaves obtained their freedom, especially in Asante was to join the Basel Mission Church. The chiefs often protested strongly to the British administration that their subjects were deserting their duties. These subjects were often the "freed" slaves, because they never protested when "free common people" joined the church. After the necessary discussions between the Chief Commissioner and the District Commissioner on the Mamponghene's petition, the Chief Commissioner stated that horn blowing in itself was not contrary to the Christian religion. The horn blowers were to go back to the chief to perform their duties but they were not to take part in "fetish ceremonies". Hereditary horn blowers who had become accepted Christians were to find replacements. In early 1928 the Chief Commissioner of the Northern Territories confessed that Indigenous Slavery still existed in his region but that

> the so called slaves are perfectly happy, generally related to their master and have no worries to making a living. I call them domestic parasites rather than domestic slaves as if they wished to leave they could always do so.[2]

In October 1927, de Graft Johnson, wrote a 19 page memorandum on the vestiges of slavery in the Gold Coast. He showed in detail the existence of indigenous slavery in the Colony, Asante, the Northern Territories and the British sphere of Togo land. He related how the freed slaves and descendants of slaves were acquired, the uses to which they were put, their rights and privileges and the close connection between chieftaincy and the indigenous institution. He also narrated the circumstances that led to the 1874 Proclamation and its effects. In the Colony, at the time of writing there were very few, if any, people alive at that time who were themselves slaves when the 1874 Proclamation and subsequent Ordinances were passed. All children born to such slaves were free, so also were slaves who had been bought and brought into the Colony. De Graft Johnson was concerned about the legal position of the children of slaves who were born before 1874 and were still alive. These people, strictly speaking and in the eyes of the law had still to be recognised as slaves. There was also the anomaly of children of the same slave parents, some born before 5th November 1874 who were still slaves and others born after 5th November 1874 who were free. In addition to the legal aspect the British administration was encouraged by de Graft Johnson to attack the issue of slave dealing more vigorously, especially in the western, central and southern portions of the Colony.

So far as Asante and the Northern Territories were concerned, de Graft Johnson opined that the Ordinances abolishing slavery in the Colony had not been applied to these territories. The conditions in these territories therefore, left much to be desired. He stated:

> In fact anyone acquainted with social conditions in the two territories would long hesitate before committing himself to a definite expression of opinion on questions touching slavery, domestic or otherwise.[3]

De Graft Johnson further related:

Today no slaves can be openly bought in the Northern Territories, but no one who has travelled to the place can unhesitatingly assert that all there are free people. There is probably not a single village where there are not to be met with some slaves or descendants of people regarded as slaves. But they all seem more or less happy since there is no longer the fear of a sudden raid and the danger of exchanging a good master for a bad or indifferent one[4]

It was de Graft Johnson's hope that with the development of a colonial economy and with time, indigenous slavery would die out within a generation or so. The governor sent copies of de Graft Johnson's memorandum to all the British officials and asked for their comments. The first to react was the Secretary of Native Affairs. He admitted that Caps. 5 and 6 of the Laws of the Colony had not been applied to Asante and the Northern Territories but slave-dealing was prohibited in Asante and the Northern Territories under Section 443 of the Criminal Code (Cap. 16). It was also true that any person in the Colony who was being held as a slave could regain his freedom by asking. He also agreed that the legal position would be improved if Cap. 6 was applied to Asante and the Northern Territories and this point should be referred to the Attorney General for his opinion. The District Commissioners in all the districts were accessible and anyone who thought he was not free had to apply to the District Commissioner. The Attorney General's reaction to the memorandum was to highly commend de Graft Johnson and to admit that people who were slaves on 5th November 1874 were still slaves but they must be a rapidly diminishing class. With respect to Asante, the Northern Territories and the British sphere of Togo land, Chapters 5 and 6 and Section 443 of the Criminal Code were in force. There was the need to go beyond the Criminal Code. He concluded

It is true that we cannot in practice abolish the actual institution of "domestic slavery"; but I am strongly in favour of expressly abolishing the legal status of slavery, including that of domestic slavery.[5]

The Attorney General prepared draft ordinances to effect the necessary changes for Asante, the Northern Territories and the British Sphere of Togo land on 9th December 1927. The Ordinances were to be cited as "The Abolition of Slavery Declaration Ordinance, 1928". In the Ordinances, the expressions "slavery" and "slave" included a reference to domestic slavery and domestic slaves. The expression "free" meant free from slavery as so defined, and from all obligations and disabilities attached to the status of slavery. The legal status of slavery was abolished. All persons born in, or entering Asante, the Northern Territories or the British sphere of Togo land were declared free. No court or native tribunal was to entertain any action, cause, matter, claim, defence or plea, founded (either expressly or by implication) on the allegation or averment that any person is, or at any time was, a slave.

SOME INFORMATION ON THE 375 RESPONDENTS

1. *Occupation*
Paramount Chiefs, Queenmothers, Sub Chiefs, Family Heads, Various traditional office holders e.g. palace officials, stool carriers; Traditional priests and Herbalists; teachers, nurses, civil servants and legal practitioners; Artisans e.g. masons, carpenters, watch repairers, auto-electricians, drivers, gold & silver smiths, blacksmiths, book-binders and seamstresses; Chop bar proprietors, transport owners; petty traders, bakers; ex-servicemen, watchmen and housewives.

2. *Regions, Towns & Villages*
Upper West – Lawra, Wa & Jirapa.

Upper East – Navrongo, Sandema, Bolgatanga.

Northern – Tamale, Bimbilla, Tuna, Daboya, Chinderi, Nalerigu.

Brong Ahafo – Chiraa, Bechem, Nkoranza, Subinso, Kranka, Nsuhia, Dormaa Ahenkro, Wenchi, Drobo, Japekrom.

Asante – Ejura, Asokwa, Kumasi, Jamasi, Atwima Nsima, Kumawu, Juaso, New Abrim, Asante-Akyem, Ejisu, Bekwai, Asante Mampong, Nsuta.

Western – Takoradi, Bogoso-Bawdie, Adiembra, Wiawso, Sefwi, Fawokabra, Aboadze, Apowa, Sekondi, Kikam Axim, Tarkwa.

Central – Cape Coast, Asebu, Winneba, Elmina, Mankessim, Brofoyedur, Twifu Mampong, Twifu Hemang, Gomoa Nyampino Traditional Area.

Eastern – Koforidua, Kwahu Praso, Kwahu Bepong, Aburi, Abetifi, Begoro,

Boadua, Kade, Akim Oda, Akim Banso, Effiduase, Asamankese, Nsawam, Nkawkaw, Suhum, Akwapim, Odumase Krobo.

Volta – Nkonya Tepo, Sovie, Lolobi Kumasi, Hohoe, Logba, Tofa, Dodi Papasi, Jasikan, Anlo, Kadjebi, Dodome Awasu, Sesa, Keta, Anfoega, Tapa Abotoase, Amedzofe, Peki Blengo, Peki Wudome, Peki Avetile, Peki Akyeadome, Peki Tsame, Adidome, Peki Adokoie, Peki Dzabati, Aflao, Avoeme.

Greater Accra – Madina, Osu, Shai, Labadi, Tema, New Ningo, Odorkor, Kaneshie, James Town.

3. Age Distribution

The range was 37-106 years. Nearly 50% were 75 years and above. The mean age was 71 years.

4. Names

Those who were willing to disclose their names on condition that it would not be made public have their names on the questionnaires. These are available for anyone interested.

5. Dates of Interviews

These are available on the questionnaires administered in the field.

6. Data Analysis

The data analysis derived from the questionnaires is also available.

BIBLIOGRAPHY

A. PRIMARY SOURCES

(I) Archival Materials
1. **Abstracts of Basel Mission** Gold Coast Correspondence, compiled by P. Jenkins, available in the Balme Library, University of Ghana, Legon.
2. **Basel Mission Archives**, Switzerland – Correspondence between Basel Missionaries on the Gold Coast and Basel, 1865-1896.
3. *Great Britain and Ghana. Documents of Ghana History 1807-1957*, London 1965, compiled by G.E. Metcalfe.
4. **Kyebi Palace Archives**, AASA/1.1/ series.
5. **Manhyia Archives**, Asantehene's Palace, Kumasi – Civil Record Books, Palaver Record Books, Divisional Court Books.
6. **National Archives of Ghana,** Accra – ADM, ACC, SCT series.
7. **Perry Castenda Library**, Austin, Texas, U.S.A. – Microfilm 11510 Reel No.2 vol. 7-13; 11510 Reel No. 3 vol. 13-15.
8. **Public Record Office**, London – Co/96 series.
9. **Ramseyer Archives of the Presbyterian Church** Abetifi – Missionary and Court Records.
10. *Records relating to the Gold Coast Settlements from 1750-1874,* Dublin 1923, compiled by J.J. Crooks.
11. **Regional Archives** Cape Coast – ADM series.
12. **Regional Archives** Ho – KE Series.
13. **Regional Archives** Kumasi – SCT, ADM series; Files C & D.
14. **Regional Archives** Koforidua – ADM series, Court Records.
15. **Regional Archives** Sunyani – ADC, GDC, RG, SY, WDC series.
16. **Regional Archives** Sekondi – ACC series.
17. **Regional Archives** Tamale – RAT series.

(II) Traders' Journals and Travellers' Accounts
1. **Atkins** J.: *A Voyage to Guinea, Brasil and the West Indies*, London 1841.
2. **Barbot** J.: *A description of the coasts of North and South Guinea*, London 1732.
3. **Beecham** J.: *Ashantee and the Gold Coast*, London 1841.
4. **Bosman** W.: *A New and Accurate description of the Coast of Guinea*, London 1705.
5. **Bowdich** T.E.: *Mission from Cape Coast Castle to Ashantee*, London 1819.
6. **Boyle** E.: *Through Fante land to Coomassie*, London 1874.
7. **Cardinall** A.W.: *Ashanti and beyond*, London 1927.

8.   **Cruickshank** B.: *Eighteen years on the Gold Coast of Africa vol. 2*, London 1966.
9.   **Daendels** H.W.: *Journal and Correspondence 1815-1817*, mimeographed at the Institute of African Studies, Univ. of Ghana, Legon 1964.
10. **De Marees** P.: *Description and Historical account of the Gold Kingdom of Guinea* (1602), translated by A. Van Dantzig and A. Jones, U.S.A. 1987.
11. **Dupuis** J.: *Journal of a residence in Ashantee*, London 1824.
12. **Freeman** R.A.: *Travels and Life in Ashanti and Jaman*, London 1967.
13. **Freeman** T.B.: *Journal of various visits to the kingdoms of Ashanti, Akim and Dahomey in Western Africa*, London 1844.
14. **Gordon** C.A.: *Life on the Gold Coast*, London 1874.
15. **Klose** H.: *Journey to Northern Ghana in 1894*, available at the Institute of African Studies, Univ. of Ghana, Legon.
16. **Pacheco** Pereira D.: *Esmeraldo de situs orbis*, translated by G.A.T. Kimble, London 1937.
17. **Ramseyer** F.A. and Kuhne J.: *Four years in Asante*, London 1878.
18. *Salaga Papers vol. I*, compiled by M. Johnson, available at the Institute of African Studies, Univ. of Ghana, Legon.
19. **Smith** W.: *A new voyage to Guinea*, London 1744.

(III) Reports
1.   **Asante Seminar,** North-western University, U.S.A. No. 1 March 1975.
2.   **British Parliamentary Papers** Nos. 60 & 62, Ireland 1971.
3.   **Ghana Law Reports** 1959-1988.
4.   **Ghana Law Reports Digest** 1989-1990.
5.   **Report of the Committee of African Forts** 1817, available in the Balme Library, Univ. of Ghana, Legon.
6.   **West African Law Reports,** 1930-1933; 1955-1959.

(IV) Newspapers
1.   Daily Graphic.
2.   Ghanaian Times.
3.   The Ghanaian Chronicle.
4.   The Pioneer.
5.   The Weekend Statesman.
6.   Weekly Spectator.

(V) Oral Sources
1.   **Ashanti Stool Histories** vols. I & II 1976, compiled by J. Agyeman-Duah, available at the Institute of African Studies, Legon.

2. **Oral Traditions of Adansi** 1969, compiled by K.Y. Daaku, available at the Institute of African Studies, Legon.
3. **Oral Traditions of Denkyira** 1970, Institute of African Studies, Legon.
4. **Oral Traditions of Dormaa** 1976, Institute of African Studies, Legon.
5. **Oral Traditions of the Fante States** – No. 1 Abrem; No. 2 Eguafo; No. 3 Komenda; No. 4 Edina (Elmina), 1974, compiled by J.K. Fynn, Institute of African Studies, Legon.
6. **Oral Traditions of Fante States** No. 6, Eyanmain, Eyan Denkyira, Eyan Abaasa, 1975, compiled by J.K. Fynn, Institute of African Studies, Legon.
7. **Oral Traditions of the Fante States** No. 7, Kwamankese 1976, Institute of African Studies, Legon.
8. **Questionnaires**, interviews, note-writing, and observation conducted in all ten administrative regions of Ghana between August 1990 and September 1992. 375 Respondents received countrywide.

B. SECONDARY SOURCES

(I) Books
Ade Ajayi J.F. & Crowder M.: *History of West Africa vol. 2*, London 1984.
Ade Ajayi J.F. & Espie I.: *A Thousand Years of West African History*, Ibadan, Nigeria 1965.
Agbodeka F.: *Ghana in the Twentieth Century*, Accra, Ghana 1972.
Al-Islam Al-Alam H.M.R.M.: *Slave Trade in Africa*, Pakistan 1985.
Amenumey D.E.K.: *The Ewe in pre-colonial times*, Accra, Ghana 1986.
Analysis of Demographic Data vol. I, Ghana Statistical Service, Accra, Ghana April 1995.
Anene J.C. & Brown G. (Eds.): *Africa in the Nineteenth and Twentieth Centuries*, Hong Kong 1981.
Anquandah J.: *Rediscovering Ghana's Past*, London 1982.
Antubam I.K.: *Ghana's Heritage of Culture*, Leipzig 1963.
Assimeng M.: *Social Structure of Ghana*, Tema, Ghana 1981.
Blake M.: *European beginnings in West Africa 1454-1578*, London 1937.
Boahen A.A.: *Ghana Evolution and Change in the Nineteenth and Twentieth Centuries*, London 1975.
Boahen A.A.: *Topics in West African History*, London 1977.
Boakye J.: *A History of West Africa vol. I A.D. 1000-1800*, Accra, Ghana 1982.
Boles J.D.: *Black Southerners 1639-1869*, Kentucky, U.S.A. 1983.
Braimah J.A. & Goody J.R.: *Salaga the struggle for power*, London 1967.
Buah F.K.: *History of Ghana*, London 1989.

Busia K.A.: *The position of the chief in the modern political system of Ashanti,* London 1968.

Casely-Hayford J.E.: *Gold Coast Native Institutions,* London 1970.

Craton M., Walvin J. & Wright D.: *Slavery, Abolition and Emancipation,* London & New York 1976.

Daaku K.Y.: *Trade and Politics on the Gold Coast 1600-1720,* Great Britain 1970.

Danquah J.B.: *Akan Laws and Customs, and the Akim Abuakwa Constitution,* London 1928.

Davidson B.: *A History of West Africa 1000-1800,* New Ed. London 1985.

Derrick J.: *Africa's slaves today,* London 1975.

Dickson K.B.: *A Historical Geography of Ghana,* Cambridge 1969.

Elkins S.M.: *Slavery – A Problem in American Institutional and Intellectual Life,* 3rd Ed. Chicago, U.S.A. 1976.

Ellis A.B.: *The Tshi-speaking people of the Gold Coast of West Africa,* London 1887.

Falola T. & Lovejoy P.E. (Eds.): *Pawnship in Africa: Debt Bondage in Historical Perspective,* Boulder, U.S.A. 1994.

Filler L.: *Slavery in the U.S.A.,* New York, U.S.A. 1972.

Fisher A.G.. & Fisher H.J.: *Slavery and Muslim Society in Africa: The Institution in Saharan and Sudanic Africa, and the Trans-Saharan Trade,* London 1970.

Frey S.R.: *Water from the Rock,* Princeton, U.S.A. 1991.

Fuller F.: *A Vanished Dynasty, Ashanti,* London 1921.

Fynn J.K.: *Asante and its neighbours 1700-1807,* London 1971.

Fynn J.K. & Addo-Fening R.: *History for Senior Secondary Schools,* London 1991.

Goodheart L.B., Brown R.D. & Rabe S.G. (Eds.): *Problems in American Civilization – Slavery in American Society,* 3rd Ed. Lexington, U.S.A. 1993.

Goody J.R.: *The Ethnography of the Northern Territories of the Gold Coast,* London 1954.

Grace J.: *Domestic Slavery in West Africa with particular reference to the Sierra Leone Protectorate 1896-1927,* London 1975.

Hargreaves J.D.: *Prelude to the partition of West Africa,* London 1963.

Hernaes P.O.: *Slaves, Danes, and African Coast Society,* Trondheim, Norway 1995.

Holt P.M., Lambton A.K.S. & Lewis B. (Eds.): *The Cambridge History of Islam vol. 2,* Cambridge, Great Britain 1970.

Hopkins A.G.: *An Economic History of West Africa,* London 1977.

Howard R.: *Colonialism and Underdevelopment in Ghana,* London 1978.

Inikori J.E. & Engerman S.L. (Eds.): *The Atlantic Slave Trade – Effects on Economies, Societies and Peoples in Africa, the Americas and Europe,* Durham & London 1992.

Isichei E.: *History of West Africa since 1800,* London 1985.

Jordan W.D. *White over Black,* Carolina, U.S.A. 1968.

Kea R.A.: *Settlements, Trade and Politics in the 17th Century Gold Coast*, Baltimore & London 1982.

Key G.B.: *The Political Economy of Colonialism in Ghana – A collection of documents and statistics 1900-1960*, Cambridge 1973.

Kimble D.: *A Political History of Ghana 1850-1928*, Oxford 1973.

Klein H.S.: *African slavery in Latin America and the Caribbean*, New York, U.S.A. 1986.

Klein M.A. (Ed.): *Breaking the chains – Slavery, Bondage and Emancipation in modern Africa and Asia*, Wisconsin, U.S.A. 1993.

Kolchin P.: *Unfree Labor, American Slavery and Russian Serfdom*, Harvard, U.S.A. 1987.

Kuada J.E. & Chachah Y.: *Ghana – The Land, the People and their Culture*, Denmark 1989.

Levtzion N.: *Muslims and Chiefs in West Africa: A Study of Islam in the Middle Volta Basin in the pre-colonial period*, Oxford 1968.

Lewin T.J.: *Asante before the British. The Prempean Years 1875-1900*, Kansas, U.S.A. 1978.

Lewis I.M.: *Islam in Tropical Africa: Studies presented and discussed at the Fifth International African Seminar, Ahmadu Bello University, Zaria, Nigeria, Jan. 1964*, London 1966.

Lovejoy P.E. (Ed.): *The Ideology of Slavery in Africa*, Beverly Hills, U.S.A. 1981.

Lovejoy P.E. (Ed.): *Transformations in Slavery. A History of Slavery in Africa*, Cambridge 1983.

Lovejoy P.E. (Ed.): *Africans in Bondage: Studies in Slavery and the Slave Trade*, Wisconsin, U.S.A. 1986.

Lovejoy P.E. & Hogendorn J.S.: *Slow death for slavery – The Course of Abolition in Northern Nigeria 1897-1936*, Cambridge 1993.

Lystad R.A.: *The Ashanti: A proud people*, New York U.S.A. 1968.

Macmunn G.: *Slavery through the Ages*, London 1983.

Manning P.: *Slavery and African Life*, Cambridge 1990.

Mcfarland D.M.: *Historical Dictionary of Ghana*, U.S.A. 1985.

Mckay J.P., Hill B.P. & Bucklar J.: *A History of World Societies, 3rd Ed.*, U.S.A. 1992.

Meillassoux C.: *L'esclavage en Afrique precoloniale*, Paris 1975.

Meillassoux C.: *Anthropologie de l'esclavage. Le ventre de fer et d'argent*, Paris 1986.

Miller J.C.: *Slavery A World-wide Bibliography 1900-1982*, U.S.A. 1985.

Miller R.M. & Smith J.D. (Eds.): *Dictionary of Afro-American Slavery*, U.S.A. 1988.

Miers S.: *Britain and the ending of the Slave Trade*, London 1975.

Miers S. & Kopytoff I. (Eds.): *Slavery in Africa: Historical and Anthropological Perspectives*, Wisconsin, U.S.A. 1977.

Miers S. & Roberts R. (Eds.): *The End of Slavery in Africa*, Wisconsin, U.S.A. 1983.

Nketia J.H.: *Drumming in Akan Communities of Ghana*, London 1963.

Nukunya G.K.: *Tradition and change in Ghana. An Introduction to Sociology*, Accra, Ghana 1992.

217

Ollennu N.A.: *The Law of Succession in Ghana*, Accra, Ghana 1960.

Ollennu N.A. & Woodman G.R. (Eds.): *Principles of Customary Land Law in Ghana*, *2nd Ed.*, Birmingham, Great Britain 1985.

Onwubiko K.B.C.: *History of West Africa A.D. 1000-1800 Bk. 1*, Nigeria 1982.

Owens H.P. (Ed.): *Perspectives and Irony in American Slavery*, Mississippi, U.S.A. 1976.

Oxford Dictionary, 2nd Ed., Oxford 1991.

Patterson O.: *Slavery and Social Death – A Comparative Study*, U.S.A. 1982.

Peoples J. & Bailey G.: *Humanity – An introduction to Cultural Anthropology*, U.S.A. 1988.

Rattray R.S.: *Ashanti Law and Constitution*, London 1929.

Rattray R.S.: *Tribes of Ashanti Hinterland*, London 1939.

Reindorf C.C.: *The History of the Gold Coast and Asante*, Accra, Ghana 1966.

Reynolds E.: *Trade and Economic change on the Gold Coast 1807-1874*, London 1974.

Robertson C.C. & Klein M.A. (Eds.): *Women and Slavery in Africa*, Wisconsin, U.S.A. 1983.

Sarbah J.M.: *Fanti Customary Laws*, London 1904.

Sarpong P.: *Ghana in retrospect*, Accra, Ghana 1974.

Searing J.F.: *West African Slavery and Atlantic Commerce*, Cambridge, Great Britain 1993.

Szereszewski R.: *Structural changes in the economy of Ghana 1811-1911*, London 1965.

Thornton J.: *Africa and the Africans in the making of the Atlantic World 1400-1680*, U.S.A. 1992.

Tourist Map of Ghana, National Atlas Development Centre, Accra, Ghana 1995.

Trimingham J.S.: *History of Islam in West Africa*, London 1962.

Trimingham J.S.: *History of Islam in East Africa*, London 1964.

Trimingham J.S.: *Islam in the Sudan*, London 1965.

Trimingham J.S.: *Islam in Ethiopia (2nd Ed.)*, London 1965.

Trimingham J.S.: *The influence of Islam upon Africa*, London 1968.

Ward W.E.F.: *A History of Ghana*, London 1966.

Warren D.M.: *The Akan of Ghana*, Accra, Ghana 1986.

Watson J.L. (Ed.): *Africa and Asian systems of slavery*, Berkeley, U.S.A. 1980.

Webster's Desk Dictionary of the English Language, New Jersey, U.S.A. 1983.

Wilks I.: *Asante in the Nineteenth Century*, Cambridge 1975.

Wills A.J.: *The story of Africa from the earliest times*, Hong Kong, 5th Impression 1981.**Wolfson** F.: *Pageant of Ghana*, London 1958.

(II) Articles in books, periodicals and conference papers
1. **Addo-Fening** R., 'The background to the deportation of King Asafo Adjei and the foundation of New Juaben,' *Transactions of the Historical Society of Ghana* vol. xiv No. 2 1973.
2. **Agri** B., 'Slavery in Yoruba society in the 19th Century,' in Miers & Kopytoff, *Slavery in Africa*, Wisconsin, U.S.A. 1977.
3. **Agyeman-Duah** J., 'Enstoolment procedures of Ashanti chiefs,' *The Pioneer*, Jan. 10 1990.
4. **Aidoo** A.A., 'Women in the History and Culture of Ghana,' *Research Review*, vol. 1. No. 1 1985, Institute of African Studies, Legon.
5. **Amenumey** D.E.K., 'Geraldo de Lima: A Reappraisal,' *Transactions of the Historical Society of Ghana*, vol. IX 1968, Legon.
6. **Andah** K., 'The role of women in agriculture,' *Proceedings of Seminar on Ghanaian Women in Development*, National Council on Women and Development, Accra, Ghana vol. 1 1978.
7. **Arhin** K., 'Succession and gold mining at Manso-Nkwanta,' *Research Review*, vol. 3 No. 3 1970, Institute of African Studies, Legon.
8. **Arhin** K., 'The Ashanti Rubber trade with the Gold Coast in the Eighteen-Nineties,' *Africa*, vol. XLII No. 1 Jan. 1972.
9. **Austin** G., 'Human Pawning in Asante 1800-1950: Markets and Coercion, Gender and Cocoa,' in Falola & Lovejoy, *Pawnship in Africa: Debt Bondage in Historical Perspective*, Boulder, U.S.A. 1994.
10. **Bame** K.N., 'Peoples in African Traditional popular culture,' *Consensus and Conflict*, U.S.A. & Ghana 1991.
11. **Bening** R.B. & Nabila J.S. 'Ghana: Preliminary Findings,' *Proceedings of seminar on Ghanaian Women in Development*, National Council on Women and Development, Accra, Ghana vol. 1 1978.
12. **Birmingham** D., 'A Note on the Kingdom of Fetu,' *Ghana Notes and Queries*, No. 9. Nov. 1966, Legon.
13. **Cohen** A., 'Politics of the kola trade,' *Africa*, vol. 36 1966.
14. **Daaku** K.Y., 'Pre-Ashanti States,' *Ghana Notes and Queries*, No. 9 Nov. 1966, Legon.
15. **Dapper** O., 'Beschreiburg von Afrika,' *Ghana Notes and Queries*, No. 9 Nov. 1966, Legon.
16. **Dumett** R., 'The rubber trade of the Gold Coast and Asante in the 19th Century', *Journal of African History*, vol. 12 1971.
17. **Dumett** R. & Johnson M., 'Britain and the suppression of slavery in the Gold Coast Colony, Ashanti and the Northern Territories,' in Miers & Roberts, *End of Slavery in Africa*, Wisconsin, U.S.A. 1988.

219

18. **Elbourne** E., 'The meaning of freedom: Britain and the Cape Colony 1799-1842,' paper presented at the *Conference on Unfree Labour in the development of the Atlantic world,* York University, Canada, 13-14 April 1993.

19. **Fynn** J.K., 'The rise of Ashanti,' *Ghana Notes and Queries,* No. 9 Nov. 1966, Legon.

20. **Fynn** J.K. 'Sources of slaves in Ghana during the period of the trans-Atlantic slave trade,' paper presented at the *World Conference on Slavery and Society in History,* Kaduna, Nigeria, 26-30, March 1990.

21. **Fynn** J.K., 'The Etsi of Ghana,' Dept. of History, Legon.

22. **Fynn** J.K., 'Borbor Fante,' Dept. of History, Legon.

23. **Gasper** B., 'Slave importation, Runaways and Compensation in Antigua 1720-1729, in Inikori & Engerman, *The Atlantic Slave Trade,* Durham and London 1992.

24. **Goody** J., 'The Akan and the North,' *Ghana Notes and Queries,* No. 9 Nov. 1966, Legon.

25. **Goody** J., 'Slavery in Time and Space,' in J.L. Watson, *Asian and African Systems of Slavery,* Berkeley & Los Angeles 1980.

26. **Hagan** G.P., 'Ashanti Bureaucracy,' *Transactions of the Historical Society of Ghana,* vol. XII 1971, Legon.

27. **Holden** J.J., 'The Zabarima Conquest of North West Ghana Part I,' *Transactions of the Historical Society of Ghana,* vol. vii 1965, Legon.

28. **Holden** J.J., 'The Samorian impact on Buna: An Essay in Methodology,' *African Perspectives,* Cambridge 1970.

29. **Jewsiewick** B. & Bawele M.M., 'The social context of slavery in Equatorial Africa during the 19th & 20th Centuries,' in Miers & Kopytoff, *Slavery in Africa,* Wisconsin, U.S.A. 1977.

30. **Johnson** M., 'Ashanti east of the Volta,' *Transactions of the Historical Society of Ghana,* vol. viii 1965, Legon.

31. **Johnson** M., 'The slaves of Salaga,' *Journal of African History,* 27, 1986.

32. **Klein** A.N., 'The two Asantes: competing interpretations of slavery in Akan-Asante culture and society,' in P. Lovejoy, *The Ideology of Slavery in Africa,* Beverly Hills, U.S.A. 1981.

33. **Klein** M.A., 'Slavery, the slave trade and Legitimate Commerce in the late Nineteenth Century in Africa,' *Etudes d'histoire Africaine,* 2, 1971.

34. **Klein** M.A., 'The Study of slavery in Africa,' *Journal of African History,* 19, 4, 1978.

35. **Klein** M.A. & Lovejoy P.E., 'Slavery in West Africa,' in Gemery & Hogendorn, *Uncommon Market,* New York, U.S.A. 1979.

36. **Kyerematen** A., 'The royal stools of Ashanti,' *Africa, the Journal of the International African Institute*, vol. xxxix, No. 1 Jan. 1969.

37. **Lovejoy** P.E., 'Indigenous African Slavery,' *Historical Reflections/Reflexions historiques*, 6, 1, 1979.

38. **Mcsheffrey** G.M., 'Slavery, Indentured Servitude, Legitimate trade and the impact of abolition in the Gold Coast 1874-1901: A reappraisal,' *Journal of African History*, 24, 1983.

39. **Miller** J.C., 'Lineages, Ideology and the history of slavery in western central Africa,' in Miers & Kopytoff, *Slavery in Africa*, Wisconsin, U.S.A. 1977.

40. **Obichere** B.I., 'The social character of slavery in Ashanti and Dahomey,' *Ufahamu*, 12, 1983.

41. **Perbi** A.A., 'Slavery: The Asante State Viewpoint,' paper presented at the *World Conference on Slavery and Society in History*, Kaduna, Nigeria 26-30 March 1990.

42. **Perbi** A.A. 'Mobility in pre-colonial Asante from a Historical Perspective,' *Research Review*, Institute of African Studies, Legon, vol. 7 Nos. 1 & 2 1991.

43. **Perbi** A.A., 'The abolition of Domestic Slavery by Britain: Asante's dilemma,' *Legon Journal of Humanities*, vol. 6 1992.

44. **Perbi** A.A., 'The relationship between the Domestic Slave Trade and the External Slave Trade in Pre-Colonial Ghana,' *Research Review*, Institute of African Studies, Legon, vol. 8 Nos. 1 & 2 1992.

45. **Perbi** A.A., 'The Legacy of Indigenous Slavery in Contemporary Ghana,' *Faculty of Social Studies Bulletin*, Legon vol. 1 No. 1 1996.

46. **Perbi** A.A., 'The acquisition and use of female slaves in pre-colonial Ghana,' *Universitas*, Legon (forthcoming).

47. **Person** Y., 'Samori and resistance to the French,' in Rotberg & Mazrui, *Protest and Power in Black Africa*, New York 1970.

48. **Poku** K., 'Traditional roles and people of slave origin in modern Ashanti – A few impressions,' *Ghana Journal of Sociology*, 5, 1, 1969.

49. **Romer** L.F., 'On the Negroes Religion in Guinea,' translated by I. Odotei in *Research Review*, Institute of African Studies, Legon, vol. 3 No. 2 1987.

50. **Savitt** L., 'Historiography,' in Miller & Smith, *Dictionary of Afro-American Slavery*, U.S.A. 1988.

51. **Scarborough** W.K., 'Slavery – The white man's burden,' in Owens, *Perspectives and Irony in American Slavery*, Mississippi, U.S.A. 1976.

52. **White** G., 'Domestic Slavery and other forms of Servitude in Africa: A Comparative Perspective,' *Africa Caribbean*, vol. 8 Dec. 1982, Jamaica.

C. DISSERTATIONS & THESES

1. **Addo-Fening** R., Akyem Abuakwa 1874-1943: A study of the impact of missionary activities and colonial rule on a traditional state, Ph.D., Univ. of Ghana, Legon 1980.

2. **Akoto** A.O., History of Akwamu, B.A., Univ. of Ghana, Legon 1974.

3. **Amissah** P., The history of the Asafo Company of Elmina, B.A., Univ. of Ghana, Legon 1975.

4. **Amissah-Koomson** K.G., The history of the Effutus, B.A., Univ. of Ghana, Legon 1972/73.

5. **Ansah** M.P., Akwamu – A study of its social and cultural institutions and their diffusion, M.A., Univ. of Ghana, Legon 1968.

6. **Arhin** K., The development of market centres at Atebubu and Kintampo since 1874, Ph.D., London 1969.

7. **Baidoo-Debey** M., The historical significance of the Elmina Pusuban, B.A., Univ. of Ghana, Legon 1979.

8. **Bonsu** A., The history of Kormantse up to the 19th Century, B.A., Univ. of Ghana, Legon 1977.

9. **Christian** L.A., The Akwamu remnant groups in the Akyem Abuakwa area, B.A., Univ. of Ghana, Legon 1974.

10. **Edwards-Idun** S.E., The treatment of slaves in the castles, B.A., Univ. of Ghana, Legon 1971.

11. **Feinberg** H.M., Elmina, Ghana: A History of its development and relationship with the Dutch in the 18th Century, Ph.D., Boston University 1969.

12. **Klein** A.N., Inequality in Asante: A study of the forms and meanings of slavery and social servitude in pre-colonial and early colonial Akan-Asante society and culture (2 vols.), Ph.D., Univ. of Michigan 1980.

13. **Mensah-Kane** C.T., Elmina: A Traditional History, B.A., Univ. of Ghana, Legon 1972.

14. **Perbi** A.A., Domestic Slavery in Asante 1800-1920, M.A., Univ. of Ghana, Legon 1978.

15. **Quaye** I., The Ga and their neighbours, Ph.D., Univ. of Ghana, Legon 1972.

16. **Wilks** I., Akwamu (1650-1750), A study of the rise and fall of a West African Empire, M.A., Univ. of Ghana, Legon 1958.

REFERENCES

Introduction
1. R.M. Miller & J.D. Smith (Eds.): *Dictionary of Afro-American Slavery*, U.S.A. 1988, Introduction.
2. P.E. Lovejoy, "Indigenous African Slavery," *Historical Reflections Reflexions historiques*, 6, 1(1979), 19-61.
   P.E. Lovejoy (Ed.): *The ideology of Slavery in Africa*, Beverly Hills, U.S.A. 1981.
   P.E. Lovejoy (Ed.): *Transformations in Slavery. A History of Slavery in Africa*, Cambridge, 1983.
   P.E. Lovejoy (Ed.): *Africans in Bondage: Studies in Slavery and the Slave Trade.*, Wisconsin, U.S.A. 1986.
   P.E. Lovejoy & J.S. Hogendorn (Eds): *Slow death for Slavery – The Course of Abolition in Northern Nigeria 1897-1936*, Cambridge, Great Britain, 1993.
3. M.A. Klein, "Slavery, the Slave Trade, and Legitimate Commerce in the late Nineteenth Century," *Etudes histoire africaine*, 2 1971, 5-28.
   M.A. Klein, "The Study of Slavery in Africa" (Review of Miers & Kopytoff Eds. *Slavery in Africa)* and of Meillassoux, Ed., *L'esclavage en Afrique precoloniale*, J.A.H. 19, 4, 1978, 599-609.
   M.A. Klein & P.E. Lovejoy, "Slavery in West Africa", in Germery & Hogendorn, Eds. *Uncommon Market*, New York, 1979, 67-92.
   C.C. Robertson & M.A. Klein (Eds.): *Women and Slavery in Africa*, Wisconsin, U.S.A. 1983.
   M.A. Klein (Ed.): *Breaking the Chains-Slavery, Bondage and Emancipation in Modern Africa and Asia*, Wisconsin, U.S.A. 1993.

Chapter 1
1. S. Miers & I. Kopytoff: *Slavery in Africa*, Wisconsin U.S.A. 1977, 3.
2. S.M. Elkins: *Slavery – A problem in American Institutional and Intellectual Life*, 3rd Ed., Chicago, U.S.A. 1976, 40.
3. W.D. Jordan: *White over Black*, Carolina, U.S.A. 1968, 64-65.
4. *Oxford Dictionary* 2nd Ed. Oxford 1991, 941.
5. Elkins, 50, 59-63; L. Filler: *Slavery in the U.S.A.*, New York 1972, 23; N.A.G. Adm II/1975; J.B. Danquah: *Akan Laws and Customs, and the Akim Abuakwa Constitution*, London 1928.
6. N.A.G. SCT 2/5/1, Criminal Record Book 2/1/79 - 4/2/84, 220-221.

7. J.D. Boles: *Black Southerners 1639-1869,* Kentucky, U.S.A. 1983, 21-22.
8. G. White, "Domestic Slavery and other forms of Servitude in Africa: A Comparative Perspective,' in *Africa Caribbean,* vol. 8. Dec. 1982, Jamaica, 39.
9. Miers & Kopytoff, 24.
10. P.E. Lovejoy (Ed.): *The Ideology of Slavery in Africa,* Beverly Hills, U.S.A. 1981, 12-16.
11. J.L. Watson (Ed.): *Asian and African Systems of Slavery,* Berkeley and Los Angeles, 1980, 2-4, 10-12.
12. A.A. Perbi "Mobility in Pre-colonial Asante from a Historical Perspective," in *Research Review,* I.A.S. Legon vol. 7 Nos 1&2 1991, 72-86. I. Wilks: *Asante in the Nineteenth Century,* New York, U.S.A. 1975, xxviii.
13. H.S. Klein: *African Slavery in Latin America and the Caribbean,* New York, U.S.A. 1986, 1-2.

Chapter 2
1. O. Patterson: *Slavery and Social Death - A Comparative Study,* U.S.A. 1982, vii.
2. J. Goody, "Slavery in Time and Space", in *Asian and African Systems of Slavery* Ed. By L.L. Watson, Berkeley & Los Angeles 1980, 18.
3. G.E. Metcalfe: *Great Britain and Ghana: Documents of Ghana History 1807-1957,* London 1964, 1-2.
4. The word "volkerwanderung" is used by Ward to describe the migrations, wars, consolidation and rise of states in Ghana during the 17th and 18th Centuries.
5. H.M. Feinberg, Elmina, Ghana: A History of its development and relationship with the Dutch in the 18th Century, unpublished Ph.D thesis, Boston University, U.S.A. 1969, iii, 126-127.
6. I. Quaye, The Ga and their Neighbours, Ph.D thesis, University of Ghana, Legon 1972, 248-249, 258-259.
7. K.Y. Daaku: *Trade and Politics on the Gold Coast 1600-1720,* Great Britain 1970, 15.
8. W. Smith: *A New Voyage to Guinea,* London 1744, 138.

Chapter 3
1. J. Barbot: *A Description of the coasts of North and South Guinea,* London 1732, 303.
2. Barbot 181, 184-185, 270-271.
3. W. Bosman: *A New and Accurate Description of the Coast of Guinea,* London 1705, 69-70.
4. Bosman 183.

5. Daaku: *Trade and Politics,* 30.
6. J. Dupuis: *Journal of a Residence in Ashantee,* London 1824, 163.
7. P. de Marees: *Description and Historical account of the Gold Kingdom of Guinea C (1602),* translated by A. Van Dantzig & A. Jones, U.S.A. 1987, 88-89
8. D. Birmingham, "A Note on the Kingdom of Fetu," in *Ghana Notes and Queries* No. 9 Nov. 1966, Legon, Ghana, 31. J.K. Fynn: *Oral Traditions of the Fante States* No. 1 Abrem, I.A.S. Legon 1974, 12.
9. O. Dapper, "Beschreiburg von Afrika," in *Ghana Notes and Queries* No. 9 Nov. 1966, Legon, Ghana, 16.
10. Barbot 189.
11. R. Addo-Fening, Akyem Abuakwa (1874 - 1943). A Study of the impact of missionary activities and colonial rule on a traditional state, unpublished Ph.D Thesis, History Dept. Univ. of Ghana, Legon, 1980, 63, 76.
12. C.C Reindorf: *The History of the Gold Coast and Asante,* Accra, Ghana 1966, 74-78.
13. Feinberg, Elmina, Ghana, 62.
14. Reindorf 123.
15. Reindorf 177
16. Reindorf 244-245.
17. M. Baidoo - Debey, The Historical significance of the Elmina Pusuban, B.A. dissertation, History Dept, Univ. of Ghana, Legon 1979, ii.
18. Baidoo-Debeyi, ii.
19. Reindorf 131.
20. Addo-Fening 26-27.
21. Reindorf 132.
22. Metcalfe: *Documents,* 14.
23. T.E. Bowdich: *Mission from Cape Coast Castle to Ashantee,* London 1819, 4.
24. Report from the Committee of African Forts 1817, Balme Library, Univ. of Ghana, Legon, 14.
25. Reindorf 163-164.
26. L.A. Christian, The Akwamu remnant groups in the Akyem Abuakwa area, B.A. dissertation, History of Akwamu, History Dept., Univ. of Ghana, Legon 1974, 5 A.O. Akoto, History of Akwamu, B.A. dissertation, History Dept., Univ. of Ghana, Legon 1974, 12-14, 23.
27. M. Johnson, "Ashanti east of the Volta", in *T.H.S.G. vol. Viii* 1965, 41-41.
28. W.E.F. Ward: *A History of Ghana,* London 1969, 120, 143.
29. Daaku: *Trade and Politics,* 31-32.
30. M. Johnson, *Salaga Papers* vol. 1, I.A.S. Legon 1965, SAL/39/2.
31. R.S. Rattray: *Ashanti Law and Constitution,* London 1929, 36.

32. Ward, 160.
33. Johnson, Ashanti, 39.
34. Johnson, Salaga, SAL/4/3, SAL/8/5.
35. Johnson, Salaga, SAL/18/11.
36. Johnson, Salaga, SAL/8/3.
37. A. Cohen, "Politics of the Kola Trade", in *Africa vol. 36* 1966, 20.
38. Johnson, Salaga, SAL/4/3, SAL/8/5.
39. J.A. Braimah & J.R. Goody: *Salaga the Struggle for Power,* London 1967, 79-80.
40. Johnson, *Salaga,* SAL/12/2.
41. Johnson, *Ashanti,* 50.
42. De Marees: *Description,* 176.
43. Barbot 270.
44. Christian, 5; Ward, 60.
45. Addo-Fening, 76.
46. Addo-Fening, 77; Reindorf 308.
47. G. Austin, "Human Pawning in Asante 1800-1950". In Falola & Lovejoy,(Eds.): Pawnship in Africa: *Debt Bondage in Historical Perspective,* Boulder, U.S.A. 1994, 122-123.
48. Barbot, 270.
49. Reindorf, 307.
50. Fynn, *Oral Traditions* Abrem, iii.
51. Reindorf, 308.
52. Johnson, *Ashanti,* 36-37; Ward, 143.
53. Reindorf, 303.
54. Reindorf, 303.
55. Reindorf, 62.
56. Ward 110-111.
57. Bowdich, 332.
58. Metcalfe, 78.
59. Johnson, *Ashanti,* 39
60. Johnson, *Ashanti,* 39.
61. R.A.K. D1092; N.A.G. Adm 11/1304.
62. N.A.G. Adm 11/1369; Adm 11/1304; Manhyia Archives, Kumasi, Palaver Record Book.
63. J.K. Fynn & R. Addo-Fening: *History for Senior Secondary Schools,* Evans, London 1991, 185.
64. Akoto, 16.
65. Akosua Bonsu, The History of Kormantse up to the 19th Century, B.A. dissertation, History Dept. Legon 1977, 31-37.

66. Quaye, 242-243.
67. J.K. Fynn, "Sources of Slaves in Ghana during the period of the trans-Atlantic Slave Trade", paper presented at the *World Conference on Slavery and Society in History,* Kaduna, Nigeria, 26-20 March 1990, 5.
68. Fynn, Sources, 5.
69. J.E. Inikori & S.L. Engerman (Eds): *The Atlantic Slave Trade - Effects on Economies, Societies and Peoples in Africa, the Americas and Europe,* Durham & London 1992, 2.
70. B. Gasper, "Slave importation, Runaways and Compensation in Antigua 1720-1729," in Inikori & Engerman 1992, 301.

Chapter 4
1. E. Isichei: *History of West Africa since 1800,* London 1985, 152.
2. R.A. Freeman: *Travels and Life in Ashanti and Jaman,* 1967, 489.
3. De Marees, *Description,* 54.
4. Birmingham, *Fetu,* 32-33
5. Bosman, 92-93.
6. Metcalfe, *Documents,* 683.
7. Wilks, *Asante,* 177.
8. De Marees, *Description,* 192.
9. London Public Record office (P.R.O.) CO 96/346 p.126.
10. R.A.T. 17/10/27, R.A.T. 11/1/23.
11. Addo-Fening, *Akyem Abuakwa,* 102.
12. R.A.K. D 234.
13. Wilks, *Asante,* 616.
14. Wilks, *Asante,* 618.
15. Dupuis, xxxviii; xxxix.
16. De Marees, *Description,* 177.
17. R.A.T. 17/10/27, R.A.T. 1/1/23.
18. De Marees, *Description,* 184-185.
19. P.R.O. London Co 96/43; Co 96/53.
20. Addo-Fening, *Akyem Abuakwa,* 80.
21. Bowdich, 75-76, 283, 289.
22. Metcalfe, *Documents,* 471-472.
23. A.B. Ellis: *The Tshi-speaking people of the Gold Coast of West Africa,* London 1887, 159, 164, 166; Metcalfe, *Documents,* 458.
24. J.H. Nketia: *Drumming in Akan Communities in Ghana,* London 1963, 193.
25. B. Cruichshank: *Eighteen Years on the Gold Coast of Africa vol. 2,* London 1966, 196-197.

26. P.R.O. London Co 96/311.
27. R.A.T. RAT/1/399.
28. C.C. Robertson & M.A. Klein (Eds): *Women and Slavery in Africa,* Wisconsin, U.S.A. 1983, 3, 5, 36.
29. Robertson & Klein, 49.
30. N.A.G. Adm 11/975.
31. Oral traditions of Dormaa, I.A.S. Legon, Ghana, Jan 1976, 34.

Chapter 5
1. R.A.T. RAT/ 399. P.3.
2. P. Jenkins: *Abstracts of Basel Mission Gold Coast Correspondence,* Univ. of Ghana, Legon 1970, 586.
3. Barbot 270.
4. Cruickshank 240, 227-229.
5. F. Boyle: *Through Fanteland to Coomassie,* London 1874, 192-193.
6. R.A. Kea: *Settlements, Trade and Politics in the 17th Century Gold Coast,* Baltimore & London 1982, 294.
7. J.J. Crooks: *Records relating to the Gold Coast Settlements from 1750-1874,* Dublin 1923, 36.
8. J. Beecham: *Ashante and the Gold Coast,* London 1841, 118.
9. Ashanti Stool Histories, I.A.S./A.S.H. 16; R. Addo-Fening, "The background to the deportation of King Asafo Adjei and the Foundation of New Juaben," in *T.H.S.G. vol. Xiv,* No. 2 1973, 213-226.
10. Addo-Fening, *Akyem Abuakwa,* 79.
11. Reindorf 93-98.
12. J.M. Sarbah: *Fanti Customary Laws,* London 1904, 123-124.
13. Sarbah 210-213.
14. Barbot 248.
15. Selected Judgements W.A.C.A. 1930-33 I, Accra, Ghana p.14; W.A.L.R. Accra, Ghana 1958, 251-253; G.L.R. 1959, 196.
16. Rattray 55.
17. W.A.C.A. 1930, 12.
18. R.A.K. SCT 24/56.
19. R.A.K. SCT 24/18.
20. R.A.K.D. District Court II, Abetifi 5/5/62.
21. Barbot 270.
22. T.B. Freeman: *Journal of various visits to the Kingdoms of Ashanti, Akim and Dahomey in Western Africa,* London 1844, 135.

Chapter 6

1. R.A.S. GDC 1/6.
2. Kyebi Palace Archives, AASA/1.1/222.
3. Kyebi Palace Archives, AASA/1.1/2.
4. R.A.K.D. Adm 29/6/41; N.A.G. Acc. No. 73.
5. Manhyia Archives, Asantehene's Court & Civil Record Book No. 25; R.A.S.K. Acc. No 3809/71.
6. Ashanti Stool Histories, vols I & II, I.A.S. Legon 1976, A.Ṣ.H. 143, 152, 172.
7. R.A.C.C. Adm 23/1/113; Cruickshank 243; R.A.S.D. Acc. 3818/71.
8. I. Quaye, The Ga and their Neighbours, Legon 1972, 227-259.
9. R.A.H. KE/ C100; Kyebi Palace Archives AASA/1.1/97; R.A.S. S/116; 58.
10. Ashanti Stool Histories I.A.S./A.S.H. 36, 46, 66, 70, 81.
11. I.A.S./A.S.H. 5, 8, 12, 86, 90.
12. I.A.S./A.S.H. 126,133, 165, 194, 16, 173, 65.
13. I.A.S./A.S.H. 102, 215.
14. I.A.S./A.S.H. 115, 134.
15. I.A.S./A.S.H. 12, 156, 134.
16. I.A.S./A.S.H. 113.
17. I.A.S./A.S.H. 109, 168, 180, 191.
18. I.A.S./A.S.H. 1, 30, 57, 91, 96, 114, 120, 164, 199.
19. I.A.S./A.S.H. 3, 15, 157, 179, 196.
20. I.A.S./A.S.H. 47, 97; Reindorf 132.
21. I.A.S./A.S.H. 21, 92, 181, 187.
22. I.A.S./A.S.H. 104.
23. I.A.S./A.S.H. 71.
24. Information on the Bantama Stool is derived from I.A.S./A.S.H. 39, 40; Wilks, *Asante* 387-397; Bowdich *Mission,* 282-283.
25. Information on the Gyasewa Stool is based on I.A.S./A.S.H. 15; N.A.G.C.S.O. 1511/31; Asante Seminar, North Western University, No. 1. March 1975, 7-15; Wilks, *Asante* 396-483; Bowdich, *Mission* 104; Rattray 121-122.
26. Dupuis, *Journal,* 55,78.

Chapter 7

1. Metcalfe, *Documents,* 165.
2. Metcalfe, *Documents,* 160-186.
3. Metcalfe, *Documents,* 160-186.
4. P.R.O. Co 96/89.
5. P.R.O. Co 96/2; Metcalfe, *Documents,* 696.

6. P.R.O. Co 96/93.

7. P.R.O. Co 96/24.

8. P.R.O. Co 96/24.

9. P.R.O. Co 96/29.

10. P.R.O. Co 96/33.

11. P.R.O. Co 96/41.

12. P.R.O. Co 96/41; Co 96/43

13. P.R.O. Co 96/72.

14. P.R.O. Co 96/115. G.C. No. 1310.

15. P.R.O. Co 96/179 Desp. No. 36; Co 96/203 Desp. No. 206; Co 96/204 Desp. No. 255.

16. P.R.O. Co 96/130 G.C. No. 3934; Addo-Fening, *Akyem Abuakwa*, 235.

17. P.R.O. Co 96/118. G.C. No. 3925; P.R.O. Co 96/6.

18. B.M.S. Correspondence on the Slave Emancipation Proceedings on the Gold Coast 1874-5, Dieterle to Basel, dd. Aburi 22nd June 1875.

19. B.M.S. Eisenchmid to Basel, dd 25th Jan. 1875; B.M.S., Asante, Mohr & Werner to the Slave Emancipation Commission of the Basel Mission on the Gold Coast 26th June 1875.

20. B.M.S. Herman Rottman to Basel, dd. Accra 30th June 1875.

21. Ibid.

22. B.M.S. Binder to Mader, dd. Basel Mission Factory, Ada, 3rd July 1875.

23. B.M.S. Muller to Basel, dd. 17th Sept. 1855 No. 1 49-50.

24. B.M.S. Widman to Basel, dd. 1st July 1875.

25. B.M.S. Asante's Report on the Boarding School in Kibi, dd. 5th Jan. 1877, No. 227.

26. B.M.S. Proposed Slave Colony Correspondence, 1893.

27. P.R.O. Co 96/43; Co 96/243; Co 96/103; Co 96/123; Co 96/185.

28. B.M.S. Binder to Mader, dd. Ada 3rd July 1875; Dieterle to Basel, Aburi 22nd June 1875; Asante, Mohr & Werner, to the Slave Emancipation Commission 26th June 1875.

29. P.R.O. Co 96/197; P.R.O. Co 96/243; Johnson, *Salaga*, 353-355.

30. P.R.O. Co 96/208. Confidential 15th Feb. 1890. C.O. Minutes

31. P.R.O. Co 96/208. Govt. HS, Victoriaborg, Accra 17th Feb. 1890.

32. P.R.O. Co 96/215.

33. B.M.S. Clerk's report for the year 1891. No. II 146.

34. B.M.S. Rosler, dd. 28th May 1893 No.1.70.

35. P.R.O. Co 96/311 D.C. Dixcove & Shama 30th Sept. 1897; D.C. Elmina, 7th Oct. 1897.

36. P.R.O. Co 96/311, D.C. Cape Coast, 7th Oct. 1897.

37. P.R.O. Co 96/311, D.C. Keta, 7th Oct. 1897; D.C. Tarkwa, 12th Oct. 1897.
38. P.R.O. Co 96/311, D.C. Saltpond, 18th Oct. 1897; D.C. Axim 12th Oct. 1897.
39. P.R.O. Co 96/311, D.C. Winneba, 20th Oct. 1897; D.C. Prampram, 30th Sept. 1897; D.C. Tarkwa, 12th Oct. 1897; D.C. Akuse, 27th Sept. 1897.
40. P.R.O. Co 96/311, D.C. Accra, 8th Nov. 1897; Commissioner of Police, Accra 14th Jan. 1898.
41. P.R.O. Co 96/255.
42. P.R.O. Co 96/321.
43. P.R.O. Co 96/337.
44. P.R.O. Co 96/311.
45. R.A.KD. 234.
46. R.A.K.D. 1906 D. 500.
47. R.A.K.D.234.

Appendix I
1. R.A.K. 735C.
2. R.A.T. RAT/1/23.
3. N.A.G. Adm 11/975 & R..A.T. RAT/1/23.
4. Ibid.
5. Ibid.
6. Ibid.